Photo: Gourab Deb

STEPHEN CURTIS is a set and costume designer for theatre and production designer for film. His extensive theatre career spans more than three decades and embraces designs for dance, drama, opera, physical theatre and musicals, including major collaborations with Australia's leading directors, choreographers, festivals and performance companies.

Stephen's many striking designs for the stage include sets and costumes for *La bohème*, *The Cunning Little Vixen* and *Lulu* (Opera Australia), *The Turn of the Screw* (Huston Grand Opera), *Shanghai Lady Killer* (Stalker Physical Theatre), *I Am Eora* (Sydney Festival), *Pygmalion* (Queensland Theatre Company), *Henry IV* (Bell Shakespeare Company), *The Venetian Twins* (Nimrod Theatre Company), sets for *The Secret River* and *The Government Inspector* (Sydney Theatre Company), *The Blue Room*, *All About My Mother* and *Tribes* (Melbourne Theatre Company), *The Alchemist* and *Scorched* (Belvoir) and costumes for *Der Ring des Nibelungen* (State Opera of South Australia).

Stephen's film production design credits include the features *Looking for Alibrandi* and Tracey Moffatt's stunningly visual *Bedevil* and *Night Cries*.

For many years Stephen has also taught design for theatre and film at both a secondary and tertiary level. He has devised workshops for teachers and students taking drama as part of their senior secondary studies, initiated and taught units in production design at the University of Technology, Sydney and theatre design at the National Institute of Dramatic Art. He developed the new degree and post-graduate curriculum in design for the Australian Film, Television and Radio School where he held the position of Head of Design for four years.

Whether teaching or designing classics, or new or devised work Stephen approaches each production with a deep conviction in the role the design has in enriching the audience's experience, and the role the designer has as a creative collaborator in developing and communicating the creative vision of the production.

STEPHEN CURTIS

STAGING IDEAS

Set and costume design for theatre

CURRENCY PRESS

First published in 2014
by Currency Press Pty Ltd,
PO Box 2287, Strawberry Hills, NSW, 2012, Australia
enquiries@currency.com.au
www.currency.com.au

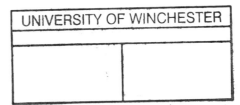

CEO: Deborah Franco
Editor and Project Manager: Paul O'Beirne
Design Concept and Designer: Katy Wall
Cover Design Concept and Designer: Vivienne Valk

National Library of Australia Cataloguing-in-Publication Data:
Author: Curtis, Stephen, 1957- author.
Title: Staging ideas : set and costume design for theatre / Stephen Curtis.
ISBN: 9780868198774 (paperback)
Notes: Includes index.
Subjects: Theaters--Stage-setting and scenery.
                Costume design.
Dewey Number: 792.025

Front cover shows Nathaniel Dean, Lachlan Elliott, Ursula Yovich, Roy Gordon, Rhimi Johnson Page and Trevor Jamieson in Sydney Theatre Company's *The Secret River*, 2013. Photo: Cassandra Hannagan. ABC Arts online ©.
Printed by the OPUS Group, Singapore.

FOREWORD

As this book of Stephen's so carefully argues, the making of theatre is an intensely collaborative experience. Too often and for too long the notion of the 'concept' of the production, the heart of its argument, the shape of its interpretation, has been seen as purely the domain of the director. In my experience at least, that interpretation gathers and changes, enriched by each of the artists who collectively and individually take responsibility for the communication of the production.

If the idea of creating a performance—putting on a show—begins with the director (it might as easily have begun with a producer, or a playwright, or an actor) it is quickly shared. It's handed on, and passed back and forth, until, in any good production, the provenance of the work is attributable to no single imagination, but is richer for all of them.

More often than not it is the designer who makes the first and most indelible mark in the process of realisation, who literally sets the stage for action. You can sit for hours considering an idea together. Or staring into a model box. Time stops in the loveliest of ways. I remember on one of our earliest collaborations Stephen and I were planted in front of the model for *Signal Driver* in the design room in the offices at the State Theatre Company of South Australia in the early '80s. Playwright Patrick White looked in. Two hours later he looked in again. 'But you haven't moved!', he cried out, fascinated and appalled.

Things do get quicker; a shorthand develops. One of the benefits of growing older is that together you get to know each other's taste and imagination. Stephen and I are linked by our childhood in the '60s. We did a production of Janáček's opera *The Cunning Little Vixen* and Stephen drew on deep memories in creating the clothes for the children's chorus who play an assortment of fox cubs, grasshoppers and frogs. We were suddenly at a 1962 Australian child's birthday party while also being in the forest of Janáček's vixen. It was a pure and beautiful play.

And on our most recent collaboration *The Secret River*, we did most of our preliminary work via email and Skype while I was doing another show in London. That extraordinary painted space, draping and curving there with its lyrical sweep towering above the characters—giving us sandstone cliffs and the river and a cathedral of Eucalypts—was conceived in a single swift gesture... But Stephen has been living on the Hawkesbury and contemplating its beauty for more than half his life. It was all there inside him. Waiting to come out.

I'm not aware of another book that so comprehensively identifies and examines the processes of theatrical design and the interactions that take place in this most human and generous of art forms—this is a resource that all theatre makers can read and learn from.

Neil Armfield,
Sydney, 2013

CONTENTS

PREFACE

This book was written for designers who design sets, and/or costumes, for live performance, and who want to discover more about how it's done. It is also for other performing artists—directors, lighting designers, performers, producers and others—who share the interests of the designer and want to learn more about thinking visually. Costume and set design are included equally as they are both important. The complex processes of interpretation and conceptual development are given equal weight to practical problem-solving, because they are equally part of what we do. The nuts-and-bolts craft is given equal place to the creative imaginative art as they are in equal measure part of our process.

I do, however, give a lot more weight to the *process*—how we do it—than to the finished result. There are a number of excellent visual surveys of performance design that show images of the completed set and costume designs as they finally appeared to the audience. However the way performance designers actually work has remained in the shadows, and my aim is to shine a bright light on our process.

I have included the voices of many other practising designers and theatre-makers because they all are passionate about what they do and have a mass of experience that they are keen to share. Most of the visual examples are from their work and demonstrate that there are many, many different ways of working.

The book is structured in several layers so that readers can find the level of complexity that best suits them. The MAIN CHAPTERS systematically cover the key steps in the design process, and the SIDEBARS in these chapters include practical tips and summaries for younger or student designers. Most chapters are followed by a CASE STUDY, following a single production through the entire design process from the first reading of the script to opening night, giving practical working samples that detail each step in the process. The FURTHER THINKING sections, highlighted in red, investigate more complex aspects of how we work, and can be read in sequence or as specialised thought-provoking topics. For readers dipping in and out of the book the arrow (⮕) symbol will direct you to related ideas or images.

I would especially like to thank all of the designers, directors and others who offered their words and work for inclusion or who advised me on the book. It is so much richer for their brilliant designs, generosity and wisdom.

Stephen Curtis

CHAPTER 1

WHAT IS PERFORMANCE DESIGN?

The Secret River (Set Designer Stephen Curtis, Costume Designer Tess Schofield)

This chapter explores the many ways our design can enrich a production. We look at the key creative questions: what is performance design? What does the designer do?

You go on a journey together, a journey to find the visual voice of the production. You never know where you'll end up—it's never a straight line. Each show has its own way of revealing itself. Jacob Nash, designer

Performance is a brilliantly multi-faceted art form. Performance artists have, over thousands of years, found incredibly varied ways to express their ideas through dance, drama, acrobatics, mime, street theatre, street parades, revue, performance art, puppetry and circus. Despite their diversity these many forms all have two things in common: the performance event is always live and there is always an audience. Live performance is *for* the audience.

Performance design has its roots in ritual. We can imagine its origins by looking at the song and dance storytelling still performed by the Australian Aboriginal people of the Western Desert *Jila* Country: the ground is prepared, bodies painted and ornamented, and special objects fashioned by the performers to tell the ancestral stories of their people.[i] Today our culture is more specialised and individual artists take on the roles of preparing the space and characters for the performance event. These artists are the *performance designers*: the *costume designer*—who visualises and creates everything that the performers wear (the costumes) and the *set designer*—who visualises and creates the on-stage performance space (the set). It also includes the important work of the lighting and sound designers, but here we are focusing on the *physical design*—elements that can be seen and touched, performed in and on. That is our work as performance designers.

Performance designers are visual artists, but unlike many other visual artists who work alone we work *collaboratively* as part of a team. The artwork that we create—the live performance event for an audience—is the combined creative work of the writer, director, performers, the creative team (including ourselves as designers), and the production team who realise our designs.

Our process is incredibly variable. It is intuitive and intellectual and creative and technical. It is based on *interpretation* (translating the words and ideas of the production to the stage), *collaboration* (working closely together), and *experimentation* (systematic trial and error). For each production we will be working with a completely new combination of ingredients—new script, different venues, directors, performers… all kinds of differences. We will never have worked exactly the same way before and we will never work exactly the same way again. To the casual observer the huge variability in our process from one project to the next can appear somewhat chaotic, or appear to lack discipline. It is true that it is difficult to apply defining rules to a process that is so variable. However, this book aims to help us see and understand the method in the madness and to map out a coherent design process, whether it be for drama, dance, physical theatre or any other performance genre, or for any performance venue, or for any set of performers or any creative team... or for any of the many other variables. This process is shaped by some basic principles that guide what we do as performance designers.

WHAT IS PERFORMANCE DESIGN? WHAT DOES THE DESIGNER DO?

WE ILLUMINATE THE PRODUCTION. In essence the role of the entire team of collaborative artists working on the production is to use our skills and imaginations to create a brilliant performance event. As designers our visual interpretation and invention will be important factors in enriching the audience's experience of the production—making the production sharper, clearer, more enjoyable, more meaningful, more moving, more challenging, more entertaining, more enlightening. Illuminating!

1.1 Stephen Curtis's set model for *The Secret River* (➡ *pages 222, 224 for more on this production*).

1.2

WE HELP TO TELL A STORY. We all like a good story, and performance (even at its most abstract) is often framed around a story. Our design can help to define the events, context and characters of the story, and it can help to provide dramatic tension and suspense and build the action to a powerful dramatic resolution. We can think of our designs as storytelling with pictures.

1.3 Kim Carpenter's set model artwork for *The Book of Everything* (➡ *page 10 for more on this production*).

1.4

WE HELP TO MOTIVATE AND SHAPE ACTION. Our set designs can create a play space (literally a *playground*) for the performers to dramatically move and physically express themselves while our costumes move with the performers and magnify, extend or shape their physical gestures. Our designs can actually motivate the performers to move and play dramatically, energetically, acrobatically, balletically with slap stick physicality or precise formality.

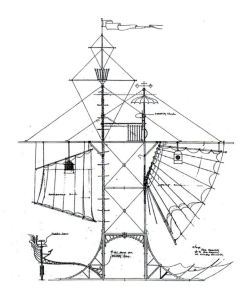

1.5 Andrew Carter's set design drawing for *Blood Vessel* (➡ *page 23 for more on this production*).

1.6

WE GIVE THE PRODUCTION A TANGIBLE STYLE. How will we tell our story, engage our audience, draw them in and communicate our ideas? The way we do this is all about style: the production style and concept, the script's literary style, and the visual style of our designs. We can choose to be 'conventional' and stick to the conventions of the script, or to explore, experiment and innovate—to find new ways of telling stories, engaging and entertaining our audience and opening them up to the production's ideas. We have the whole international history of art, culture and theatre to draw on to inspire us. Our stylistic experiments as designers will help shape the next generation of live performance.

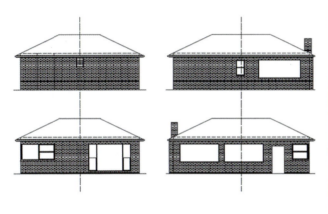

1.7 Robert Cousin's set design for *The Season at Sarsaparilla* (➡ *see page 46 for more on this production*).

1.8

WE HELP TO CREATE FOCUS WITHIN A SCENE. We can use our design to help 'direct' the audience's eyes to where we want them to look, and where their eyes go, their imaginations follow.

1.9 Bill Haycock's ballet designs for *Turandot* and *Madama Butterfly*.

1.10

WE COMMUNICATE IDEAS. As designers we convert the ideas in the script and the director's concepts into tangible, physical, visual *things* that the audience can actually see and the performers can use. Live performance is always visual, and the audience will absorb a lot of the production's meaning from what they see. The set and costume design will have a powerful influence on the audience's interpretation. Our designs will also be a powerful tool to communicate the production's ideas to the entire production team, so everyone has a clear picture of the show we are making together.

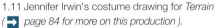

1.11 Jennifer Irwin's costume drawing for *Terrain* (➡ *page 84 for more on this production*).

1.12

WE ENGAGE THE AUDIENCE AND MAKE THEM WANT TO WATCH. The audience may have bought their tickets and come to watch, but it is up to us to get them hooked and make them want to keep watching—to draw them deeper and deeper into the live performance experience. Our designs can inspire, amuse, provoke, move or entertain the audience, but we can never let them—even for a minute—be bored.

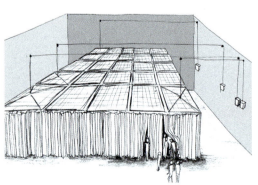

1.13 Joey Ruigrok van der Werven's concept drawing for *Monstrous Body* (➡ *page 66 for more on this production*).

1.14

WE SOLVE PRACTICAL PROBLEMS CREATIVELY. Performance design is a balancing act of creativity and practicality. Right from the beginning our imaginations will be tailored to practical solutions—we need to be able to actually build our invented world. Our designs will need to work for the script, the director and the performers; they will need to work for the audience, and will need to be within budget and within the production's technical resources. We can be at our most creative when our designs help to solve practical problems.

1.15 Anna Tregloan's set design for *Journal of a Plague Year* (➡ *page 114 for more on this production*).

1.16

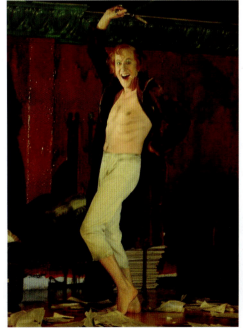

1.17 Tess Schofield's costume design for *Diary of a Madman* (➡ *page 176 for more on this production*).

WE USE DETAIL TO COMMUNICATE INFORMATION: WHEN, WHERE, WHO, WHAT AND WHY. As designers we can be like a crime fiction writer—carefully planting clues (important, subtle, potent pieces of visual information)—that helps the audience 'get the picture' and understand when and where the action is happening, who the characters are, what they are doing and why they are doing it. We can choose to make important information clear, and like a great detective novel we can also choose to tantalise the audience and stimulate their imaginations by making some of the clues intriguingly subtle.

1.18

WE BUILD AN ATMOSPHERE OR MOOD. The audience will have an instinctive emotional response to the production, which will be possibly the most powerful factor in shaping their interpretation. The special mood or atmosphere we conjure and express through the costume, set and lighting design has the power to shape and shift the audience's emotions—from joy to deepest sorrow.

1.19 Pip Runciman's designs for *Romeo and Juliet*
(➡ *page 177 for more on this production*).

1.20

WE CREATE A WHOLE WORLD. A wonderful thing happens when the lights go down at the start of a show. While their bodies remain seated the imagination of each audience member goes for a virtual journey into the *world* of the production. This illusory world is made up of a multi-layered mix of characters, action, context, mood and ideas. As set and costume designers we work closely with the director, performers and the rest of the creative team and production team to construct this imaginary world for the audience's imaginations to enter.

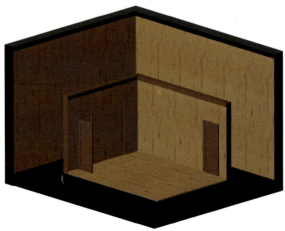

1.21 Claude Marcos's 3D set renderings for *The Trial*
(➡ *page 190 for more on this production*).

1.22

WE REVEAL CHARACTER. It is the performers who are at the heart of the live performance experience. Our role is to support them in the development and expression of their performance. Our costumes and sets will reveal and communicate aspects of their character to the audience. What motivates their characterisation needs to also motivate our designs so all three elements—performance, setting and costume work together and make perfect sense.

1.23 Bruce McKinven's costume design for *Gwen in Purgatory* (➡ *page 206 for more on this production*).

1.24

THE PERFORMANCE DESIGNER IS RESPONSIBLE FOR EVERY PHYSICAL THING ON-STAGE: HOW IT LOOKS AND HOW IT WORKS. This really is the bottom line. Our design will be successful when we have holistically managed the whole process so that every element looks good and works well. There is always a way of it doing both!

Performance design is a rich and multi-layered creative enterprise. In this book we progress one step at a time, breaking each creative process down into straightforward tasks. Even so, sometimes the complexity can seem overwhelming. At these times we can remind ourselves that our job is simply to help make a great production—a brilliant performance event that adds something to the lives of the audience. I invite you to take up the challenge.

The Book of Everything (Designer Kim Carpenter)

This chapter outlines the key steps in the design process and looks at getting ourselves organised—collecting together everything that we will need to begin our design journey.

ALSO IN THIS CHAPTER—FURTHER THINKING: Collaboration and the Creative Team, page 18

The moment I have finished reading a new script a knot of energy forms in my belly and just keeps growing. I know that deep in my subconscious there is a design solution even though I haven't the faintest idea of what it might be! Dan Potra, designer

Our design builds step by step. With each decision we advance to the next stage as we gradually shape our design to the needs of the production. The process might include steps to the side and backwards as we explore different design possibilities. Sometimes we go full circle in our effort to work out the best solution. We will each have our own individual way of going about it, shaped by our background, skills and personalities, and our individual process will also change as we adapt to our director and creative team and the needs of the production. However, the steps described here can be taken as a guide, and these are the steps we will follow through this book.

THE DESIGN PROCESS		
INTERPRETATION	**GETTING ORGANISED**	Collecting together all of the resources and information we will need: script, venue plans, timeframe and deadlines, budget, venue, cast, creative team, music (➡ *This chapter*).
	SCRIPT INTERPRETATION	Analysing the 'script' for the information that will help us develop our interpretation: how it feels, what it means and how it works (➡ *Chapter 3, page 23*).
	RESEARCH	Feeding our imaginations with research, especially pictorial research, also gives us material to share with the creative team (➡ *Chapter 4, page 46*).
	CONCEPT DEVELOPMENT	The creative team consolidates their interpretation and design framework. Script interpretation, research, production style and visual style all come together into the concept: how we want our audience to see, feel and understand the production (➡ *Chapter 5, page 56 and Chapter 6, page 79*).

| EXPLORATION | EXPERIMENTATION | We test different approaches to the design by experimenting with alternate design interpretations, using design sketches and pre-visualistion tools, such as sketch models and preliminary costume drawings (➡ *Chapter 7, page 98*). |
| | DESIGN DEVELOPMENT | We begin refining the detail of the designs, making sure every element of the design works together towards a cohesive production concept. We carefully consider how space, character and light work to shape the design (➡ *Chapter 8, page 114, Chapter 9, page 154 and Chapter 10, page 177*). |

DESIGN REALISATION	DESIGN DELIVERY	The resolved and completed designs are presented to the production company in the form of costume design drawings, set construction drawings, scale model, plans, elevations and working drawings. This material becomes the blueprint for production (➡ *Chapter 11, page 190 and Chapter 12, page 206*).
	PRODUCTION	The designs are realised by the production team: costume, prop and set makers, scenic artists, wig-makers, makeup artists, milliners, sculptors and other specialists. Their work will be creatively overseen by the designer and managed by the production manager (➡ *Chapter 13, page 218*).
	REHEARSAL	During rehearsals the designer is attentive to how the design is brought into play by the performers, adapting the design to their needs. The designer acts as a vital link between the production workshops and the rehearsal room.
	PRODUCTION WEEK	All of the production elements come together for the first time and are refined and coordinated in a process of technical rehearsals and dress rehearsals.
	OPENING NIGHT	At long last our designs are complete and able to help engage the audience and enrich their understanding and enjoyment of the production.

On a conventional drama production this whole process might happen over 3–6 months but it can be as short as several weeks, and on a complex production may take as long as a year or more.

*After I have been given the job—that's when I sit down at a clean desk,
go through my notes, jot down ideas, look for 'jumping off' points... and
the process begins.*   Pip Runciman, designer

HOW DO WE BEGIN?

Why are we designing this production? What do we have to offer? Sometimes
we take on a project because the script is great and has something really worth
communicating, or it is an opportunity to work with new people, or rekindle
an established working relationship, or because it presents a new creative
challenge, or a combination of all of these. Sometimes the reasons can be more
pragmatic, but in any case a clear motivation is a great start.

Are we designing the whole production? Or will the design be split between
costume designer and set designer?

Who are the other members of the creative team? Are they people we have
worked with before? It is always a good idea to figure out how they like to
work. Amazingly, many people have never consciously thought about how
they work. You might talk about this with your director, or work it out by
observing what they do or don't respond to. It is also a good idea to find out
whether the director likes to consider several different approaches, or settle on
one approach early on. Do they like to see design ideas as preliminary design
sketches or sketch models? Or do they like to sift through masses of pictorial
research together with us? Do they like to keep a firm, controlling hand on the
process? Or do they have a more open, collaborative style? Do they like a lot of
time to make decisions, or are they quick and decisive? Do they already have a
clear sense of where they want to go with the production, or do they want to use
the design process to work through multiple potential solutions? The creative
team can also discuss how we all like to work so we can tune our methodology
to each other's needs and all work together happily and creatively. I would
always encourage my director to meet with the whole creative team as a group
early on in order to get everyone started on the same page and help build a
strong collaboration.

What is the script for the project? Is it a classic? If so, is it a new adaptation?
Is it a translation? If so, is it a good translation? Is it a new play? If so, is it an
early draft that's likely to change, or a final draft? Will the writer be involved in
developing the production? If it is a devised work without a script, is there an
outline concept or other document, such as a storyboard, that will act as a guide?

If it is an opera or musical or other form of music theatre, does the musical
score already exist? If so, we will need a copy straightaway so we can listen and
respond to it as part of our design process.

Where is the production being staged? Is it a venue we are familiar with? Is
the venue a good choice for this production? Will the production tour to other

venues? If so, are they very different formats from the space for which you are initially designing? We will need to get scale plans and elevations of all of the venues for which we are designing. Our production manager should supply these, but many venues also have PDF and computer-aided drafting (CAD) versions on their website that we can download to get started.

Who are the cast? Are we already familiar with the cast? Is the director familiar with them? Are they a strong cast or has the director made some compromises? Are some roles still to be cast? If so, when will casting be complete? We will need photographs (ideally full figure) of each cast member to help us start thinking about costume design.

What is the potential audience for this production? Will the audience influence the production style?

DESIGN PHASE			
Week 1 • Read the script. • Record first impressions. • Get organised. • Preliminary research. • First creative meeting with director.	**Week 2** • Script interpretation. • Analysis and brainstorming. • Deep research. • Creative meeting to share and discuss research and analysis.	**Week 3** • Exploring design concepts, production style and visual style with design sketches, sketch models and costume roughs.	**Week 4** • Continue exploration and experimentation. • Creative meeting to share and get feedback on design options. • Agree on design concept and stylistic approach.
Week 5 • Specific research. • Design development. • Creative meeting to confirm the design approach.	**Week 6** • Preparation of final designs. • Presentation model and costume drawings.	**Week 7** • Continue preparation of final designs. • Creative meeting to resolve detail. • Design documentation: construction and working drawings, lists.	**Week 8** • Completion of the design delivery package. • Design delivery. • Budget and resource meetings.
PRODUCTION PHASE			
Week 1 • Pre-production. • Design consultation with production manager and heads of department. • Resolve any remaining design issues.	**Week 2** • Pre-production. • Brief the production team in detail.	**Week 3** • Rehearsals start. • Design presentation to company. • Supervise designs. • Production meeting.	**Week 4** • Rehearsal week 2. • Supervise designs. • Production meeting.
Week 5 • Rehearsal week 3. • Supervise designs. • Production meeting.	**Week 6** • Rehearsal week 4. • Supervise designs. • Production meeting.	**Week 7** • Production week. • Bump-in set and lighting (the installation of the set, costume and lighting elements into the performance venue). • Plot lights. • Technical rehearsals.	**Week 8** • Dress rehearsals. • Previews. • Opening night.

DESIGN TIMELINE

GET ORGANISED: CHECKLIST

- What is my motivation?
- Director. Do they have a strong sense of where they want to go with the production or will they use the design process to experiment with interpretations?
- Director's availability. When will we meet?
- Design roles combined, or split between costume and set designer
- Who are the other members of the creative team?
- Script: classic, new, translation, draft, devised?
- Music score: existing, being composed? Available as a recording?
- Venue plans, 'tech specs'
- Visit the venue with the director and take photographs
- Touring? Touring plans.

- Cast: casting completed or still underway?
- Cast photographs
- Cast measurements
- Audience: old, young, mixed? Audience expectations?
- Timeframe/important dates: design deadline, start of rehearsal, opening night
- Design schedule
- Budget: overall budget and budget allocations to each design area
- Resources: existing set/costume making workshops or will these be set up for the production?
- Other resources, including the skills and experience of the production team

What is the timeframe for designing the show, and getting it all prepared for opening night? By discussing the timeframe with our director early on we can work out how regularly we should meet and how available the director is to meet over the design period. We can also discuss deadlines and agree on a schedule of what we both expect to achieve.

What is the budget? Is it realistic? Does our director know and understand the budget framework and understand design options that may or may not be possible within the budget? There is no point developing designs that are more ambitious than the budget or resources allow. (Although there usually *is* a way to realise an idea if it is good enough!)

What production resources are available to us? Is there a production team of set, prop and costume makers already set up? Or will the design be 'farmed out' to freelance makers? If so, who will manage this process? How 'hands on' will we need to be?

Often, when we take on the design of a show not all of the information we require will be confirmed or available. But if we know what information we need, we can keep asking until we get it.

With all of this information under our belt we are ready to begin our design journey.

A production timeline will help us structure the design process, schedule creative meetings and meet design deadlines. An 8-week design period and 8-week production period might look something like the DESIGN TIMELINE opposite, although in practice we may have a design period of anything from half to double this time.

Pygmalion: designer Stephen Curtis
Case Study — Stage 1:
Getting Started

This double-page case study is the first in a sequence that follows the production of George Bernard Shaw's satirical drama *Pygmalion*, directed by Michael Gow and designed by Stephen Curtis for the Queensland Theatre Company. We will track progress on this production through the whole design process from the very beginning shown here—where we see important 'getting started' information—right up to opening night.

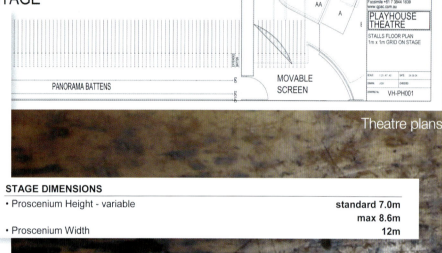

Theatre plans

STAGE DIMENSIONS

• Proscenium Height - variable	standard 7.0m
	max 8.6m
• Proscenium Width	12m

AR STAGE/
HEARSAL   SOUNDDOOR   MAIN STAGE

SETTING LINE

ORCH PIT/
FORESTAGE

QPAC

Queensland Performing Arts Centre
Cnr Grey & Melbourne Sts
South Bank Queensland Australia
Telephone +61 7 3840 7444
Facsimile +61 7 3844 1839
www.qpac.com.au

PLAYHOUSE
THEATRE

STALLS FLOOR PLAN
1m x 1m GRID ON STAGE

VH-PH001

PANORAMA BATTENS

MOVABLE
SCREEN

QPAC

Please confirm all critical measurements on site.

PLAYHOUSE

STAGE FACILITIES

STAGE
- Fixed Proscenium Arch with adjustable header
- Main Stage, Forestage, Rear Stage, OP Side Stage
- Single Purchase Counterweight Flying System operated from prompt side of stage and forestage
  Note - Setting Line is the back of Proscenium Arch
- To allow for the use of trapdoors and heavy machinery, the stage floor is not sprung
- For dance productions a 30mm thick portable *Biltflor* sprung dance floor with black *Tarkett* covering is available

STAGE DIMENSIONS
• Proscenium Height - variable	standard 7.0m
	max 8.6m
• Proscenium Width	12m
• Apron Depth (from setting line)	1.2m
• Forestage (Orchestra Pit) Lift Depth along centre line	3.4m
• Load-in door dimensions (from dock to stage)	8.8m x 3.7m
• Height of Stage Level from auditorium floor	910mm
• Stage Depth to last flying line from setting line	11.9m
• PS proscenium to fly rail PS	6.5m
• OP proscenium to OP side stage wall	19.3m
• Clear height from stage floor to fly floor over	8.8m
• Distance between PS & OP fly floor	21.0m
• Distance from setting line to sound curtain	13.3m
• Distance from setting line to back wall of rear stage	22.4m
• Setting line to House Curtain	410mm
• Stage to underside grid	22.9m
• Stage to grid floor	23.0m

REAR STAGE
• Width of Rear Stage (wall to wall)	17.3m
• Depth of Rear Stage from sound isolation door	
• Clear height of Rear Stage	
• Manual winch lines in Rear Stage (500kg WLL)	
• Clear height under winched battens	

SIDE STAGE
- Width of Side Stage from fly floor over
- Depth of Side Stage
- Clear height of Side Stage

VENUE HIRE KIT
Queensland Performing Arts Centre

Tech specs

Melanie - Eliza
Robert - Higgins
Bryan - Pickering
Chris - Freddy
Keith - Clara
Kaye - Mrs Higgins
Penny - Mrs Pearce
Chris - Doolittle
Carol - Mrs Eynsford Hill

Christopher Hunter - Clergyman/doctor
Peter Marshall - Host/Taxi driver
Brad McMurrayTayler - Bystander/Nepommuck
Andrea Moor - Parlourmaid, Hostess

Melissa Agnew (Dialect)
Tony Brumpton (Sound)
Francesca Savage (Asst. Dir.)
David Walters

Kylie Degen MM
Staycee ... 2nd
Jodie Roche SM

Simon - Prod. Tech.
David - Tech Co-Ord.
Sam - Sound Tech
Julian - Prod. Asst.
Terry - Carpenter
John Pearce - Head Mech
Peter Sands
Kate Snyder - Wardrobe Trainee

Cast list

SUIN PLAYS

BARKER'S
BOOK STORE
35

Bernard Shaw

Pygmalion

Script

Design Presentation	Tue, 30 November 10
Rehearsals	Mon, 14 February 11
BBQ	Thu, 17 February 11
Play Briefing	Mon, 28 February 11
Bump-In	Mon, 14 March 11
Previews	Mon, 21 March 11
Previews	Tue, 22 March 11
Previews	Wed, 23 March 11
Opening	Thu, 24 March 11

Schedule

Schedule part A

Item 1 – the Production
The Production is **Pygmalion** written by George Bernard Shaw, to be directed
Gow and to be presented at the **Playhouse**, Queensland Performing Arts Ce
QLD.

Item 2 – Dates and deadlines

Design Presentation	Tue, 30 November 10
Rehearsals	Mon, 14 February 11
BBQ	Thu, 17 February 11
Play Briefing	Mon, 28 February 11
Bump-In	Mon, 14 March 11
Previews	Mon, 21 March 11
Previews	Tue, 22 March 11
Previews	Wed, 23 March 11
Opening	Thu, 24 March 11
Audio Described Performance	Sat, 2 April 11
U 30 Night	Sun, 3 April 11
Night with the Actors	Thu, 7 April 11
Close	Sun, 10 April 11

Item 3 – Production budget

	Materials/Services	Labour(Weeks)	Labour(Hour
Set & Furniture	$23,500	20	760
Properties	$5,000	4	152
Scenic Art		5	190
Wardrobe	$25,000	41	1,558

Item 4 – Special Events
PLAY BRIEFING - you must attend the Play Briefing, in the Bille Brown Studio fro
7.30pm.
NIGHT WITH THE ACTORS – if available and required, you may be invited to at

d billing practice is to credit all creative team memb
ammes, media releases and press ads larger than 15c
he right to discretionary billing on all other press adve
rials

wing billing: Designer Stephen Curtis

Item 3 – Production budget

	Materials/Services		Labour(Weeks)	Labour(Hours)
Set & Furniture	$23,500		20	760
Properties	$5,000		4	152
Scenic Art			5	190
Wardrobe	$25,000		41	1,558

Hullo Stephen,

I've got a week and a bit until this show i'm doing for the brisbane festival opens. i go back up home north thursday week. how do you want to time tackling pygmalion? the deadline is probably before the end of the year so it might be time to at least start thinking about when to talk and/or get together. once this show is out of the way i'm free. i am coming to sydney on october 6 for a bell shakespeare launch so we could certainly meet then. but that's over a month away. anyway, your call.

talk soon

mg

Email from director

For me the most compelling part of working on a new script or any piece of theatre is the creative development period—sharing stimulating conversations with the director, composer and choreographer. It's this phase that makes theatre special, where your ideas can be expanded—at times be reinvented—through exchange with your artistic collaborators. This is what separates the theatre artist's experience from the independent artist's experience (writer, painter, musician, sculptor)... Kim Carpenter, designer, director

FURTHER THINKING
COLLABORATION AND THE CREATIVE TEAM

Collaboration is team work. In theatre-making we work closely together with a group of people like players in a sports team—all working towards the end result of the live performance for an audience. Our team is called the *creative team* and consists of the director, writer, designers (set, costume, lighting and sound designers), composer, choreographer, stage manager and cast, and may also include specialists such as audio-visual designers and fight choreographers. As with a sports team every member of the creative team needs to be trained up to play their own position and also to be highly aware of everyone else's role and how we all fit and work together. There might be individual strong players or team members with brilliant specialist skills, but the end result—a win or a great show—is not dependent on any one player, but on how well the team works together.

A sports team will train together for a whole season or possibly for years, and some creative teams also work this way. Great work can come from these tight-knit relationships. More often the creative team is pulled together for a particular project, and we need to be able to get up to speed and mesh together quickly.

Every team needs a captain, and in the creative team this is the director. The director might not be the 'strongest player'—sometimes the writer or a performer or a designer might make the biggest creative contribution, but it is the director who leads and guides the process and keeps the creative vision on track right up until show-time. A project can be derailed by an individual member of the creative team insensitively pushing their own agenda. Equally a project can fail to reach its potential if a team member is not able to contribute 100 per cent, or chooses not to participate fully.

While the roles and responsibilities of each member of the team will be clearly understood, the roles need not be clearly defined, and responsibilities frequently overlap.

Throughout the production process creative team members will offer up contributions which might then be taken up and developed by others. When the process is working well there is a lot of creative give and take. In the end it is everyone's combined efforts that make the eventual performance for a live audience a real work of art.

THE BOOK OF EVERYTHING, DESIGNER KIM CARPENTER

2.1

2.2

Kim Carpenter's design drawings (2.1 and 2.2) and production images (2.3 and 2.4) for *The Book of Everything*. Kim began his career as a designer and now also devises and directs projects, mainly for young audiences. He creates multi-media works which tap into the rich creative immediacy of the child's imagination, using a combination of live performance, projection and puppetry. Kim began his design process for *The Book of Everything* with a treasured personal memento—a childhood notebook of his mother's—which he developed into the key storytelling device of a huge pop-up book.

2.3

2.4

Collaboration: the combined experience of many makes a good idea great.
Bruce McKinven, designer

THE CREATIVE TEAM: WHO DOES WHAT?

THE DESIGNERS. Through looking at what performance design does (➡ *Chapter 1, page 1*) we understand our role as designers within the creative team. The roles of set and costume designer may be combined or separate, depending on the scale of the production and the producer's or director's preferences. When the roles are separate the set designer and the costume designer will work closely together to develop the design, as well as working closely with the rest of the creative team.

THE DIRECTOR heads the creative team and is responsible for the overall artistic vision of the production. They will nurture, shepherd and guide the interpretation, exploration and conceptual framework for the production. They may have chosen the script or devised the concept for the production in collaboration with the production company / producer; they will select the creative team and cast the performers; they will guide the design process and are responsible to the production company for the feasibility of the production concept of which the design is an important part; they will rehearse the performers and bring together the creative contributions of the entire team into a cohesive whole. As designers we will work very closely with the director throughout the entire development, pre-production and production period, right up to opening night (➡ *Further Thinking, page 40*).

THE WRITER will play an active part in the creative team when the script is a new one. In this case the script will often still be in development and the writer is likely to use the design process as a way of testing and developing the script. This process will often continue into rehearsal with some script changes happening in response to the way the production comes together. As designers we may be actively engaged in the script development, or we may only have contact with the writer through the director. As the script develops we will need to accommodate these changes within our design.

THE CHOREOGRAPHER will devise and direct dance or movement elements in the production such as the dance sequences in a musical. In the case of a ballet or dance work in which the whole work is choreographed the choreographer will also fulfil all of the director's roles, and will be the head of the creative team. Design for dance requires us to work closely with the choreographer to develop design concepts that respond to their language of movement.

The production may also include a **FIGHT DIRECTOR** who will choreograph fight routines. We will work closely with the fight director in the choice of weapons, and how they are worn and used so we retain the desired look while making sure that the performers are safe at all times.

COLLABORATION FOR STUDENTS

The collaborative nature of theatre presents a challenge for students undertaking individual design projects, where you are acting simultaneously as director and designer. This means that you will not have the resource of other minds to bounce ideas off and give you creative feedback.

It is a good idea to set up a small support network which can help fill this gap. This network might be made up of your subject teacher or another teacher in the school with whom you have an affinity, and/or parents, friends or siblings who can be encouraged to have an understanding or interest in your project. They will need to read the script and have their own opinions on it. Alternatively you might seek out a theatre professional to act as a mentor.

Choose your script carefully! You will be working many long hours with this script so make sure your script is one you connect with.

COLLABORATION SKILLS

- Know your own role and contribute 100 per cent.
- Understand the roles of the other team members and respect their contributions.
- Learn to speak the same language: a shared understanding of the ideas, concepts and the words you all use to describe what you are doing ensures everyone knows what's going on.
- Communicate positively, with clear objectives.

THE COMPOSER/SOUND DESIGNER will create all of the audio components of the production which may be an operatic score, songs in musicals or a dramatic underscoring of music or sounds. In the case of opera where music is such an important component the **CONDUCTOR** will have an important creative contribution and as well as 'directing' the orchestra will often collaborate with the director on the creative vision for the production.

THE LIGHTING DESIGNER uses light to shape the mood and atmosphere of the production as well as creating dramatic transitions and focus. They are an important member of the visual design team, and our creative collaboration with them will ideally begin early in the design process. They may be joined by an **AUDIO-VISUAL DESIGNER** (AV designer) when the production includes projection. As projection is usually both a scenic and lighting element we will collaborate closely with the AV designer to integrate all visual design elements (Chapter 10, page 177).

The creative team is often narrowly defined to include only those listed above, but I would also include:

THE PERFORMERS may be actors, dancers, physical theatre acrobats and gymnasts, singers, mime artists, burlesque or circus performers. They will work closely with the director and/or choreographer to develop the performance. They are at the centre of what we do, and we will work closely with them through rehearsals to develop our design so that it supports their performance (Further Thinking, page 172).

THE STAGE MANAGER manages the rehearsal room and facilitates the director's and the choreographer's work with the performers. They will also run the production in performance, calling performers' entrances, lighting and sound cues, and generally 'managing the stage'. We will work with the stage manager and their team of **ASSISTANT** or **DEPUTY STAGE MANAGERS** (ASMs or DSMs) from rehearsals through to opening night: they will be our eyes and ears in the rehearsal room, letting us know how aspects of the design are working and if modifications are required. We share all information that influences how the show will work on stage. The ASMs will often also source props for rehearsal and for the production and we will brief them and coordinate this process.

One of the tricks of being a good designer is to maintain as much flexibility as you can within the structures of how companies work. All production departments will try to lock down the physical elements of production as early as possible because it makes it very much easier for them to do their job. One of the difficult things to say after the second preview might be: 'Actually, it should all be pink' or 'I think she should be wearing a wedding dress.'
Ralph Myers, designer[ii]

WAYS OF WORKING

The makeup of the creative team will depend on the kind of production we are designing and the kind of production company that is producing the work. Some companies work as a collective, where roles and responsibilities are shared and swapped, and the whole team shares in the profit (or loss) of the production. Small companies may engage a creative team but employ no other production staff so as designers we may be single-handedly production managing, set and costume building, rigging lights and anything else that needs doing, possibly even performing. Some groups have a more experimental way of working and the design may be developed collaboratively through rehearsals. Larger companies may be subsidised (government-funded) or commercial and these tend to have more defined crew roles and responsibilities and very defined production processes. They will set out the design delivery dates and how, when and where the production will be built and rehearsed, and these terms are likely to be stipulated in our contract. These defined roles and processes help with forward planning, budgeting and cost-effective crew management. They organise what could otherwise be an unruly process—described by one production manager as 'like herding cats'. But when too rigidly applied these management strategies can run counter to the explorative, innovative and experimental nature of theatre-making. We often strive for a balance between the right amount of structure and the right amount of creative freedom. This may be something that we negotiate openly with the creative team and the production company.

CHAPTER 3

INTERPRETING THE SCRIPT

Blood Vessel (Set Designer Andrew Carter, Costume Designer Nikki Raffin)

This chapter investigates the process of analysing and interpreting our script—leaving no stone unturned in the discovery of design information.

ALSO IN THIS CHAPTER—FURTHER THINKING: The Director–Designer Partnership, page 40

This moment of your first [reading]… should be unforgettable…
The loss of this moment is irreparable because a second reading no
longer contains the element of surprise so potent in the realm of
intuitive creativeness. Constantin Stanislavski, director[iii]

We are at the beginning of our design journey, ready to start the creative process of interpretation. The script* is the basis for our interpretation. Until the script is interpreted into actions and images it is merely words on a page. Unlike a novel or a poem the script is a work of art written to be performed for an audience, and our task is to imagine the words *off* the page and *onto* the stage for the audience to experience.

Every design decision will be a valid response to the script, so we need to get to know it well. There are many, perhaps infinite interpretations of a script. How will we know if our interpretation is 'right'? A deep understanding of the script—based on a detailed script analysis with our director—is the best foundation for a valid interpretation.

Interpreting a script can seem to be a daunting task if we are doing it for the first time, but we can see it as an adventure; exploring new, unfamiliar territory with the same delight and discovery that an audience brings to the production when they see it for the first time.

When we start analysing the script we are asking lots of questions: Is there a story? What are the themes? What are the main events? How is the story told? Does the playwright have a clear point of view, position or message? Who are the main characters? What is their relationship to each other? Is there an event or moment that changes the course of action? Where does it take place? What does it feel like? What don't I understand? What don't I know?

It can be hard to know where to start. There are many different ways to start and many different tools that a designer can use to achieve an understanding of the script. Designers, directors, performers or anyone else starting this process of script interpretation can try any or all of the approaches discussed here,

* A written script will usually be in the form of a text divided into scenes with lines spoken by named characters. Information will be conveyed through this spoken dialogue and/or in action. There may also be stage directions, and descriptions of characters and the setting (as in the *Pygmalion* script in the case study on pages 38–39 of this chapter). The script may be in a published format or still in draft form hot off the playwright's printer. In the case of music theatre such as opera or musicals the 'script' will include the musical score and lyrics. In the case of dance the music may *be* the 'script'. In devised work, where the production develops through rehearsals, the 'script' may consist of the director's notes, key images they have in mind, a storyboard or a set of themes they are interested in exploring. For an event designer the 'script' may be little more than a promotional title. All of these documents can be thought of as the script and will become the basis of our interpretation through a process of analysis and exploration.

YOUR FIRST READING

Put aside *undistracted* time for your first reading. Make sure you read it right through in one sitting, just as the audience will experience the production in performance. Read it for your own enjoyment.

Switch on your imagination and try to imagine you are watching the production as you are reading it. If it is a music theatre production listen to the music in the same way. Let it really go to work on you.

You may want to put some effort into recording your first impressions after your first reading. The best way to do this is visually: a quick expressive colour sketch or collage. Otherwise jot down words or phrases that occur to you while you are thinking about the script. Try to capture your emotional response—how the script makes you feel, the mood or atmosphere and how it *affects you*.

ELEMENTS OF DRAMA

The Greek philosopher Aristotle (384–322BC) identifies six Elements of Drama: plot, thought/theme, character, diction, song/rhythm, and spectacle. These elements have become a basic analytical tool in theatre. Contemporary Drama courses extend the list of elements to include: **theme**, **plot**, **audience**, **dialogue**, **stagecraft**, **convention**, **genre**, **character/role**, **music**, **spectacle**, **dramatic structure**, **contrast**, **symbols**, **focus**, **rhythm**, **space**, **movement**, **sound**, **time**, **mood/atmosphere**, **pace**, **pause** and **actor–audience relationship**.

experimenting to find out which approach reveals more to them. If you are a methodical thinker and list-maker you might want to start with the script breakdown. If you are more of an abstract thinker you might focus on what the script means. If you are tuned in intuitively and emotionally you might want to start with what the script feels like. In practice, most designers would use a number of these interpretive tools simultaneously, or favour one approach as the one that works best for them. Different scripts and production processes also require different approaches.

The analytical tools used here are based loosely on the Elements of Drama (➡ *Box, above*). I have grouped them into three areas of analysis, or layers of understanding.

- *What the script feels like* takes in mood, atmosphere and instinctive responses.
- *What the script means* takes in themes, images and symbols.
- *How the script works* includes dramatic structure, focus, style, genre, conventions, spectacle, character and space.

Like a detective, we are looking for clues to understanding. The more carefully we look, the deeper our understanding of the script will be.

All artistic form is an indirect expression of feeling.

Susanne Langer, philosopher[iv]

ANALYTICAL TOOLS

WHAT IT FEELS LIKE *mood, atmosphere, emotional response, intuitive response*

The instinctive or emotional responses we have to a script when we first read it (or in the case of music theatre, first hear it) are possibly the most powerful factors in shaping our interpretation. The first reading of the script is a treasured moment. We only get to read the script for the *first* time once. Every successive reading will yield a deeper understanding, but the first reading is perhaps the closest to the audience's reaction—fresh, open, inquisitive, unsure of what lies ahead. We can ask two kinds of questions at this first reading: what is the mood or atmosphere of the script (chaotic, oppressive, cold, light, tranquil…?), and how does the script make us feel (delighted, amused, thoughtful, angry, sad…?). It is not hard to see how the answers to these questions will influence the kinds of images we will use to express our interpretation of the script through the design. If during our first reading we noted the word 'chaotic' for example this throws up images of confused, broken surfaces, swirling energy, harsh contrasts of light and shadow. Putting word pictures together begins the process of refining our early impressions and helps us develop a language to talk about the production with our collaborators. The combination of the words 'chaotic + oppressive + hot' for example connotes quite a different visual world to the combination 'cold + oppressive + static '. As we translate the script into feelings and moods we can start to imagine what these feelings *look like*, and start to put together a collection of visual images: textures, spaces, colours… the beginning of a visual language to describe the world of the script. Although inherently subjective, these emotional responses can be our design's first building blocks. When we are designing for music theatre (such as opera or musicals) our response to the music is likely to be primarily emotional, and this strong response will be a major influence on the way our design takes shape.

We will often have strong, intuitive visions or mental pictures during our first reading. Our early ideas are often our best—they are spontaneous and fresh. Even if our deeper analysis of the script takes us in a different direction they are a great first start, so record those first impressions in scribbles or squiggles, collage or notes, or however you can.

Message? Message? What the hell do you think I am, a bloody postman?
Playwright Brendan Behan, on being asked what was the message of his play *The Hostage* [v]

WHAT IT MEANS *themes, images, symbols*

Playwrights almost never tell us directly what the script 'means'. What the playwright wants to say is usually buried within the script so we need to work it out, based on our intelligence, imagination and experience. Good scripts

3.1

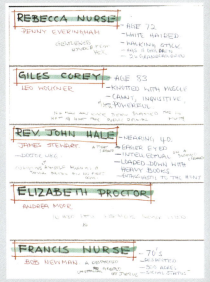

3.2

3.3

3.4

3.5

Robert Kemp's costume drawing (3.1), costume breakdown (3.2), research image (3.3), scale model (3.4) and production photo (3.5) for *The Crucible*. Robert uses the forest as a powerful symbol of the dark forces of the unconscious that underpin Arthur Miller's drama. Robert juxtaposes his forest against bare pine floorboards and 1950s costuming of a puritan simplicity to evoke the interplay of the rational and irrational, the conscious and the unconscious, good and evil. We can also see in his character breakdown how scripted information begins to shape his interpretation.

will always have a range of possible meanings, and the meaning will change as the perceptions and values of the audience change. A production of Arthur Miller's *The Crucible*, for example, would have been understood quite differently when it was first produced (in the USA at the time of Senator McCarthy's anti-communist witch hunts) from a production staged today. Great plays are open to many interpretations, and will speak to audiences across time and within many cultures. Many of Shakespeare's plays, for example, are forever in production all around the world because their themes are universal and complex and are interpreted in new ways that continue to have meaning. Sometimes scripts from the past will be rediscovered because their themes have a particular cultural relevance today.

The meaning of the script might be conveyed in the dialogue, in action, in the subtext, in images, in the dramatic structure… We are looking for meaning anywhere and everywhere!

Let's start analysing the script's meaning using the tools: *themes*, *images* and *symbols*. We will come back to some of the more obvious factors (for example, character, time and place) when we look at the *script breakdown.*

THEMES: The central theme will almost always deal with an aspect of the universal human condition (such as humankind and fate, love, loneliness, loss of innocence) or the working out of a political, social or moral problem (such as injustice, the struggle between right and wrong, humankind's incompatible ideals). Often these universal themes will be expressed in terms of characters' individual conflicts, problems and situations. In the early stages of our script analysis identifying the themes of the script will always be something of an over-simplification but it is an important basic step.

As designers we need to look for ways the theme is expressed physically in the script. Is the theme expressed through an element of setting or a physical action? Does one character especially embody a theme? Do other characters reinforce or counterbalance this? In Shakespeare's *Romeo and Juliet* the theme of division or separation is one of the play's many interconnected themes. The theme of cultural, personal and spiritual separation is evoked *physically* through Shakespeare's use of walls, windows, gateways, extreme differences in height and other barriers. The theme is also expressed in *character* through the personality differences that divide the volatile Capulets and the relatively restrained Montagues—the poetic introspective Romeo at odds with the volatile Tybalt. It is suggested in *action* by the physical separation of the lovers in the balcony scene, in Romeo's banishment and in Juliet's false death all of which divide the lovers. And it is Juliet and Romeo's final separation from life that eventually brings the divided community together. It is exciting for us as designers to discover the way themes are made concrete and physical in this way. Here we are working with directly visual material sometimes referred to

SCRIPT ANALYSIS FOR DESIGN IDEAS

Why bother analysing a script? Why not just follow the written description at the beginning of the script?

There often *are* descriptions in the text, and they are sometimes very detailed. They might be how the playwright imagined the world of the play when they wrote the script, or they may be a description of the design from the play's first production. In either case these descriptions may have little relevance to today's audience. These days playwrights tend to keep their stage directions and descriptions of characters and settings to an absolute minimum, acknowledging that there is no fixed 'way' to stage their script. The creative team is encouraged to find their own visual interpretation from *within* the text, and to tailor this interpretation to the specific time, place and audience of their production.

- THEMES are the 'big ideas' explored in the script; the central ideas that unify the whole work. There might be a single or multiple themes; the theme may be simple or complex. The themes will be introduced early, and will be developed with more complexity and subtlety as the script unfolds.

- IMAGES are the 'mental pictures' the playwright uses to give tangible shape to their themes. (For example, Shakespeare employs three different images of the theme of light when Romeo says: 'But soft! What light through yonder window breaks?/ It is the East, and Juliet is the sun!/ Arise, fair sun, and kill the envious moon,' *Romeo and Juliet* II:II: 2–4.)

- SYMBOLS are elements in the script that explicitly represent an abstract idea or concept. (For example, a skull = death; a locked box = a secret.)

as *visual metaphors*. It is easy to see how these thematic elements can be translated into ideas for set, costume and lighting design. (The *Romeo and Juliet* concepts on pages 86, 88 and 90 illustrate how three designers have translated the script's visual metaphors into design ideas.)

In the case of music theatre, themes will be communicated musically, and there may be particular musical motifs that are linked with particular characters or thematic situations (known as *leitmotif*). If we are designing events, or other performances that do not have a formal written script the themes are likely to be explicit in the title, storyboard or synopsis.

IMAGES: Designers are visual thinkers and often respond to images and symbols first. We are particularly looking for recurring images, or a strong central image around which the work can be built. As our understanding of the script develops, we can progress from identifying the key images to observing how they are developed and used throughout the script. Continuing with our *Romeo and Juliet* example, we can tune into Shakespeare's constant poetic use of opposites—the way he juxtaposes the sun and moon, heat and cold, light and dark, high and low, love and hate, life and death. The recurrence of these images of opposites reaffirms a central theme of the play: *the unifying of opposites*. While Shakespeare's plays are jam-packed with images other plays may be built around a single image: in *The Crucible* Arthur Miller develops and explores the central image of the witchhunt to great dramatic effect, using it as an allegory of the anti-communist hysteria of his time, and on a deeper level exploring timeless themes such as intolerance, jealousy and the struggle of the rational against the irrational.

3.6

3.7

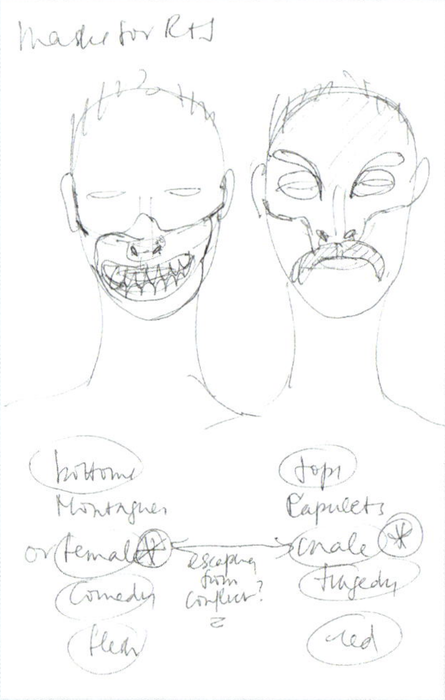

3.8

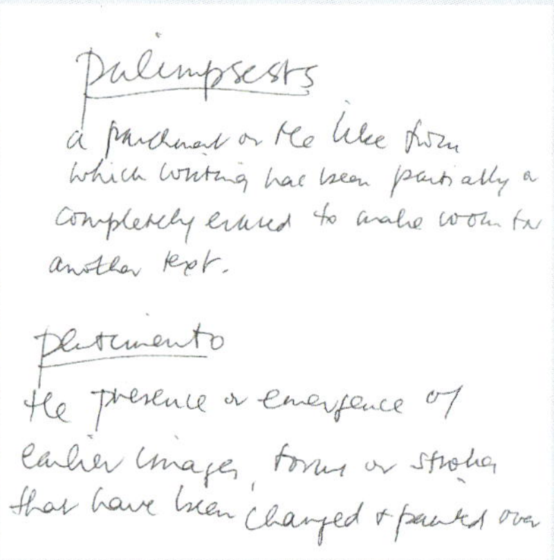

[handwritten sketches and notes: two face masks, labeled]
Master for R+J

bottom
Montagues
or female
Comedy
flesh

escaping
from
conflict?

top
Capulets
male
tragedy
red

3.9

[handwritten notes]
palimpsests
a parchment or the like from
which writing has been partially or
completely erased to make room for
another text.

pentimento
the presence or emergence of
earlier images, forms or strokes
that have been changed & painted over

Bill Haycock's preparatory collage (3.6, 3.7),
sketches and notes (3.8, 3.9) for *Romeo and
Juliet.* Bill has recorded his instinctive first
impressions of Shakespeare's *Romeo and
Juliet* in what he calls a 'concept collage'.
Already key ideas such as an aesthetic
richness (a response to the poetic richness
of the language of the script), the clash of
opposites (represented here in the dynamic
combination of blue and orange, and in the
exploration of psychological opposites in
the form of masks) and an interest in the
way surfaces can tell stories (palimpsest/
patina) are identified and recorded. Visual
memos such as these may be shared with
our director, or may remain part of our own
personal exploration.

DRAMATIC STRUCTURE: KEY TERMS

Plot: The narrative sequence of events and actions.

Subplots: Secondary plots introduced to complicate and enrich the main plot.

The climactic structure*

Exposition: The storytelling elements of character and plot are established; the story may be triggered by a significant event (catalyst) or a dramatic 'problem' that will need to be resolved.

Rising action: Twists and turns in the plot and subplots develop the themes of the script in complex ways to draw us deeper into the drama.

Climax: The most dramatic point. Events play out to a crucial turning point or reversal of fortune.

Falling action: The consequences of the reversal of fortune are played out with more complications and suspense.

Denouement: The final resolution or catastrophe which resolves the conflict and solves the problem set in the exposition.

Episodic structure: The episodic structure uses a series of self-contained scenes that may be only loosely connected. They may be put together out of chronological time sequence.

Musical structures: Sometimes a playwright might base their structure on a classical music structure such as a theme and variations, sonata or quartet.

Cinematic structure: Many short scenes (often set in many different locations) are 'cut' together in an unbroken sequence like in cinema.

Postmodern structure: An 'anti-structure' which may be complex, fractured or incomplete, or inconclusive.

* Freytag's 'pyramid' climactic structure: Gustav Freytag: *Die Technik des Dramas*, 1863

SYMBOLS: For the designer as for the audience there will always be a degree of subjectivity in reading images within a script; we will each have a slightly different sense of their meaning depending on our background—and this is a major factor in the rich process of interpretation. Symbols, however, are images that have a particular explicit meaning, universally understood by the whole audience. Playwrights usually use symbols cautiously so that their meaning does not become too obvious. Designers might choose to convert an image from the script into a physical symbol when the creative team wants the audience to clearly feel or understand an idea or concept in the production, as with Robert Kemp's use of the symbol of the forest (➡ The Crucible, *page 27*).

HOW IT WORKS *dramatic structure, focus, style, genre, conventions, the world of the play, spectacle, character, space*

Designers are usually practical people. We deal creatively with making things work. This area of analysis deals with the 'mechanics' of the script. There are a number of tools we can use to analyse how the script works. We might begin by using each of these tools separately, and then pull together our complete understanding later on.

What is the structure of the script?

DRAMATIC STRUCTURE is the shape of the script, and the design will be influenced by this shape. Usually a script will be broken up into units: scenes and /

or acts. These units are 'chunks' of storytelling, action, character development or thematic exploration. They are like chapters in a novel or verses in a song. It is worth investigating why the playwright has broken the script up as it is. Are they working within the accepted structure of their era? Are they adapting or playing with a common structure? Or are they creating their own structure?

Historically dramatic structure has developed over centuries of theatre, from the Greeks who favoured no break in the dramatic action, to the five-act structure used by Shakespeare, to the four-act structure developed by naturalists such as Ibsen in the late 1800s, to the three-act structure of many of the 20th century plays to the two-part structure of much of today's writing which is often shaped around the best dramatic point to place the interval. Contemporary playwrights may also experiment and develop their own individual structures.

Usually the audience will not consciously be aware of the dramatic structure, but for the designer, tuning in to it can help us think about how the script works and how we can help make it work.

A designer is looking first for the overall dramatic shape.

- Does it build steadily to a climax (climactic structure)?
- Is it made up of a number of self-contained episodes (episodic structure)?
- Is it a series of variations on a theme (a 'musical' structure)?
- Or made up of many short scenes in different locations ('cinematic' structure)?
- Or is the structure loose, fragmented or unpredictable (post-modern structure)?

We are also looking for the relationships between acts or scenes. Is one scene very different from the others? Do scenes at the end mirror those at the start? Are some scenes variations on others? Does the action move back and forth between two or three locations? Are there breaks in time, such as seasonal changes or flashbacks? Are there scenes of parallel action where we are watching two events play out simultaneously? If there is a climax where is it? By looking for the answers to these questions we are able to work with the dramatic structure. Our design can emphasise and amplify key aspects of the playwright's structural vision.

How does the script move?

PACE AND RHYTHM is concerned with how the script moves from one moment to the next: how fast or slow the narrative unfolds, and whether it slows down or speeds up at different points. Is it a gradual unfolding? Is the rhythm broken by slow sections or pauses where we are asked to be thoughtful and take stock? Is the rhythm regular and predictable, or do some scenes or characters within scenes break the pattern? Does the script erupt dramatically at some point? Is it a slow build to a climax that needs to be carefully sustained, or is the climax abrupt? Are there events that take us by surprise? The design can translate this

JOURNAL OF A PLAGUE YEAR AND *THE HAM FUNERAL,* **SET DESIGNER ANNA TREGLOAN, COSTUME DESIGNER FIONA CROMBIE**

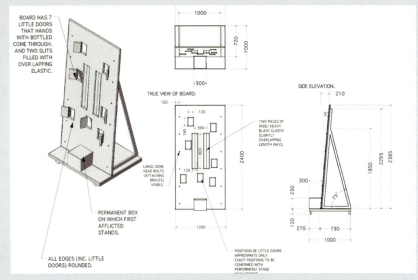

3.13

3.10

3.11

Anna Tregloan's set designs—CAD truck construction drawings for *Journal of a Plague Year* (3.10) and 3D Models for *Journal of a Plague Year* (3.11) and *The Ham Funeral* (3.12), which played in repertory— each playing on alternate nights, sharing the same core set elements with an ensemble cast. In her approach to designing these two productions Anna combined an astute eye for focusing and dramatising key moments in the drama with the practical need for fluidity within and between the two productions. She developed a series of easily moved trucked scenic elements, such as the bed, puppet booth and central raised stage platform that helped to establish the theatrical style of the two productions, and helped serve specific action and to distil a series of strikingly memorable images.

3.12

3.14

energy and give it physical shape. The design might subtly change as the play unfolds, or begin as a simple statement and become more disjointed or complex as the play develops; we might jump abruptly from one scene to the next or flow smoothly between scenes; we might swing back and forth between two opposing worlds, or be able to see all of the places where action happens all of the time; we might see a character gradually transform, or abruptly change as a result of a crisis. If it is a play (like one of Shakespeare's) that needs to move quickly from one scene to the next to sustain the dramatic pace, the design will need to provide for rapid scene changes that drive the energy of the plot forward.

What is the form and genre of the script?

FORM AND GENRE describe the literary style that the playwright is working within. The terms are often used interchangeably, but here I use the term *form* to describe the broadest shape: tragic or comic drama, music theatre, physical theatre, dance, circus, revue, street theatre. The form of the script will be obvious from the outset. I use the term *genre* to describe a more precise subcategory that has specific shared features. It might take more investigation to determine the genre: if the form is comic drama is the genre farce, or a comedy of manners? If it is a tragedy is the genre epic or melodrama? If it is an opera is it *opéra bouffe* or an operetta. You don't need to be an expert in literary analysis or be able to fully understand the technicalities or the genres' definitions, but it is helpful to broadly know where your script 'fits' stylistically. You might want to compare your script with others by the same writer, or other writers from the same era to get a sense of how genres work (➡ *Appendix A for a list of forms, genres and conventions, page 232*).

Playwrights in the past tended to work within the genres of their time, and it is useful to work out whether they are following the conventions of that genre as they were then understood. *Conventions* are defining stylistic characteristics; they are not rules to be followed, they are simply part of the script's dramatic language that the original audience would have unconsciously understood. For example, Shakespeare's audience understood the convention of the *aside* in which the actor speaks directly to the audience, and we all accept the convention in musicals that characters will break into song to express their feelings. The director may choose to work within the genre's conventions, to play with the conventions or to subvert them completely (➡ *Chapter 5: Precedents of Production Style, page 60*).

Contemporary and recent playwrights may experiment and develop their own unique form, but with scripts from any time past or present it is important for the designer to understand the form within which the playwright is working and to find a design style that complements it.

What are we supposed to be focused on?

FOCUS describes what the playwright wants the audience to pay attention to at any particular moment. As we get to know the script better, we can start to see how the playwright draws our attention to key elements within each scene. Is it the entrance of a major character? Do we see two characters who represent opposites together on stage for the first time? Is a central image introduced or developed? Is one speech particularly important to how the play unfolds? Does the focus shift from one character to another as the power-play unfolds? Our design can subtly or boldly help to direct the audience's eyes to where the focus needs to be (➡ *Further Thinking: Focus, page 113*).

Making a real impact on the audience

On a broader level, the designer is looking for key points or highlights in the script when all of the ingredients of a production coalesce into a potent expression of the script's ideas. I use the term *theatrical moment* to describe these key defining points. 'A *moment* is a game-changer. EVERYTHING is different after the moment.'[vi] A highly focused theatrical moment may be at the play's climax, but there could well be others that help to capture the audience's attention and keep them hooked. In Shakespeare's *Romeo and Juliet*, for example, the first meeting of the young lovers, the balcony scene, the separation and the final coming together of the warring families over their dead bodies are all significant theatrical moments around which a design could be structured. The brawl, Capulet's ball and the death of Tybalt and Mercutio are also moments—in this case moments of dramatic spectacle—and our design might be structured around moments such as these, interspersed with moments of intimacy.

A successful design will be a solution to presenting the *whole* play, but in the early phases of the process finding the key *theatrical moments*, and working to express their full potential can be a dynamic way of understanding and working with the script. The key theatrical moments can work as stepping stones that guide designers and the audience through the script's complex structure.

Let's get down to detail: the script breakdown

Directors, actors and almost anyone else working towards a deep understanding of the script would find an analysis of mood, meaning and how the script works useful. However, there are two areas for further investigation that are of particular importance to the designer: *space/setting* and *character.*

All of a designer's analysis and understanding about the play as a whole will ultimately be expressed through the set, prop and costume designs; they are the physical design—what the audience actually *sees*. If you are a systematic thinker who loves detail you might want to begin your analysis of the script here.

We will need to do a detailed reading or 'breakdown' of the script for specific information to inform these areas. We are working like a psychologist and a detective looking for any information about:

TIME: period/year, season, time of day. Time might be sequential or non-sequential: look for flash-backs or flash-forwards, or breaks in time.

SOCIAL CONTEXT: class and culture, politics and economics.

SETTING: locations, exits and entrances, quality of light. Places may be concrete, specific locations or poetic or abstract places that represent a state of mind or mood.

CHARACTER: age, gender, occupation, status, relationship to other characters, personality traits, doubling of roles, character development, scripted costume changes. Characters may be based on actual personages, or inventions of the playwright; they may be universal types or stereotypes or highly individual.

PROPS: hand props, furniture, costume props, set dressing—anything the characters physically use.

This is the minimum information a designer would need to begin designing a production. You might want to use a highlighter pen to mark information as you come to it in the script, or make separate lists for settings, props and character information. If you choose to make lists these will form the basis of organising your design and will be useful to yourself and the production team later on.

The information that is given in the dialogue is the most important to note, as this will be the information that the audience will hear. The audience will only be aware of the information in the stage directions if your production makes these instructions visible to the audience in the form of the set, costumes or the actors' performances. After you have scoured the dialogue for every design clue, you can go back over the stage directions and really investigate them for information that helps you. There might be aspects of the original playwright's stage instructions that fit with the interpretation you are evolving with your director or there may be details that spark an interest—revealing a way of staging the scene or thinking about a character that hadn't previously occurred to you. In his script *Pygmalion* George Bernard Shaw includes incredibly detailed descriptions of the settings and characters. He did this because he wanted his plays to be staged as realistically as possible as he was reacting against the shallow theatricality of the theatre of his day. When designing this play for a contemporary audience with a different theatrical background I initially skimmed over the stage directions and then ignored them completely while I focused on the information in the dialogue and investigated my emotional response to the script, what it means and how it works. Later, when I was well underway with the design I went back and read his stage directions very carefully and found information that helped me develop design detail relevant to our design (➡ *Case Study* Pygmalion – *Stage 2, pages 38–39*).

We discover different things with every reading. It is a good idea to re-read the script, either in part or as a whole, regularly during the design process to test your design ideas against what the script says. I aim to know the script at least as well as my director, so that I can connect their ideas to what I know in the script.

Script analysis is not something we do in isolation. By sharing insights with our collaborators we enrich each other's understanding of the script.

DESIGN INFORMATION FROM THE SCRIPT

So having completed our SCRIPT ANALYSIS what design information do we have to work with?

- Word pictures that describe the **mood** and **atmosphere**, and our emotional responses.
- **Mental pictures** imagined in our 'mind's eye'.
- A clear idea of what the playwright wants to communicate—**what we think it is 'about'**.
- A solid grasp of the **form and genre** the script is working within and whether the script follows conventions or has its own style.
- A shortlist of **themes**—identifying **central images**, **visual metaphors** or **symbols** that give physical shape to the themes.

- An understanding of how each scene relates to other scenes and how the **dramatic structure** shapes our experience of the drama.
- A sense of how fast or slow the action moves (**pace**), when and how the **rhythm** changes and the effect this has on the drama.
- A moment by moment understanding of what we should be **focused** on in every scene ...
- ....and the big, intense or **theatrical moments**.
- We know **when** and **where the script is set**, including the **social context**.
- We know each **character** in detail, and how they relate to each other.
- And we know what **props** are used by the characters in their actions.

Our combined knowledge will feed the interpretation and help to build the production concept.

While we focus our attention on the detail through the script breakdown it is important not to get lost in the detail—we want to be able to see the forest *and* the trees. We need to remember that there are big-picture issues concerning the characters, settings and their relationship to each other. We can tune into the big picture by using some of the other script analysis tools such as *focus*, *structure* or *theme*. Playwrights often communicate their ideas through their characters and settings, so it is worth investigating what these elements signify. Does one character embody a theme, image or idea? Who represents the opposite? How subtle or extreme are the contrasts? Can several characters be meaningfully grouped, and what are the defining qualities of the group? Do any of the characters have their own special place on stage that communicates the kind of person they are? Does the space change as they do? How intimate or epic are the spaces? To keep the big picture in mind while making detailed observations (such as the style of jacket a character might wear, or the sort of chair they may sit in) is one of the most vital challenges for a designer throughout the process.

A thorough script analysis covering the areas outlined above, when accompanied by a visual research process that feeds the imagination, could occupy one-third of the designer's time in pre-production, with the remaining time split between developing the designs and producing the resolved designs. During these later phases, the designer will be constantly experimenting and testing design possibilities against what they know about the script. A deep understanding of the script is the basis of a fruitful design process and a superior design, which enhances the production and results in a richer experience for the audience.

Case Study
Pygmalion— Stage 2:
Script Analysis

This sample script page from *Pygmalion* shows a 'breakdown' of the script looking for design information: time, social context, setting character and props. Information may be obvious or 'hidden'—requiring reasoning and deduction.

PYGMALION ACT ONE

THE DAUGHTER. Did you try?

FREDDY. I tried as far as Charing Cross Station. Did you expect me to walk to Hammersmith?

THE DAUGHTER. You havnt tried at all.

THE MOTHER. You really are very helpless, Freddy. Go again; and don't come back until you have found a cab.

FREDDY. I shall simply get soaked for nothing.

THE DAUGHTER. And what about us? Are we to stay here all night in this draught, with next to nothing on? You selfish pig –

FREDDY. Oh, very well: I'll go, I'll go. [*He opens his umbrella and dashes off Strandwards, but comes into collision with a flower girl who is hurrying in for shelter, knocking her basket out of her hands. A blinding flash of lightning, followed instantly by a rattling peal of thunder orchestrates the incident*].

THE FLOWER GIRL. Nah than, Freddy: look wh' y gowin, deah.

FREDDY. Sorry [*he rushes off*].

THE FLOWER GIRL. [*picking up her scattered flowers and re placing them in her basket}*]Theres menners f'yer! Te-oo banches o voylets trod into the mad. [*She sits down on the plinth of the column, sorting her flowers, on the lady's right. She is not at all a romantic figure. She is perhaps eighteen, perhaps twenty, hardly older. She wears a little sailor hat of black straw that has been exposed to the dust and soot of London and has seldom been brushed. Her hair needs washing rather badly: its mousy colour can hardly be natural. She wears a shoddy black coat that reaches nearly to her knees and is shaped to her waist. She has a brown skirt with a coarse apron. Her boots are much the worse for wear. She is no doubt as clean as she can afford to be; but compared to the ladies she is very dirty. Her features are no worse than theirs; but their condition leaves much to be desired; and she needs the services of a dentist*].

THE MOTHER. How do you know that my son's name is Freddy, pray?

Specific location in London. (There are so many of these references that London becomes a character in the play.)

Character note.

It is raining.

Time: night. Windy? Bleak?

Costume note, flimsy evening clothes?

(We can choose to follow or ignore stage directions.)

Lightning used to focus important action—a special 'theatrical moment' when the main character is introduced.

Scripted props

Mud?

She sits? On what?

Again we aren't obliged to follow these stage directions, but there is so much wonderful detail here! This is how Shaw imagined her at the time he wrote the play (1913–14)

Character note: Freddy's relationship to the Mother.

Scene breakdown

ACT I — COVENT GARDEN / ST PAULS - taxi/rain

INTERLUDE #1 — ELIZA'S LODGINGS ANGEL COURT — empty birdcage

ACT II i — HIGGINS' LABORATORY - next day

INTERLUDE #2 — SPARE BEDROOM / BATHROOM - bath

ACT II ii — HIGGINS' LAB

INTERLUDE #3 — LESSON? ELIZA CHANGING? Shopping spree?

ACT III — MRS HIGGINS CHELSEA APARTMENT - weeks later

INTERVAL

INTERLUDE #4 — EMBASSY BALL - 6 months later

ACT IV — HIGGINS' LABORATORY - later that night

INTERLUDE #5 — ELIZA'S BEDROOM → STREET → LONDON SQUARES - taxi

ACT V — MRS HIGGINS' CHELSEA APARTMENT

Costume plot: a scene by scene character breakdown

ACTOR	CHARACTER	ACT 1	INTERLUDE	ACT 2/1	INTERLUDE	ACT 2/2	INTERLUDE	ACT 3	INTERVAL	INTERLUDE	ACT 4	INTERLUDE
		Covent Garden	Taxi	Higgins'	bathroom	Higgins'	bedroom	Mrs Higgins'		embassy ball	Higgin's	bedrm/street
Melanie	Eliza	* #1	*	#1A	* naked QC	* #3	* # 3	* #4 QC		* #5	* #5	* #6 QC
Robert	Professor Higgins	* #1		* #1A		* #1A		* #1		* #2	* #2	
Bryan	Colonel Pickering	* #1		* #1A		* #1A		* #1A		* #2	* #2	
Chris S	Freddy Eynsford-Hill	* #1						* #1				* #1 QC
	Embassy Guest									# 2		
Kerith	Clara Eynsford-Hill	* #1						* #2				
	Embassy Guest									* #3		
Kaye	Mrs Higgins							* #2				
	Embassy Guest											
	Bystander	* #1								* #3		
Penny	Mrs Pearce			* #2	* #2	* #2						
	Embassy Guest									* #3		
	Bystander	* #1										
Carol	Mrs Eynsford-Hill	* #1						# 1A				
	Embassy Guest									* #2		
Chris B	Mr Doolittle					* #2						
	Embassy Guest									*#3		
	Bystander	* #1										
Chris H	Taxi Driver											
	Bystander	* #1	* #2 QC									
	Embassy doorman									* # 3		
	Policeman 2											* #4
Peter	Bystander	* #1										
	Embassy Host									* #2		
	2nd Taximan											* 1A
Brad	Bystander	* #1										
	Neppomuck									* #2		
	Policeman 1											* #3
Andrea	Bystander	* #1										
	Embassy Host									* #3		
	Parlormaid							* #2				

I know I rely hugely on my designer to create a conceptual unity in the work—to challenge me to eliminate unnecessary detail and deliver a vision that is resonant, practical and beautiful... My own rule for when a design is working is that I can feel myself wanting to play in it, because if I want to play in it the audience will as well. Neil Armfield, director

FURTHER THINKING
THE DIRECTOR–DESIGNER PARTNERSHIP

Now that we have come to terms with the script we are ready to begin developing our design interpretation—what we want the script to communicate and how we want to communicate with our audience.

It is impossible to talk about how an interpretation is developed without first looking at the relationship between the director and their designer. It is a central relationship in the creative development of a production, and for the design to develop creatively it needs to work well. There are many ways that it can work, but like every good relationship it will be based on respect, trust and good communication.

In our first meetings we will have worked out how we each like to work, and how we can best work together. We will have laid the foundation for our collaboration and begun sharing our ideas, considering one design possibility and then another as we have analysed the script. Soon we will also be poring over research images together. We might make many discoveries by consciously weighing up one approach over another, and we might make big leaps through intuition and by giving expression to our instinctive responses. We are gearing up—ready to firm up our interpretation and make decisions about the production concept and style.

In my experience most directors use the design process as a way of working out their conceptual approach to the production. The conceptual interpretation actually takes physical shape *through* the design, and directors generally rely on their designers to make the concept concrete. They rely on our specialist imaginative and practical skills as designers to turn ideas into things. A director might come to the process with a fully resolved idea of how they want to present the production (though this is rarely the case); more often they will begin their process with their designer in a more open-ended way—perhaps with some research images of their own, some personal insights into the script, or a set of ideas that they want to explore. They may have begun casting and may be quite advanced in developing their interpretation of the script. Or they might start empty-handed; just beginning their thinking on the production. They may or may not have a clear sense of how they want to present the production. Whatever the case, it is our job as designers to draw out the director's vision and enhance it with our own imaginative response—to find ways to develop and express the director's ideas in forms that the audience will actually *see*: the sets/spaces, costumes/characters and lighting/mood. There are no definitive rules about how this process should work, and every time we do it, it will work differently. If our director has a clear idea of how the production will work and has a visual imagination and good visual language then our job may be relatively straightforward, but if our director does not yet have a strong conceptual idea, or does not have a good visual imagination or strong visual language then the process will be very different: more explorative, supportive, reflective and sustaining.

… in working with directors it's often about listening to what's needed rather than what's wanted… 'I need a chair' may really mean 'I think they need to sit down or have an option not to always be standing'…

Bill Haycock, designer

It is important for us to remember that no matter how much we contribute to the process, it is the director's vision that holds it all together. The ideas expressed in the design will be the same ideas that will be carried through all the other aspects of the production, and it is the director's job to make sure it all comes together in a coherent way. It is part of our job as designers to make sure that the design 'fits' with all of the other production elements.

The best way for a designer to contribute to the interpretational process is to *show things* to the director. We are trying to convert words (the script and the director's words) into physical objects (sets, costumes, props). Showing examples of the shape the ideas could take will give the director a way of seeing what we are both thinking. We might show things by sharing research images, early design sketches, music, film references, fabric swatches, sketch models, shared trips to the art gallery, Photoshop visualisations, storyboard frames… *anything visual that helps to get the ideas out of our heads and into a physical form.*

I believe it is important to give the director *options*, so they can make clear choices about which is the best solution for their production. I know that some designers don't agree with me on this, and argue that giving directors choice only confuses them! It is true that in conversations with young designers the most common complaint about directors is that they are indecisive—unable to make up their mind about which is the best option. It is also true that in conversations with directors who are working with young designers the most common complaint is that the designers don't bring enough to the table—they don't bring enough material that they are committed to or enough options to explore. It is worth taking some time to really consider what's going on here. Clearly the solution to both of these issues (if they *are* an issue for you) lies in the *way* we offer our director choices.

- Offer options that are *real* options—you need to be able to present each choice as a valid response to the production.

- Propose each choice in the context of your interpretation—make it clear how each idea reveals some aspect of the production's meaning. Strong options will strongly support your own and the director's interpretations.

- With each choice that you offer ask questions that give you clear answers: Are we on the right track here? Is this how you imagined it? Is this what you meant when you said…? Do you prefer X or Y? Why?

- You might want to offer choices in some aspects of the design, but not in others that you already feel strongly committed to. Explain your reasons and let the director feel the confidence of your vision.

- Be prepared to let go of an idea if it does not form part of the director's vision of the production.

- Don't be afraid to let the director know which option/s feel the best to you, and why. You can lead the decision-making process through your own considered responses.

- Try to learn something from the options your director 'discards'—discovering what your production is *not* can be a useful step in establishing what it *is.*

- Give your director time to respond if they need it. Encourage them to take some of your design material away with them to think about.

- Affirm your need for clear decisions within your agreed timeframe, and keep following up with your director—they may need more information or clarification.

- Be clear in your own mind what you need decisions on, and what you can wait for.

A FRAMEWORK FOR WORKING TOGETHER

- Set up a trusting, relaxed relationship where you both feel confident in each other's abilities.
- Establish a common language by talking about other productions you have both seen, what you like and don't like in theatre, sharing your views on culture and life generally.
- Talk about how you each like to work and establish a process that will work for you both.
- Discuss the design timeframe, deadlines and agree on when, where and how you will meet.
- Share your first impressions and establish common ground.
- Confidently offer all your ideas; even the least promising ones—they may become important springing-off points.
- Share your insights from your script analysis, and follow up all leads. Reach agreement on key points of interpretation.
- Share your research material, and really interrogate the connections you both make to key images.

- Visit the theatre together and discuss the potential actor–audience relationship, scale, focus, sightlines and how the production will work in this space.
- Explore possible approaches to the production style, and establish the production style for your production.
- Establish the production concept in clear terms you all understand and check that each element of the design fits within the conceptual framework.
- Start working with the 'big picture' and progress towards resolving the design in greater detail.
- Offer options: design choices, multiple possibilities, variations, versions A, B, C and D.
- Test all your design ideas against the specifics of how your director wants to stage particular moments in the production: entrances, action, character development, focus within a scene, transitions, lighting.
- Use all of the visual tools at your disposal to communicate your design intentions: sketches, models, storyboards, fabric swatches.

- Be prepared for some aspects of the design to fall into place later, and talk about this with your director so you both know what you are working towards.
- Keep designing while they are thinking. The fact that the design process is still proceeding can help motivate the process, and will also mean you are able to offer up new options.

DESIGN MEETINGS are important stepping stones in the design process. They can be short and sweet or roll on for hours; they might be regular or intermittent; they might be when we need them or when we are least ready for them; they might be via telecommunications if either party is interstate or overseas; they might be the sole focus for either one of us, or part of a busy overlap of productions where we are just grabbling a few minutes together. However they happen we can make them more productive with good preparation, and by having a clear sense of what we want the meeting to achieve before it starts. It might be worth making the objectives explicit at the outset; the director may have a different goal, but if we each know what is expected we can usually achieve both their objectives and our own.

By the end of every meeting it needs to be clear what the next steps will be, and what is expected of everybody in the meantime.

BLOOD VESSEL, **SET DESIGNER ANDREW CARTER**
CONCEPT DEVELOPMENT

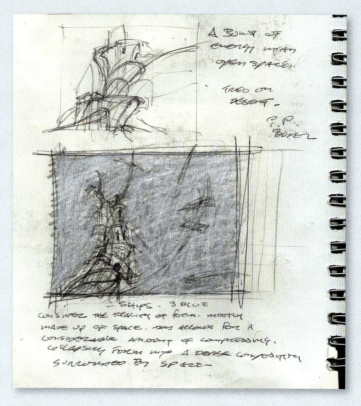

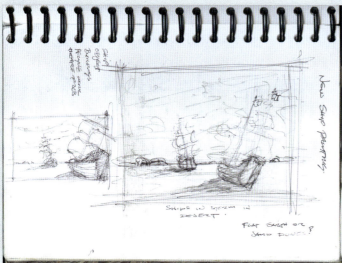

Andrew Carter's early set design conceptual sketches and construction drawings for the outdoor physical theatre production *Blood Vessel*.

These drawings became the basis of the production concept as he developed it with his director Rachael Swain. We can see the evolution of Andrew's design ideas around the visual metaphor of the ship as he and Rachael progress from loose ideas to specific solutions to the practical demands of the show. '... it became a type of adult playground—sails were hoisted and bits of it served as acrobatic supports or integrated lighting positions…'

During Blood Vessel *rehearsals we would 'road test' the visual ideas physically and conceptually allowing the metaphoric and physical nature of a design concept to find its fullest potential. Andrew would sketch constantly as we worked through the complexity of a visually imaginative and completely self-supporting structure designed for large-scale outdoor production—involving projection, aerial performance, gas fire effects, pyrotechnics and hard core touring. In the end Andrew's contribution to the dramaturgy of the work was significant and his background in engineering critical to its realisation.* Rachael Swain, director

Rachael and I would meet and talk for days. Our sources would often come from very obscure places, not always related to the themes. It could be a piece of poetry, music or a narrative from history. Because Blood Vessel *was concerned with the topic of settlement, immigration and the notion of relocation in people's lives, we looked at patterns of movement, modes of transport and natural ways of 'getting around'—the wind, sails, currents, boats and all the mystery and romance of sea travel. Rachael and I shared a common passion for the natural evolution of things and mostly were not concerned with being too judgmental about what eventuated. In the end it was a presentation of social evolution but done in an ethereal, poetic way that let the human body, music and design, tell the story.* Andrew Carter, set designer

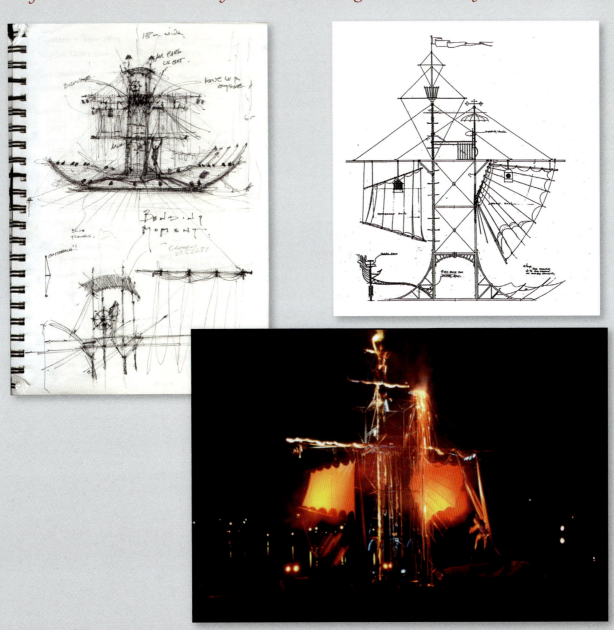

RESEARCHING TO FEED OUR IMAGINATION

The Season at Sarsaparilla (Set Designer Robert Cousins, Costume Designer Alice Babidge)

Our research process can take us far, wide and deep. In this chapter we look at why and how we research, and how we can use our research material to feed the creative process.

When you research left of centre—far beyond the commonplace—
you are rewarded tenfold...

Judith Hoddinott, designer, drama teacher

One of the joys of performance design is that each time we start a project we are exploring a completely new world; meeting new characters in completely new situations. The script guides us in this exploration and our research inspires us.

WHY RESEARCH?

By researching deeply and widely we are doing four important things.

- Feeding our imaginations. We are visual artists and visual imagery stokes our creative furnace.
- Providing ourselves with visual images that help us share our design ideas with our collaborators. Showing an image makes it much easier for our director to see what we are talking about.
- Providing ourselves with specific visual source material that helps us develop the detail of our designs: who the characters are, when and where they are. We become 'experts' in their specific cultural niche.
- Deepening our understanding of the background of the script—cultural, political and social issues or ideas that influenced the playwright and may influence our audience.

Research is easy. It should be pleasurable and stimulating and useful. I suggest you start early and dip into your picture file frequently. It is a good idea to research while you are doing your script analysis as the two processes inform and enrich each other, and the aesthetic pleasure of immersing yourself in inspiring imagery helps to balance all the analytical 'head' work.

WHAT ARE WE LOOKING FOR?

We are particularly looking for *visual* information. A picture is worth a thousand words, and with a few great pictures we almost don't have to open our mouths.

We may want to start by casting our research net wide, looking for images that capture:

- the mood or atmosphere of the script
- visual qualities such as colours, textures or images that express our early impressions
- particular themes identified from our script analysis

- conceptual ideas developed with our director
- other places or times the script could be set
- architectural references, spaces and environments
- costume references, real people
- visual styles such as brutalism, impressionism, fantasy, surrealism and expressionism that might influence how we present our design ideas to the audience (➡ *Further Thinking, page 74*).

Anything that helps to stimulate our imagination and clarify our design vision is useful.

Alternatively we might want to begin by researching the context or 'world' of the script as it was imagined by the playwright. Think of this as any aspects that would influence the way people live or dress:

- the period in which the script is set
- the location(s) in which it is set
- the cultural background of the characters.

We can also research the background to the script: the times in which it was written: social, political or cultural events that influenced the playwright, and other scripts and/or writers from the same period. The playwright's personal life circumstances and philosophy and critical writing about their work may also be useful.

Even if our script is set in our own time we can't assume that we do not need to undertake research. Research can help us zone in on the particular culture or subculture at work in the script. This subculture may be very different from our own background. The audience also knows their own time very well, and it will register with them immediately if aspects of our design don't ring true.

Reflecting on the way people live today can also make us more aware of the subtle mix of periods and subcultures that are always at play in any era. A teenager, for example, might be wearing the most current fashion, but their parents will be wearing clothes influenced by previous trends and their grandparents' clothes will be influenced by even earlier fashions. Similarly, the spaces in which we live and work reflect a range of periods and cultural influences. When we are researching it is a good idea to be quite broad in how we define the period and cultural background of our script to take account of this range.

Our research can be more specific and targeted as we tailor it to our own production concept:

- the specifics of the world of our production
- design detail relevant to the set and costume designs
- samples of fabrics and set materials you may actually use in your completed design.

WAYS OF RESEARCHING

When we start researching we often don't really know what we are looking for. So how can we start? There is no 'best way' to start. Different designers will be turned on by different kinds of material, but you could try:

THEMATIC RESEARCH: Your script analysis will have identified several themes. Pick one of these and look for as many different visual versions of this theme as possible. For example, with *The Crucible* we might be interested in the theme of a divided community. We might explore the way a highway, river or railway track can divide a community or the way clothing such as uniforms visually segregate one group from another. There will also be non-literal, metaphoric possibilities, such as images of a knife slicing... a torn page... a cracked footpath...

FREE-RANGING RESEARCH: Go to the Q (quarto) and F (folio) section of the photography and art books in a good library and pull out one book after another, just flipping through them while you are thinking about some aspect of the script. When an image makes you stop and have a second look bookmark it and move on. When you have a stack of bookmarked pages, go through them and look for common threads or visual themes.

BACKGROUND RESEARCH: This is the easiest kind of research, so you might want to start here. Look up the playwright. Find out what was influencing them: the politics of their time, the current of social and cultural events. If the script is based around a particular social, political or personal issue research this issue so that you understand the forces at work in the drama.

WHERE CAN WE LOOK?

The knack with research is to cast the net wide: look in as many different places as you can, and when you have found a reference source that inspires you, go in deep. You will find that different research sources are good for different phases of the design process, but they will all be worth investigating.

- First-hand (primary) research is the best kind. Your phone-camera is your best research friend because you have a camera with you wherever you go. Photograph places, people, objects or surfaces that inspire you. These images are of real value because they interpret the world of the script through the world you and the audience live in.

- Talk to people who may have experienced aspects of the script's subject matter. These first-hand experiences really help immerse you in the project and make it real.

- Exhibitions of art, design, fashion or costume in galleries and museums will expose you to some of the best-quality research material, and with each visit you will also be exposed to other cultural references that may help you think 'outside the box'.

- Visiting buildings that are of the period, or inspire you because of the way they use space, or their surfaces, or sense of scale can be a great way to start to visualise the spaces the characters might inhabit.

- Fabric swatches and architectural samples are great ways to start really coming to terms with colour and texture.

THE SEASON AT SARSAPARILLA, SET DESIGNER ROBERT COUSINS, COSTUME DESIGNER ALICE BABIDGE

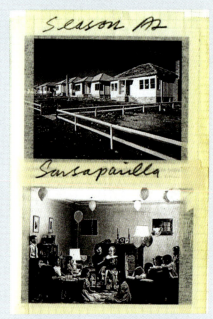

4.1

4.2

4.3

4.4

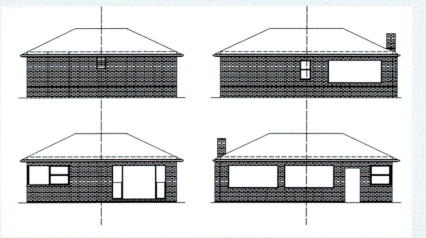

4.5

Extracts from Robert Cousins' research journal for *The Season at Sarsaparilla* (4.1–4.3), set construction drawing (4.5), rehearsal and production photographs (4.4, 4.6). Robert's research for *The Season at Sarsaparilla*, took him back to old family photographs and the memory of his own childhood home, photographing in the streets that playwright Patrick White re-imagined as the iconic Australian suburb of 'Sarsaparilla', and exploring period real estate advertising. His painstaking recreation of a brick veneer suburban home, based on this research, was installed in the rehearsal room, where the director and cast explored simultaneous projection as a way of recontextualising and reinterpreting the idea of a suburban reality. In the theatre the house was set up on a revolve, with projection screens at each side of the stage, and took on a hyper-real, dreamlike presence.

4.6

- Books are still the best secondary source of imagery. A well-stocked library, especially one at a tertiary institution that teaches design subjects, is a goldmine. The Q (quarto) and F (folio) large-format picture books are particularly useful as they have large high-quality images that you can really immerse yourself in:
    - photography {Dewey call no 770s}
    - art, by art movement {700} or by individual artists {759}
    - history of architecture {720}
    - history of costume {391}
    - fashion design {746}
    - interior design {747}
    - furniture design {749}
    - graphic arts {760s}
    - decorative arts {745}

- The internet is convenient; you can cover a lot of territory quickly and the images are easy to save, but you need to work hard to get really useful images. You need to be very precise with your search title and start using the higher-end picture libraries to get past the obvious, lacklustre and clichéd.

- Magazines are useful because they tap into popular culture at its most current, and they are often cheap enough that you can tear out the images that inspire you.

- Advertising images can be inspiring. The best ones will often distil quite complex ideas into visual images that are easily understood.

- Photo albums or memoirs from the period provide more personal, 'real' references and can be a treasure trove of detail.

- Films are a useful point of reference, particularly when considering visual style and genre. You can use your computer to take screenshots of DVDs so these references are easy to share with your collaborators.

Histories of architecture, interior design and costume are useful as an overview of a period, but are often quite narrow in their focus and tend to only show us what was in fashion (especially with the wealthy). To understand these limitations take a minute to consider the difference between the clothes worn by models in fashion magazines today and what we see people actually wearing on the street. If we designed a contemporary production using only fashion references it would not feel 'real'. Photographic collections give us a much better idea of the way people really lived, and observing real people in real life is even better.

You cast quite a wide net and gradually pare it back until you end up with the key elements.

Pip Runciman, designer, about researching her production of *Romeo and Juliet*
(➜ *Romeo and Juliet* Concept, pages 86–87)

HOW DO WE USE IT?

The key here is that we do use it. There is no point assembling a great body of research material if it stays unused in a pile under our desk or stored in our computer. Make your images go to work for you.

- Select 'key' images—the ones that really inspire you—and keep them handy.
- Pin up the best images in your workspace so you can keep referring to them and they become part of your design process.
- When you get 'designer's block' flip through your research file to stimulate a fresh line of thinking.
- Assemble a research folder that is organised in a way that best suits you: feature the images that you are most likely to refer to in discussions with your collaborators. Make sure you know where everything is. You might want to create categories, for example, divide the folder by character or scenes. The folder may be digital if your laptop or tablet are familiar tools, or it might be a ring binder that you keep adding to.
- Make sure you have your research folder with you at every design meeting with your director and other collaborators. Have the folder open and 'talk to' the images you have collected so your collaborators can really *see what you mean.*
- Filter out the images that are no longer relevant so the folder truly reflects the production you are designing. But don't throw them out. You never know when that picture of the rusted mediaeval hinge or the snakeskin gloves or the desolate space under a freeway fly-over will come in handy!
- Key research images will become important references for the production team as they set about making the costumes, props and sets for the show. Our research images will be a valuable resource for them—providing specific detail or useful background information.

We might spend a week or more intensively researching at the start of our process. Soon we will have a selection of images that start to represent the *visual language* of our design approach. Our particular feel for tone, texture, colour, atmosphere and style will be evident when we lay out our key images on our workbench. Our images will reflect back to us how our design ideas are taking shape, and we will be able to use our images to share this perspective with the rest of our creative team.

We can find ourselves in unusual places having curious conversations in the quest to source the most valuable research material. As a costume designer I have called on a tattoo parlour, the NSW Forensic Office, the Church of England in the UK and travelled through the Pitjantjatjara Lands studying Australia's Indigenous for an upcoming play. Julie Lynch, designer

4.7 Costume designer Julie Lynch uses a large-format folder for her research on *Noises Off*, keeping all of her reference material organised and at hand to share with her director, other designers, the cast and the costume production team.

Case Study
Pygmalion — Stage 3:
Research

Finding inspiration in museums, books, games, films,
period magazines, on-line and in life.

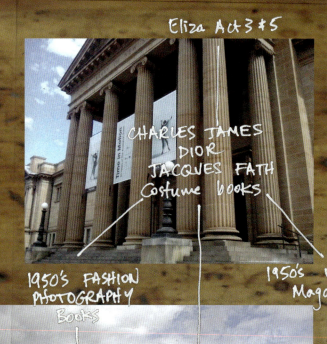

Eliza Act 3 & 5

CHARLES JAMES
DIOR
JACQUES FATH
Costume books

1950's FASHION
PHOTOGRAPHY
Books

1950's
Mags

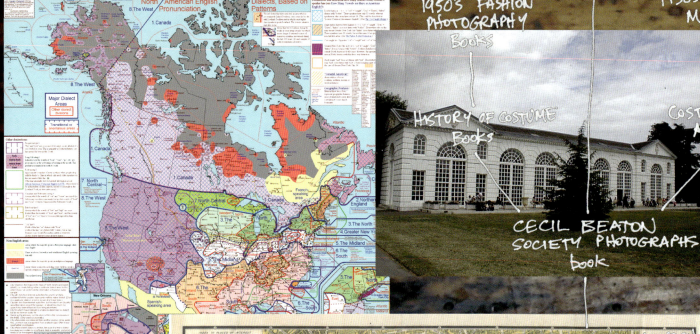

HISTORY OF COSTUME
Books

COSTUM
A/t

CECIL BEATON
SOCIETY PHOTOGRAPHS
book

GREAT HOUSES OF LONDON
interior design books

20th CENTURY
CLASSICAL
REVIVAL
interior design books

GEORGIAN
ARCHITECTURE
Adam, Wyatt
architecture

1920's & 1930's CINEMAS

KEW GARDENS
GLASSHOUSE

Mrs Higgins' Ottoman

Higgins, Act 2

VINTAGE MENS
TAILORING MANUAL
Specialist library

WILLIAM MORRIS
ARTS & CRAFTS MOVEMENT
Books

THE ENGLISH
GENTLEMAN
book

ENGLISH ECCENTRICS
book
online search

...BITION
...

...NGUAGE DIALECT MAP
...ual Museum browsing

GEORGE BERNARD SHAW
playscript preface/online

...ON ETHNOGRAPHIC MAPS
online search

VINTAGE MAPS OF LONDON
online search

...NOPOLY BOARD
GAME

LANDMARKS OF LONDON
Hanover Square
St Pauls Covent Garden

...Colour Coding Class
Boundaries

COLONNADED PORTICO OF
LOCAL PUBLIC BUILDING
Photographic 'recce'

Act one Set

PYGMALION RESEARCH NET
THEMES AND CONCEPT

- Ethnographic language map (museum). Showing the division of the country into language zones – just as Professor Higgins does
- Monopoly board game (personal collection). The colour-coding of the British class system (dark blue = wealthy, brown = poor)

THE 'WORLD'

- Cecil Beaton society photographs (book, personal collection). The eccentric Sitwell family – link to Higgins
- *Enlightenment* film (watched again on DVD). An insight into the English class system; 1930s period was a dead-end
- London landmarks (internet). St Paul's, Covent Garden, Chelsea
- August Sander (photographs book, personal collection). Clear delineation of class in clothing; 1920s period was a dead-end
- Dorothy Parker, New York satirist (radio documentary). Insight into 1950s high society
- Irving Penn (photographs book, personal collection). Tradespeople photographed in the 1950s – link to Doolittle
- Fashion of the '50s (museum costume exhibition). Insight into 1950s clothing as a signifier of class and confirmation of the choice of 1950s as the period for this production.

VISUAL STYLE

- Monochrome fashion image (tear-out from fashion magazine). Strong colour-coding of scenes affirmed
- Various artists books (library and personal collection). David Hockney (dissecting society), Matisse (clear colours), 'Eric' 1950s fashion illustrator (graphic style)

DESIGN DETAIL

- 1920s street map of London (found on internet, and sourced as hardcopy). Basis of artwork for the set
- 1950s fashion designers Dior, Fath books (personal collection and library). Specific reference for Eliza and other guests at the embassy ball and Mrs Higgins
- Kew Gardens glasshouse (internet). Reference for Act III windows
- 1920s and 1930s cinemas book (library). Reference for classical revival furniture, leading to design of the ottoman and Higgins' club chair
- William Morris (books and online references). Arts and Crafts furniture, leading to design of Higgins' table
- Museum furniture (visit to two museums). The idea of Higgins as a cultural bowerbird
- Silk satin fabric swatch (from fabric wholesaler). Search for the perfect shade of red for Eliza's ball gown
- 1950s knitting patterns – specific reference for Clara's twinset
- Humphrey Spender, photographer (book, library). Specific reference for Covent Garden workers, leading to Eliza Act I and Doolittle
- Voice-recording equipment (on-line). Prop references for scripted props used by Higgins
- Many, many more strands to the *Pygmalion* research 'net'.

Madama Butterfly (Designer Bill Haycock)

This chapter examines different stylistic approaches to forging our own unique way of visually communicating our ideas.

ALSO IN THIS CHAPTER—FURTHER THINKING: Developing a Visual Language, page 74

Every production creates its own grammar,
its style handbook. Once set, those rules must be adhered to.

James Waites, theatre critic [vii]

How will we tell our story, engage our audience, draw them in and communicate our ideas? Do we want to set the production in a world the audience will recognise, or in an imaginary place? Do we want to play on the audience's emotions or challenge and provoke them, or just 'make 'em laugh'? Do we want the production's meaning to be absolutely clear, or more open to interpretation? Do we want to strip everything back to bare essentials, or create a rich, detailed stage picture? Do we want to work with the style the playwright uses or develop our own way of telling the story? The choices are endless. How do we decide?

At the time of writing my theatre-going took in a realist family drama, a severely minimalist revival of a classic, a new play shaped around a powerful visual metaphor, a dance work that playfully mixed styles, a performance installation shaped by new technology and a poetic/atmospheric classic. Is any one of these choices of production style more valid than another? Why has the director chosen one approach over another?

When we ask these questions we are talking about the *style* of the production. Style is the *way* we communicate our ideas to the audience, and we are now ready to explore the options and make some decisions about the way *we* want to communicate *our* ideas on this production to *our* audience.

Style is an incredibly variable, controversial and misunderstood ingredient in our work as theatre-makers. Some designers think that designing is all about style while others regard style as almost a dirty word. Style is talked about in the vaguest possible terms: 'a little bit abstract... not really realistic... minimalistic... kind of stylised...'. What are we trying to communicate when we describe our designs in such imprecise ways? Certainly we can make our intentions clearer by backing up these vague and almost meaningless terms with some strong reference images, so we can say 'as real as this Larry Burrows (documentary) photograph... as stripped back as this Jeffrey Smart painting... deconstructed like the Bilbao Guggenheim Museum... stylised like this art deco textile'. But we can go further: by seeing style as an expression of culture, by learning where styles come from and how they relate to each other we can meaningfully discuss style options, weigh up the choices, intelligently mix stylistic approaches or evolve our own unique stylistic interpretation.

There are a number of different ways of talking about style—it has different meanings in different contexts. We might talk about the *literary style* of the script, or our own *personal design style*, or the *visual style*, or the *conceptual/production style*. All four kinds of style interconnect and influence each other, and all four kinds of style come together in the design, and become part of the way we communicate to our audience.

THE SCRIPT'S (LITERARY) STYLE is the style that the playwright is working within, more accurately known as the *form and genre*. Over thousands of years performance has slowly evolved from ritual, to Greek tragedy and comedy, to mediaeval liturgical drama and passion plays, to commedia dell'arte, to the complex dramas of Shakespeare, to court masques, revenge tragedies and comedies of manner, to melodramas, to realist dramas and on and on to our own time. At any time in this evolution of performance the audience would have understood that there was basically only one way to 'do' performance. Theatre-makers were generally limited to the form and genre of their day, and these forms and genres each had their own set of 'rules' (conventions) that the audience would have understood. But theatre has evolved because there has always been someone prepared to bend the rules or experiment with different approaches in the quest for a better way to connect with their audience. Sometimes this process was led by writers, at other times by directors, theoreticians, actors, producers or designers.

We will have identified our script's literary style—its form and genre—as part of our script analysis. Our design will be a sensitive response to the literary style but we might adopt it, adapt it, subvert it or mix it with other forms or genres, rather than being conventional and simply following the conventions (➡ *Chapter 3, page 23 and Appendix A, page 232 for more on the playwright's style: forms, genres and conventions*).

I tend to 'cast' designers in much the same way I would cast an actor. If it feels like it will play to their strengths, or at least that there will be an interesting point of intersection between the energy of the designer and the heart of the work. Neil Armfield, director

OUR PERSONAL STYLE is like our own design fingerprint. Every designer will have their own particular way of going about designing a production. Just as for any other visual artist our social and cultural background, our tastes, skills, methodology and perceptions will be reflected in our work, sometimes subtly, sometimes unmistakably. Some designers are known for a particular way of using texture or colour or space or detail, others for a particular aesthetic and others for working in a particular theatrical form. Our personal design style will influence how we communicate our ideas to our audience, as will the personal style of the director and other members of the creative team.

THE 'STYLE WARS'—1880–1920

Illusionism was the established theatrical style for four centuries up to the 1880s. Audiences were spectators, happy with the make-believe that painted trees were a forest and painted bricks were a wall. Theatre was popular, entertaining and contrived.

In the mid-1880s **realism** swept through the arts and revolutionised how people saw the world. Influenced by psychology and the new technology of photography it took over theatre, led by writers such as Ibsen and Chekhov and director Stanislavski's ground-breaking work with actors. The *illusion* of reality was out, and psychologically true and photographically detailed 'slice-of-life' realism was in. Productions were based on careful observation of human behaviour and real life. Theatre was changed forever.

Barely had the 'fourth wall' of realism been erected than by 1910 the pioneering designers Edward Gordon Craig, Adolphe Appia and Robert Edmond Jones were tearing it down in favour of **metaphor**: suggestion instead of description, the poetic instead of the literal, the universal rather than the specific, elevating the spirit rather than reproducing the everyday. Their movement was to become known as New Stagecraft and it encouraged the audience to engage imaginatively with the stage world.

Hardly had the curtain gone up on the beautifully atmospheric New Stagecraft productions than by 1920 the new kids on the block—Brecht, Piscator and Meyerhold—were reinventing theatre again. Their highly **dynamic** theatre experiments built productions up from the bare essentials in their efforts to actively engage, challenge and provoke the audience: harsh white light exposed the workings of the production, rudimentary constructivist structures replaced representational sets and emblematic costumes replaced period accuracy. Their quest to regain the primal power of ceremony and ritual were taken up by Kantor and Grotowski, and then later by Peter Brook, Robert Wilson and companies such as Théâtre du Complicité, and Cheek By Jowl.

Personal style is something that develops over time. It will be shaped by our background and the things we find easy (or not) and the opportunities we experience (or don't experience). It is by definition a very individual quality and there is little value in generalising about it here other than to make one observation: remarkably we can be the last to recognise our own style—to us it is just the most natural way to design. Others will recognise it in us; in fact directors will employ us on the basis of their perception that our style is the right one for a particular production. You might want to consider whether to develop your understanding of your personal style by comparing your work to other designers, or you may just prefer to happily and unselfconsciously continue to do what you do well.

THE VISUAL STYLE is the visual language of the production—the way it *looks*. Visual style is the way artists and designers communicate their ideas. It is the visible 'skin' of the production.

When we explore different possibilities of visual style we will consider different degrees of reality and unreality, abstraction or exaggeration, varying degrees of theatricality, or we might experiment with different visual approaches, such as impressionism, brutalism or expressionism. As visual artists this is our language. It is the language of tone, texture, colour, form, contrast, balance and focus, and it makes sense for us to know how to 'speak' this language and use it to communicate the ideas of the production. It is such a big area of what designers do that I have given it its own section (➡ *Further Thinking, page 74, and Appendix B, page 234*).

THE PRODUCTION STYLE is the overall conceptual approach. It is the director's language—the 'big picture' of how the production will communicate its ideas to the audience. In past times there would typically have been one prevailing production style, and writers, directors, designers and performers would all have worked within that style (for example commedia dell'arte or melodrama) and would all have been working to the same set of rules. Today there is no single set of rules that we all have to follow. We are able to draw on the best of performance traditions from all over the world and from all of history. What an amazing rich, deep pool of experience to work with!

PRECEDENTS OF PRODUCTION STYLE

For most of the past the way of presenting theatre has been a slow progressive development. Occasionally fierce rebellion and a sense of urgent exploration have led to a rapid turning over of one style for another. The four decades from 1880 to 1920 were such a time (➡ *Box, page 59*) and in many ways the furious explorations of those forty years has established the stylistic framework for us today—four essentially different pathways to presenting a production. I use the terms *illusionist, realist, metaphoric* and *dynamic* to describe these four pathways—four 'big picture' ways to tell our story and communicate with our audience. Fifty years later, in the 1970s and '80s *post-modernism* added a fifth pathway.

5.1

Inigo Jones's design drawings for an illusionistic court masque: *Salmacida Spolia*, 1640. The courtiers were dressed as deities and in a spectacular finale were revealed in a series of clouds above the stage. The stage is framed by sliding wings of perspective scenery representing 'a great city'.

5.2

Hugh Colman's set model for the ballet *Swan Lake*. 'This "traditional" *Swan Lake* grew from a response to Tchaikovsky's music which [choreographer] Stephen Baynes and I felt was deeply, perhaps irrevocably, connected to its 19th century influences, in particular the whole Romantic movement and its ideas about the place of man in nature.' Hugh Colman, designer

ILLUSIONISM invites the audience to pretend that what they see is real when they know that it is not. The audience is invited into a game of theatrical make-believe, and this style has in fact become synonymous with the term 'theatrical'. Illusionism celebrates the 'art' of artificiality and was *the* style of European theatre for four centuries up to the end of the 19th century with cloths and flat scenery painted to depict architectural and natural settings in pictorial 3D. Illusionistic trompe l'oeil painted scenery is no longer the prevailing theatrical style but illusionism is still alive and well in classical theatre traditions such as romantic ballet and opera and in contemporary performance in the form of projected pictorial scenery and photographic digital scenery. Illusionism might be chosen as a production style when the director wants to declare the theatrical artifice of the script or explore themes such as pretence and deception. It will often be used in an ironic or metaphoric way, when an overt sense of theatricality is required. For the designer much of the challenge of illusionism is the skill of the illusion—to cleverly draw the audience into the make-believe.

REALISM aims for an exact representation of life through the accumulation of closely observed detail. The audience is drawn into a complete world—a microcosm in which they 'identify' and empathise with the characters because they believe that the characters and their world are as real as themselves. We now take realism for granted in film, where it has a stylistic stranglehold, but in theatre our attitudes to realism are ambivalent, to say the least. Almost from its inception realism has been under attack for limiting the imaginative potential of

5.3
Shaun Gurton's scale model for *Red*. *Red* portrays the real-life artist Mark Rothko at work in his studio with the intense and exacting documentary reality of a 'bio-pic', making realism a logical choice for the creative team. The detail in Shaun's 1:25 scale model acts as a visual template for everyone involved in the production.

5.4
The Lower Depths, Moscow Art Theatre 1902. Set designer Viktor Simov, working under Stanislavski's direction, recreated the impoverished conditions of a Russian shelter for the homeless in painstakingly realistic detail.

the production and stifling the theatrical heart of performance. But despite ninety years of ongoing criticism realism is still alive and well. Why is this? Audiences seem to like it—they feel connected to the characters and understand the exact context. Is this a bad thing? Some scripts only make sense if we understand the specific situation the characters are in, for example a particular subculture or moment in history, and realism would be a logical choice for a director for such a production. For designers realism is all about getting the detail right. Even a spare realist design will be absolutely specific and carefully observed in the detail (➡ *Further Thinking, page 128; Box, page 95*).

METAPHORIC is my catch-all term for production styles that suggest and evoke rather than literally represent. The metaphoric approach frames the production around symbolic, metaphoric, poetic, atmospheric or emblematic elements that aim to express the ideas in elemental and universal terms. The set design will often be a physical representation of the production's 'big idea'. The audience is encouraged to imaginatively engage with the production by 'reading' the metaphor, leading to a deeper understanding of the themes and ideas. Some commonly explored metaphors are the trap, the dream, the game, the stage within a stage, the machine and heaven/hell. Metaphoric productions dominated Western theatre for the whole of the second half of the last century and often had a quality of being 'stripped back' to simpler more expressive forms.

Some highly regarded designers in this mode include Adolphe Appia, Robert Edmond Jones, Edward Gordon Craig, Jo Mielziner and Josef Svoboda. For the director the metaphor can act like a visual 'hook' that grabs the audience's attention and puts them in a receptive frame of mind. It is also a very clear way of making a directorial statement about the work—offering the audience a specific line of interpretation. For the designer part of the challenge is negotiating how subtle or distinct the metaphor should be.

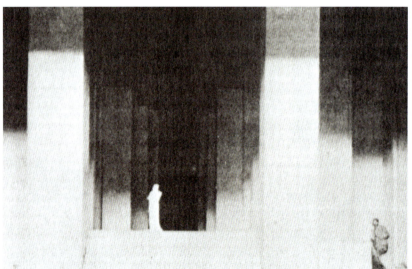

5.5
Director/Designer Edward Gordon Craig's scale model for the final scene in the Moscow Art Theatre's production of *Hamlet*, 1913. Craig's non-representational, modular set designs and highly influential writings on theatre, together with those of Adolphe Appia, are regarded as forming the foundation of modern theatre design. They 'called for a simplicity, suggestion, abstraction and grandeur within the context of a three-dimensional sculptural setting that would unify the performer and the stage space'. [viii]

CHOOSING A PRODUCTION STYLE

The director may begin the design process having already decided on the production style, or it may evolve through the design process. If you are a student designing a project you will be the one who decides on the production style for your project. In any case the designer will be actively involved in shaping the production style to the specific needs of the production. What are our options?

ILLUSIONISM: Make-believe and pictorial fantasy: see images 5.1 and 5.2.

REALISM: Photographically real: see images 5.3–5.5.

METAPHORIC: Framed around a poetic, metaphoric image: see images 5.6 and 5.7.

DYNAMIC: 'Raw theatre' stripped back to functional and expressive essentials: see images 5.8, 5.9, 5.13 and 5.14.

POST-MODERN/MIXING STYLES: Juxtaposing elements to add layers of meaning: see images 4.4 and 4.6.

Some other strategies of production styles include:

- resetting the period
- contemporising (setting it now)
- mixing periods within a production
- swapping it into a different genre or a hybrid mix of different genres
- total theatre: mixing media
- mixing cultures.

Our director might use different terms, or have their own understanding of production style. The best way of reaching a common understanding is to show each other examples. We might refer to other productions, films or artworks to help share our understanding and begin to shape the production style for our production.

DYNAMIC productions assume quite a different approach to the audience. The audience is seen as active participants in the performance rather than passive spectators. The audience of a dynamic production is challenged or provoked to think about what the production has to say—Brecht referred to this as 'tears from the brain'. There are many individual practices of dynamic production but they have important things in common. They will often work to renegotiate the actor–audience relationship by physically setting up the performance space in a way that forces the audience into a more active role.

In dynamic productions the stage picture is not so much stripped back, as built up from an empty space with the use of very basic, functional elements that are there because, and only because, they help the production work. For the director a dynamic approach will often involve a degree of collaborative experimentation through rehearsal, and the way of staging the production might be the result of improvisation, trial and error or theoretical exploration. For the designer the process is an open-ended one, often being intensively involved in the development of the whole production through the rehearsal process. The design will often have a dramaturgical function: shaping the actual meaning of the production. Some of the best-known models of dynamic theatre were each shaped by the individual philosophies of their director:

- Bertolt Brecht: 'Epic Theatre'
- Antonin Artaud: 'Theatre of Cruelty'
- Jerzy Grotowski: 'Poor Theatre'
- Peter Brook: 'The Empty Space'
- Tadeusz Kantor: the set conceived as a 'Machine for Acting'.

A work of art can influence only through the imagination. Therefore it must constantly stir the imagination… Schopenhauer[ix]

5.6
Sally Jacobs' design for Peter Brook's *A Midsummer Night's Dream*, Royal Shakespeare Company, 1970. This highly influential production stripped the setting back to a simple white box in which performers drew on the language of circus, and the stage lighting and technicians were left exposed.

5.7
Dale Ferguson's set and costume designs for the opera *A Midsummer Night's Dream*. Dale uses metaphoric, scenic and costume elements to suggest the fantasy forest of the fairies Oberon and Titania. Spidery runnels of paint evoke upside-down forest foliage and webs of forest creatures; Oberon 'flies' overhead; a huge sweep of fabric evokes Titania's dreamy bower while her translucent trailing costume is wafted by the child-fairies.

Bertolt Brecht's highly influential 'epic theatre' style aimed to jolt the audience into a state of active interpretation. He built the production up from bare essentials and evolved a sophisticated minimalist aesthetic by using elements such as skeletal constructivist sets, emblematic costumes, exposed lighting and stage machinery, projected text and the half curtain.

5.8 Karl von Appen's design for Brecht's *The Caucasian Chalk Circle*, Berliner Ensemble, 1954. These drawings were an important pre-visualisation tool for Brecht, and helped shape his staging solutions.

5.9 Jerzy Gurawski's design for Grotowski's production of *Kordian*, Theatre of 13 Rows, 1962. The audience members are integrated into the setting and become 'patients' in the mental hospital.

POST-MODERNIST productions promote the juxtaposition of conflicting and often incongruous elements from various cultures and historical periods. This mixing of styles and elements is intended to encourage the audience to see from multiple perspectives—aware of their whole cultural history, and the place of the production within that history. Post-modernism encourages multiple ways of interpreting. Post-modernist productions reject the idea of stylistic unity that underpins illusionist, realist, metaphoric and dynamic productions.

This mixing of styles is something that theatre-makers have been doing for a long time—long before the post-modernist label was invented. We have put together ingredients from various unrelated sources, combining elements from popular culture, other art forms, other genres and mixed together visual styles. A very common example of this is a production in which *realistic* period costumes are worn by actors performing *naturalistically* like contemporary people in *abstract* sets—three contradictory styles so commonly fused together that most audiences would take it for granted.

Post-modernism now gives us a framework for consciously mixing styles in this way, and a language to do this in a more sophisticated and deliberate way that is more aware of its effect on our audience (➡ The Season at Sarsaparilla, *page 50*).

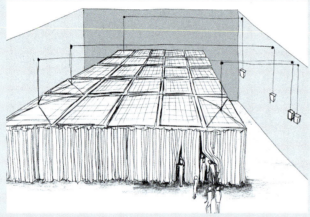

5.10 and 5.11

5.12 and 5.13
Joey Ruigrok van der Werven's concept drawings (5.10, 5.11) and production images (5.13, 5.14) for *Monstrous Body*. Joey and Gravity Feed Collective created a dynamic and ever-changing labyrinth of translucent plastic screens which were raised and lowered on pulleys in a series of choreographed reveals and conceals. The visual and aural environment was shared by performers and audience, and the audience became active participants in the performance.

STYLE STRATEGIES

There are endless ways directors and designers mix and play with style to evolve their own way of communicating their ideas. Some of these strategies are so popular that from time to time they may set a fashion for a particular way of 'doing' theatre.

Playing with period: Directors working with a classic text may look for another historical period in which to set the production—a period that will make the script's themes clearer to today's audience. They might identify a period of social or political change that fits with their view of the script. (For example, Nazi Germany and Totalitarian Russia have been popular candidates for Shakespearean tragedies in the past.)

The political manoeuvring in Richard III strikes me as shockingly up to the minute, up to the latest headline… It leaps off the page like some pacy political thriller, and it's for this reason I decided on a contemporary setting. A certain vital energy flows down our modern corridors of power, an energy captured well by TV series such as the neo-Shakespearean The West Wing. *In Shakespeare's day power came dressed in ermine and purple, topped by a crown; now it wears a well-cut, single-breasted suit, but the dynamism is the same.*

Simon Phillips, director [x]

RICHARD III, COSTUME DESIGNER ESTHER MARIE HAYES, SET DESIGNER SHAUN GURTON

5.14 and 5.15 *Richard III*, Melbourne Theatre Company 2010, director Simon Phillips, set designer Shaun Gurton, costume designer Esther Marie Hayes. This production used a modern setting and costumes to bring a contemporary understanding of political game playing to Shakespeare's tragedy (➡ *page 201 for more on this production*).

PICCADILLY CIRCUS CIRCUS, DESIGNER DAN POTRA

5.16 and 5.17
Storyboard drawings for Dan Potra's design proposal for *Piccadilly Circus Circus*. Dan's lively drawings capture the excitement of the 'total theatre' event as he visualises each stage of the performance—incorporating aerial physical theatre using telescopic cranes, wires and nets with music and spectacular lighting effects.

More often, a director might 'contemporise' a classic, choosing to set it in our own time, with the intention of helping the audience identify with its characters and issues by relating them to their own lives (➡ Richard III, *page 67*).

These are relatively unified ways of playing with period, but a director and designer might also decide to *mix periods within a production* , for example, clothe one character in a particular period, and other characters in different periods. Mixing period in a looser, non-literal way such as this might be adopted as a production style to highlight differences in attitude between characters, or link ideas across time, or just to free up the audience's perceptions (➡ Servant of Two Masters, *page 162*).

Playing with form and genre: A director might choose to present a script in a completely different genre from the one in which it was written—as a way of encouraging the audience to 'see' it in a new way. This is most often done with classics or scripts from a realist tradition, for example a 'kitchen-sink' realist drama presented as an epic tragedy… or vice versa. The audience is asked to 'read' the production with both frames in mind—to see the characters and situations in both contexts simultaneously to give a new twist to the script.

Or the director might create a 'hybrid' work by combining different forms (perhaps from other art fields) such as combining contemporary dance with martial arts, cinematic noir thriller with circus, or commedia dell'arte with rap.

For the designer, playing with historical period, form or genre can be a great creative challenge, and the excitement of this challenge translates into a production that creatively challenges and excites the audience.

'Total theatre': This is a 'multi-media' production approach that combines multiple forms and techniques of theatre and media in an integrated way.[xi] For example, mime, dance, dialogue, acrobatics, song and music might be combined to make a unique new work. Today mass-appeal events such as rock concerts and arena spectaculars are often conceived in this way and will add projection, and scenic, costume and lighting effects to the mix. For the designer, these productions make effective collaboration within the creative team even more important.

The blank space: A director may decide to strip the stage space back to bare essentials, perhaps to return to the core ingredients of performance—just the performer and the audience—or because they reject a style of theatre where the design tries to say or do too much. These spaces are never really blank. When a production is stripped back in this way any and every object in the space becomes highly focused, whether it be a yellow parka, a bunch of balloons or a performer's simple gesture. For the designer, resolving the exact nature of the 'blank' space is vital: is it a constructed blank box…? the raw walls of the theatre…? a black or white space…? Aesthetic consideration of every detail is crucial.

Intercultural: These are productions in which non-Western production styles such as Japanese Kabuki and Nōh, Chinese Opera or Indian Kathakali are mixed with Western theatre practices. Eastern theatre has tended to retain many of its traditions, and extensively uses illusion and symbolism in ways that can inspire Western theatre practice. For designers the question is: how can we mix elements of other cultures without appropriating?

The decorated stage: Sometimes the director just wants a good-looking show! For some forms of theatre (especially revue and variety) this would be a natural production style choice. For the designer the challenge is sustaining the audience's interest and enjoyment with high-class visual inventiveness.

Starting points: A director's stylistic starting point might be determined by something other than the script, for example, a site-specific performance space (such as a building site or shopping centre), a new technology (such as interactive projection) or the performance style of a key performer (such as casting a 'star' stand-up comedian in a drama). As designers we will work with the director to evolve the production style and the design from this starting point.

PLAYING BY THE RULES

We are designing in interesting times. Unlike any other time in history there is no orthodoxy—no single set of rules or conventions that are driving our art. Many of the revolutionary techniques evolved in the past have now been assimilated into mainstream performance design. We are free to explore the innovations of past theatre-makers, other artists, scientists and others to find the best design tactic. We are free to draw on the theatrical traditions of other cultures. We are free to continue the ongoing process of exploration and experimentation—to push the boundaries and find our own solutions to connect with our audience. Where will your explorations of style take us?

Within this freedom there is also structure. Once the production style for our production has evolved it becomes an informal 'set of rules' or principles that guide the way the whole production develops. These agreed principles are often referred to as the *theatrical language* of the production, and may be thought of as 'in this production we will do it *this* way'. Each member of the creative team will need to understand and play by these stylistic principles so that every design element and every other element of the show 'fit together' into a coherent whole. This does not mean that the production needs to be completely unified—there might be moments or images that are powerful and significant *because* they stand out from the rest of the show, or the production style might be based on deliberately mixing disparate elements. But the rules guide the creative team aesthetically, conceptually and ideologically so that the performance holds together and makes sense to the audience. A production that breaks its own rules is likely to confuse the audience, who will then start to disengage from the performance. When a production makes sense to the audience they will have no trouble accepting even an extreme interpretation or choice of production style. A confident and coherent production will take the audience with it.

LULIE THE ICEBERG, **DESIGNER KIM CARPENTER**

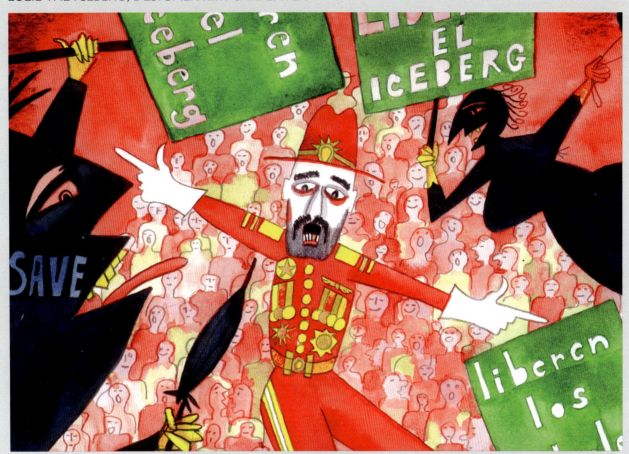

Drought-stricken country - 3D puppet

A Latino Dictator commands his minions to exploit Lulie for water to save their country.

5.18–5.20

Kim Carpenter's coloured design rendering (5.18), storyboard frame (5.19) and
production image (5.20) for *Lulie the Iceberg*. Kim's productions for children
utilise a sophisticated combination of projection, digital animation and puppetry,
live music, dance and performance. His disarmingly simple theatrical language is
rigorously carried through into every element of the production.

Case Study
Pygmalion — Stage 4:
Developing the Production Style

Exploring and developing a metaphoric production style and a very graphic visual style for *Pygmalion*, with costume and set roughs and Photoshop storyboards and notes from Director Michael Gow.

Pygmalion — First thoughts

Interested in Shaw's expanded second version for the seques between the acts.

He says they can't be shown unless in cinema or theatre with advanced technology — but can be done if whole production **not** realistic.

So: maybe a more mechanistic approach? Meyerhold approach — revolve? flown elements?

Allow for if these interludes or at least² an overall cinematic fluid production.

Because —
Eliza as very young the play-thing of much older more powerful people, Higgins, Pick. & Doolittle.

The machine is London? Y Woolf's Mrs Dalloway: the streets of London a machine, a prison. The Monopoly B.Board as reference

Director's notes

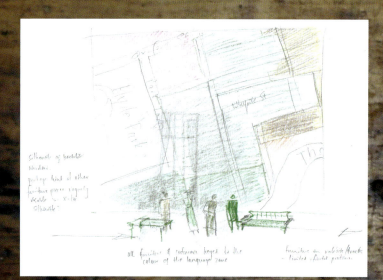

Set roughs

Photoshop storyboard

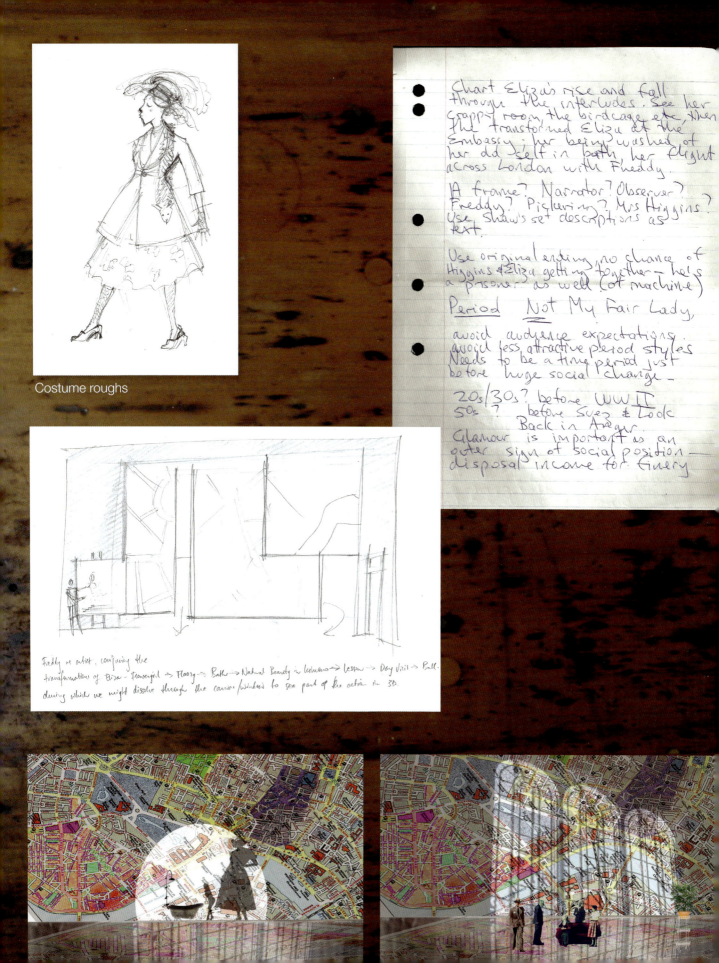

Costume roughs

Chart Eliza's rise and fall
through the interludes. See her
crappy room, the birdcage, etc, then
the transformed Eliza at the
Embassy: her being washed of
her old self in bath, her flight
across London with Freddy.

A frame? Narrator? Observer?
Freddy? Pickering? Mrs Higgins?
Use Shaw's set descriptions as
text.

Use original ending, no chance of
Higgins & Eliza getting together — he's
a prisoner as well (of machine)

Period   Not My Fair Lady,

avoid audience expectations.
avoid less attractive period styles
Needs to be a time period just
before huge social change —
20s/30s? before WWII
50s? before Suez & Look
Back in Anger.
Glamour is important as an
outer sign of social position —
disposal income for finery

Freddy as artist, conjuring the
transformation of Eliza — Flowergirl → Floozy → Bath → Natural Beauty in kimono → Lesson → Day visit → Ball.
during which we might dissolve through the canvas/window to see part of the action in 3D.

A stage designer is an artist—part of a tradition thousands of years old that serves to throw fresh light on the nature of human existence. It would be arrogant and self-indulgent to ignore or dismiss this tradition. Not only do you run the risk of repeating what others have already discovered, but you cut yourself off from a rich visual language gradually developed by all of the artists preceding you.

Robert Kemp, designer

FURTHER THINKING
DEVELOPING A VISUAL LANGUAGE

We have looked at the literary style of the playwright, and the director's production style, and at our own personal style as creative artists, but it is *visual style* that is specifically the designer's tool. Visual style is the creative vocabulary of designers and other visual artists. If we have a good 'visual vocabulary' we can talk about and use our design elements in an informed way: when we say 'more abstract' or 'less idealised' or 'more expressionistic' we will know what we are talking about and will be able to effectively communicate our design intentions with our director and other collaborators.

WHY WE NEED TO THINK ABOUT VISUAL STYLE

It is difficult for us from our contemporary perspective to understand the grand historical sweep and evolution of visual style—the way that artists in each generation have forged a particular visual language to express their ideas. In the distant past a style or fashion might last for centuries. With advances in travel and communication in the 18th and 19th centuries the pace of cultural change quickened and a stylistic trend might have endured for a number of decades and would become known as a 'movement'. By the mid-20th century the pace accelerated to such a degree that trends in design fields such as fashion, architecture or interior design might have lasted for only a few years, and today may survive only a matter of months. The post-modernist movement of the

1970s and 1980s also changed our thinking about visual style as an absolute, definable factor and instead advocated the juxtaposition of styles of the past in ways that encouraged us to re-evaluate our cultural heritage. Today styles of all kinds are chopped up and blended together in a great cultural soup which at its best can be like a wonderful meal of exciting flavours combined in new ways, and at its worst can be like making a 'smoothie' from anything and everything within reach in the refrigerator. In a relatively recent development not only historical styles from our European cultural heritage, but every possible national or ethnic style is now part of the mix—to be 'used' in almost any combination with anything else.

Our understanding of style is made more difficult by the lack of a language to discuss it. Art history today is rarely taught as a continuum from the ancient world to the modern, encompassing everything in between, and even the basic awareness of style as a continuous response or reaction to what has gone before is not understood. If we look at the way fashion has evolved over our own lifetime we can see how a style is created by a trend-setting group or individual, is then picked up by the most fashion-conscious, is gradually adopted into mainstream fashion, by which time it is rejected or reworked by the next group of innovators. This process of innovation, response and reaction has in fact been the driving force behind the evolution of style over centuries.

I grew up around art and creating images, going to exhibitions every week—learning how to see a story within an image. It's become a natural part of my life.
Jacob Nash, designer

Why does any of this matter? Isn't it okay just to use our intuition to pick and choose styles that suit our purpose? Absolutely, this is fine, but having a conscious awareness of why and how we are using style will help us communicate these choices with our collaborators, will help us consider the pros and cons of one style over another, and will help us tailor the stylistic choices to the specific needs of the production. It will help give us command and control of this important design tool and fit the look of the show to its production style and concepts. It will also help us understand and appreciate that our stylistic choices are shaped by the culture of which we and our production are part, and will in turn help to shape that culture.

STYLE CHOICES

Let's look at a few different ways of thinking and talking about visual style, and consider some art references that help us visualise these choices. Art movements that correlate to stylistic choices are shown in red.

We can think of visual style in terms of being abstract or less abstract:

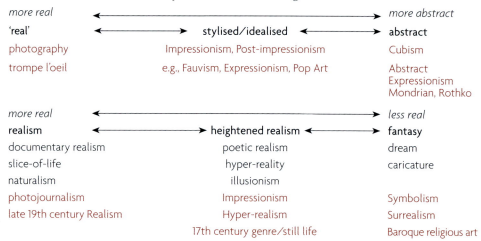

more real ←————————————————————————→ *more abstract*

'real'	←→ stylised/idealised ←→	abstract
photography	Impressionism, Post-impressionism	Cubism
trompe l'oeil	e.g., Fauvism, Expressionism, Pop Art	Abstract Expressionism Mondrian, Rothko

more real ←————————————————————————→ *less real*

realism	←→ heightened realism ←→	fantasy
documentary realism	poetic realism	dream
slice-of-life	hyper-reality	caricature
naturalism	illusionism	
photojournalism	Impressionism	Symbolism
late 19th century Realism	Hyper-realism	Surrealism
	17th century genre/still life	Baroque religious art

Or we can think of realism as a 'neutral' central state, and the further away from the centre, the more stylised we become. At the extremes of stylisation we have fantasy. If we are led from the centre by our emotions we move towards romanticism, and if we are led in the opposite direction by our reason we move towards classicism:

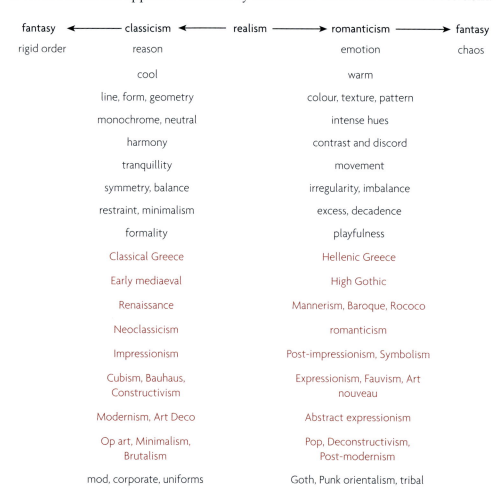

fantasy ←— classicism ←— realism —→ romanticism —→ fantasy

rigid order	reason		emotion	chaos
	cool		warm	
	line, form, geometry		colour, texture, pattern	
	monochrome, neutral		intense hues	
	harmony		contrast and discord	
	tranquillity		movement	
	symmetry, balance		irregularity, imbalance	
	restraint, minimalism		excess, decadence	
	formality		playfulness	
	Classical Greece		Hellenic Greece	
	Early mediaeval		High Gothic	
	Renaissance		Mannerism, Baroque, Rococo	
	Neoclassicism		romanticism	
	Impressionism		Post-impressionism, Symbolism	
	Cubism, Bauhaus, Constructivism		Expressionism, Fauvism, Art nouveau	
	Modernism, Art Deco		Abstract expressionism	
	Op art, Minimalism, Brutalism		Pop, Deconstructivism, Post-modernism	
	mod, corporate, uniforms		Goth, Punk orientalism, tribal	

Typically culture develops from a relatively 'pure' aesthetic form and evolves to become more and more complex and ultimately 'decadent', only to be rejected and replaced by yet another simpler, pure form. The forces of political and social change are strongly linked to these cultural patterns. In revolutionary periods of radical change design forms tend to be stripped back to basics and have a formal ('classical') rigour. Conversely periods of stability and growth are often characterised by a creative 'flowering' in which design forms become more complex and idiosyncratic ('romantic').

USING VISUAL STYLE CHOICES TO DESIGN

We can use these stylistic patterns as designers by aligning the moods and themes of the project with corresponding movements in art and culture. This can help us identify architectural forms, period costume silhouettes, uses of colour or light, mood and many other visual qualities that in turn can help us shape our design.

To demonstrate how this can work let's investigate some of the (many possible) themes and moods of Shakespeare's *Romeo and Juliet* and see how we might apply our understanding of visual style to give them shape.

Themes	Possible style references
sensuality and passion	Baroque, Romanticist, Fauve artists e.g., Tiepolo, Rubens, Delacroix, Matisse
romantic idealism	Symbolist and Romanticist fantasy artists e.g., Redon, Freidrich, Rousseau, Chagall
repression	Look for extremes of order and structure e.g., Minimalism, Brutalism, Fascist classicism
rebellion	Investigate periods when art violently rejected orthodoxy e.g., Neo-classicism, constructivism, punk
collision of opposites	Work two opposite styles against each other, e.g., corporate vs Goth, Bauhaus vs pop

Moods	
spiritual bliss (the lovers' first meeting)	early Mediaeval, early Renaissance, Islamic art, Klimt
anger, rage (the fight where Tybalt is killed)	Expressionists/Abstract Expressionists: Kandinsky, Pollock,
sombre beauty (the final death scene)	Morandi, Rothko, de Chirico Minimalism, Classicism

Performance designers are great magpie borrowers, picking and choosing from the vast treasury of cultural assets as it suits our needs. (Grotowski[xii] calls this 'artistic kleptomania'—think about it!) We might be designing a tough contemporary action drama one month, and a poetic, contemplative dance work the next. Each production requires us to develop a visual language that works for that production. If we understand how style has evolved out of culture: how it reflects the politics, values, economics and spiritual perspective of a particular time and place we can start to apply this understanding to enrich our designs. Seen in this way we can appreciate that performance design is an integral part of the continuum of culture; part of what makes culture tick.

It was written for a generation gasping for air after the stifling Victorian and Edwardian eras of rigid morality and social rituals, dark over-decorated interiors, constricting clothing, ornamentation and artistic naturalism all topped off by the horrors of World War I. Just as Coward's characters are outrageously modern, witty, irreverent and bursting with life, so too were the artists of the day. The Fauves, represented by artists like Raoul Dufy, for example were excitedly throwing vivid paint over canvases in grand unrestrained gestures. Like Coward, they were reacting to an oppressive past. The option to use aspects of this work or the spirit of this work to underscore Coward's dialogue was like having another set of colours at my disposal.

PRIVATE LIVES, **DESIGNER ROBERT KEMP**

5.21 and 5.22 Designer Robert Kemp describes how his understanding of art and culture informed his design thinking for *Private Lives*. Production images for Act 1 (blue) and Act 2/3 (red) of *Private Lives* draw inspiration from French Fauve artist Raoul Dufy to create a lively world for Noel Coward's comedy of manners.

CHAPTER 6

DEVELOPING OUR DESIGN CONCEPT

Terrain (Costume Designer Jennifer Irwin, Set Designer Jacob Nash)

This chapter explores the creative and practical factors that the creative team will consider, and how all of these factors come together in devising the design concept.

ALSO IN THIS CHAPTER—FURTHER THINKING: The Actor–Audience Relationship, page 92

*As a director, I'm not particularly interested in high-concept theatre or the question of what I am doing **to** a work… I prefer to think of what the material is doing **to me** and what it's doing to the creative team and the cast. We're looking for the essence of the world of that play…*

Sam Strong, director [xiii]

DEVELOPING A CONCEPT

Our script analysis has given us a secure understanding of the script and our research process has opened up the visual potential of the design. There will have been a lot of discussion with the director, testing one interpretation over another. At this stage of our design process our ideas might seem like a whole lot of disconnected thoughts, references, sketches and suggestions—like a tabletop of loose jigsaw pieces. Now we are ready to link all of these pieces together and consolidate our interpretation. Often this interpretation will coalesce into a *concept* summarising the creative vision for the production. This concept (which may also be known as the *director's premise*) will be a unique vision of the script and will highlight what we most want the audience to see, feel and understand.

As you can see from the diagram opposite, there are many aspects of the production that all come together at this time like jigsaw pieces fitting together to make up the complete puzzle image. The production style will be a strong starting point (like the corner pieces and edges of the jigsaw puzzle). On any production one or two of the other factors might lead the design process and inspire us and our director to shape the design. The design might develop by working with just *focus* and *visual style* for example, or *character* and *atmosphere* using key *research* images to give shape to our ideas. We can always come back and start to explore some of the other factors in more detail later on when we need fresh inspiration, or if we hit a 'design block' and need some new insights. But however we go about pulling it all together, we will need to take all of these aspects into account at some time.

The concept might be expressed as a production metaphor centred on a key image, or a statement of intent, making the goal of the production explicit. It might be clearly articulated in a 'concept statement' or be implicitly understood from agreed aspects of the design and production. Whatever the case everyone in the production team needs to agree and understand what the concept is.

Often the concept is expressed in terms of the *'world of the play'*, a term that implies an invitation to the audience to leave the real, present-day world we all live in, and imaginatively enter the world that the characters inhabit. Much more than merely describing the play's location, the 'world of the play' is a catch-all phrase taking in period, social context, character and setting, mood

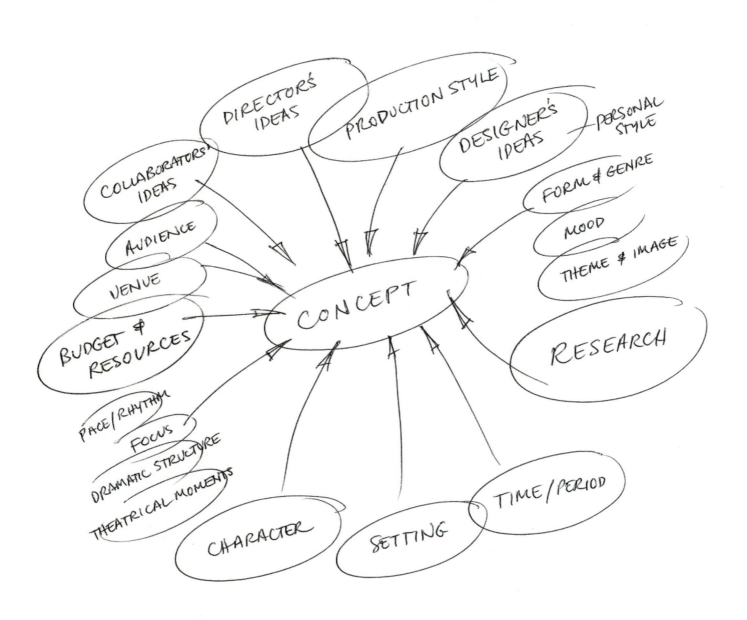

The following diagram is a mind map centered on the word CONCEPT, with the following connected labels:

- DIRECTOR'S IDEAS
- PRODUCTION STYLE
- DESIGNER'S IDEAS
- PERSONAL STYLE
- COLLABORATORS' IDEAS
- FORM & GENRE
- MOOD
- THEME & IMAGE
- AUDIENCE
- VENUE
- BUDGET & RESOURCES
- RESEARCH
- PACE/RHYTHM
- FOCUS
- DRAMATIC STRUCTURE
- THEATRICAL MOMENTS
- CHARACTER
- SETTING
- TIME/PERIOD

You can see it like this or like that. It just depends on the way you watch…You can always watch the other way.

Pina Bausch, choreographer [xiv]

and visual style. For example, different production concepts for Shakespeare's *Romeo and Juliet* (set in Verona, sometime in the past) could describe the 'world' as a hot Baroque place of privilege, passion and sensuality... or a brutalist, war-torn contemporary city where everything is in conflict... or a delicate, romantic Renaissance love story inspired by the paintings of Botticelli... or a schizophrenic world divided between the crass hard-edged materialism of the adults and the computer-game fantasy of the kids... (➡ Romeo and Juliet *Concepts, pages 86–91*).

INTERPRETATION: MAKING MEANING

We now come to one of the most important questions the creative team need to ask (and answer)—'How clear do we want the meaning of the production to be?' The debate swings back and forth. Some argue that there is no point making

DOGTROEP IN BRUGES PENITENTIARY COMPLEX, **DESIGNER JOEY RUIGROK VAN DER WERVEN, COSTUME DESIGNER YKJE HIBMA**

6.1 Production photograph: *Dogtroep in Bruges Penitentiary Complex.* Designer Joey Ruigrok van der Werven worked collaboratively with the team of performance and visual artists who made up the Dutch performance collective Dogtroep to devise this performance in a working prison in Bruges (Belgium). The production incorporated the institution's prisoners as performers, and took place in a large prison courtyard space shared by the audience. In a powerful theatrical moment at the conclusion of the work the prisoners left the shared space, exiting through a doorway which opened in a curtain of water for them to pass. As the last prisoner left, the doorway dissolved, and the water curtain formed a complete barrier between the world of the prisoners and the world of the audience. Part of Joey's design role was to develop an effective solution to realise this beautiful image.

theatre if it doesn't communicate its meaning clearly to the audience, while others argue that each member of the audience should be left to interpret the production in their own way. What do you think? What does your director think?

Will the audience's understanding be more intellectual or emotional? Will the meaning be obvious, specific and objective, or shifting, personal and subjective? Do we want the production to be 'accessible' or 'obscure'?

We can see it as a choice in how we want the audience to understand the production, or more usefully as a balancing act. Peter Brook states it beautifully: '.... a design that has clarity without rigidity; one that could be called "open" as against "shut"…' [xv]

It is a delicate balance. We have all experienced productions that have left us confused and frustrated, even angry that the production has not 'made sense', and at the other extreme productions in which it is all too obvious in the first five minutes where the production is going, as when the design 'lets the whole stylistic story out of the bag before the actors have uttered a word'. [xvi]

The design will have a big role to play in how the audience interpret the production and make meaning for themselves because we are all very used to interpreting visual information and making sense from what we see. It is often a question of how much visual information we give the audience. How much is enough? The rule 'less is more' is often applied. Meyerhold talks about leaving 'gaps' for the audience to fill with their imaginations, and Grotowski about 'leaving space for the unexpected'. These are strategies that leave room for the audience to interpret in their own way.

DESIGN PRIORITIES AND RESOURCES (BUDGET AND SCHEDULE)

Designers tend to be practical people, and we might think of the concept in terms of *design priorities*—the design elements that are most important and those that are less important. Our designs will often be the first physical, tangible, actual expression of the director's concept. It is important for us to remember that it is our work as designers that commits the intangible ideas of the script and director into actual physical things, and money will be spent in this process. I mention this very obvious point because we have quite a responsibility to make sure that the production concept is reflected in our design priorities and that the budget and resources are being used in the best way for the production.

 The concept should determine our design priorities, and in turn identifying our design priorities allows us to look objectively at the budget and resources to determine how we want to allocate time and money. If we know that particular aspects of the design are crucial then we can set about designing them in such a way that they can be realised within the budget and schedule. The production manager will be able to help us work out how to use the resources efficiently, but they will not be able to help us work out what is high priority and what is not.

TERRAIN, SET DESIGNER JACOB NASH, COSTUME DESIGNER JENNIFER IRWIN

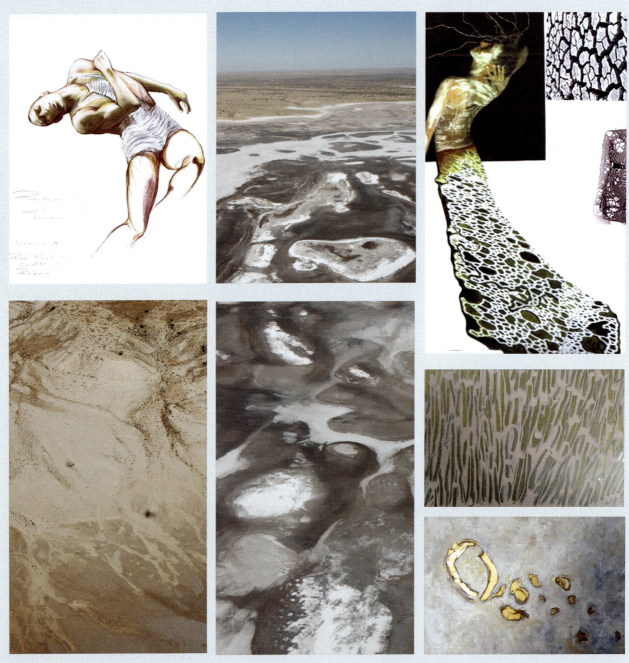

6.2–6.8 The creative team for the dance production *Terrain* (Bangarra Dance Theatre Australia's contemporary indigenous dance work by Frances Rings), including costume designer Jennifer Irwin and set designer Jacob Nash all travelled to the remote and starkly beautiful desert landscape of Lake Eyre, and it is there that their concept crystallised. In the costume design image (6.2), research images taken from the air (6.3, 6.4, 6.5), artwork for one of the evocative cloths for the production (6.6) and set concept artwork (6.7, 6.8) we see how the design team responded to the subtle and unique textures of the landscape in their design response.

Working with budgets is a skill that designers develop with experience, however there are a few guiding principles that can help to steer the process.

- Be clear on your design priorities and make sure your design reflects them.

- Begin by dividing the budget equally between costumes and sets because they are equally important. You can readjust the budget as the design develops.

- The production manager is there to help you. Bring them into the process early.

- We are not expected to know the cost of everything: estimates and informed 'guestimates' will usually be enough to guide the early design stages until the production manager undertakes a full costing.

- If there is something you need advice on, get advice. Ask lots of questions, and make sure you get clear answers.

- 'Less is more' is a good creative policy, but less is not necessarily cheaper. Sometimes a really spare design element, particularly if it involves automation, electronics or projection might be much more expensive than a big set of conventional flats, or one complex costume might be more expensive than a wardrobe of simpler ones.

- Do your research on special materials or processes you might be interested in using.

- Be flexible. Develop a number of design solutions that give you different ways of realising the concept. If you can't afford one solution you will be able to move on to another.

By this stage of the process, with the concept established and a strong sense of our design priorities and the shape the design will take, we need to know that the design will 'work' for the production: will work to express the script and director's vision, will work for the performers, will work for the audience, and that we can make it work within the resources at our disposal. Our next step is to explore and test design solutions that will achieve these goals.

*****

Pages 86–91 present three different productions and three different concepts for Shakespeare's *Romeo and Juliet*. Each of the three designers (Pip Runciman, Bill Haycock and Stephen Curtis) has worked with their director to devise their own ways of visually conveying their interpretation, using tools such as storyboards, concept sketches, plans, costume sketches and sketch models to communicate their concept. Each has explored visual metaphor in their interpretation to create a distinct world.

COMPARE THREE CONCEPTS:
ROMEO AND JULIET, DESIGNER PIP RUNCIMAN

State Theatre Company of South Australia production (an adaptation by Geordie Brookman and Nicki Bloom), 2010, directed by Geordie Brookman

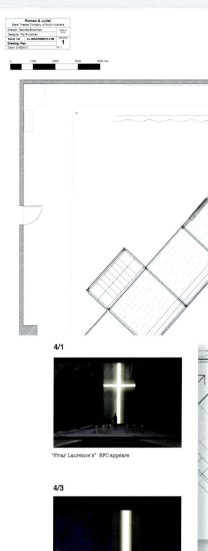

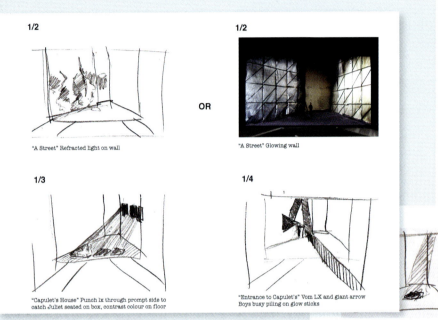

1/2

1/2

OR

"A Street" Refracted light on wall

"A Street" Glowing wall

1/3

1/4

"Capulet's House" Punch lx through prompt side to catch Juliet seated on box, contrast colour on floor

"Entrance to Capulet's" Vom LX and giant arrow Boys busy piling on glow sticks

Concept storyboards

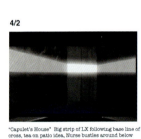

"Juliet's Chamber" Doona drop C stage

4/1

"Friar Laurence's" BFC appears

4/2

"Capulet's House" Big strip of LX following base line of cross, tea on patio idea, Nurse bustles around below

4/3

"Juliet's Chamber" Juliet enters with doona around her neck - bride silhouette.

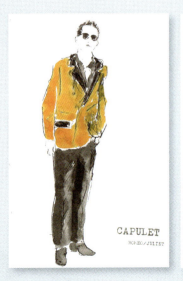

CAPULET
ROMEO/JULIET

LADY CAPULET
ROMEO/JULIET

MONTAGUE
ROMEO/JULIET

JULIET
ROMEO/JULIET

Costume drawings

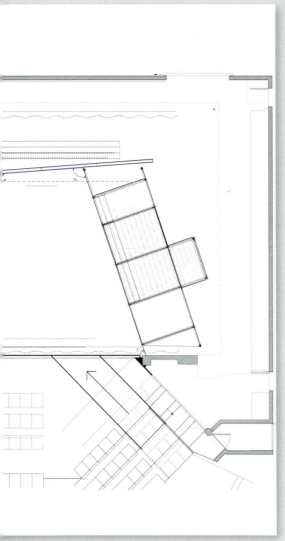

Set plan

The contrasts in the script were a big starting point: fate and chance, night and day, love and death, beauty and terror. We wanted the set to reflect these paradoxes. We wanted something that could be intimate and also vast, suggestive of a cathedral or church in its scale—a giant magic box that could be simply and easily transformed and communicate the emotional landscape of the play. Geordie [director] had the lovely idea of the prologue for the play being delivered as a eulogy—which led us to the cathedral and church as a setting. The church is a strong symbol of the paradox of the feuding Montagues and Capulets, their faith in the church and the resulting suicides of Romeo and Juliet.

Geordie wanted a set that looked solid but the actors could disappear and reappear quickly through a seemingly solid wall. Before we even started working on the design Geordie had decided that he wanted to use the voms [actor entries from the auditorium—see arrows on the plan to the left] to link the stage with the auditorium, and these really helped to shape the whole set.

Pip Runciman, designer

Production images

COMPARE THREE CONCEPTS:
ROMEO AND JULIET, DESIGNER BILL HAYCOCK

Queensland Theatre Company production, 2012,
directed by Jennifer Flowers, costume drawings,
set concept sketches, preliminary model,
presentation model and production image

Costume drawings

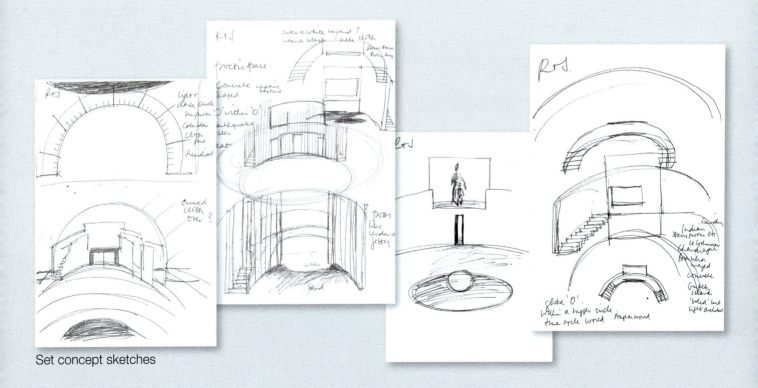

Set concept sketches

A lot of our early discussion focused on various aspects of time… how fast or slow time moves in the play depending on mood and emotional state, and the seemingly endless appeal, repetition and variations of this thwarted love story through time. This seemed to push Jennifer [director] and I away from any specifics of location or costume into a 'timeless' classic feel, drawing from both past and present—ancient/modern textured walls and costumes that were patched, pieced and scarred in an attempt to show their wearer's 'history'.

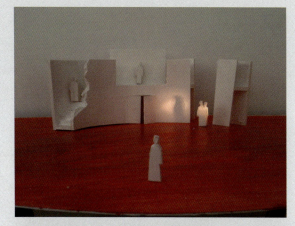

Together with these ideas came the idea of a reflective pool of water downstage centre into which a pebble fell at the start of the production with an exaggerated 'ripple' of lighting that spread outwards through the space and over the audience to include them in the fateful events that follow. In essence the concept was to 'start the clock/light the fuse' that would set the play in motion, as well as to subliminally suggest that this was a story that just kept repeating and reverberating over and over through time and in different circumstances…

The water was used in different ways—as a reflective pool, as a contrast to the hotness of the days, but most significantly as a premonition of death. Everyone who died made some connection with it… and it became the final tomb for Juliet to lie within.

Preliminary model, presentation model and production image

Bill Haycock, designer

COMPARE THREE CONCEPTS:
ROMEO AND JULIET, **DESIGNER STEPHEN CURTIS**

State Theatre Company of South Australia production, 1984,
directed by Neil Armfield, costume references, roughs and costume
drawings, set concept sketches, model and production image

Costume references, roughs and drawings

*We wanted a hot, hot space with an intense atmosphere where passions of love
and hate were at boiling point. Neil [director] wanted the world of the play to
have the feel of a contemporary sun-drenched Mediterranean piazza, with a
bleakly authoritarian feel, while never being a particular place, and always being
open to every theatrical possibility. The huge red curtain was a response to the
play's sensuality, and gave us ways to reveal and conceal, to move fluidly and
energetically from one scene to the next and when lowered and draped over the
stage to become bed and tomb. It became identified with the idea of the freedom of
the kids, as opposed to the desolate authoritarian world of the adults. We began
exploring the costuming from the perspective of the schoolyard—working from
how kids naturally behave and dress—what they might wear when they're hot,
when they go to parties, when they sleep with their lover...*

Stephen Curtis, designer

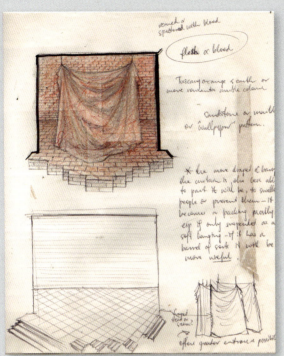

Set concept sketches

Set model

Production image

VLADIMIR: …There's no way out there. *(He takes Estragon by the arm and drags him towards front. Gesture towards front.)* There! Not a soul in sight! Off you go. Quick! *(He pushes Estragon towards auditorium. Estragon recoils in horror.)*…

Samuel Beckett, *Waiting for Godot*

FURTHER THINKING
THE ACTOR–AUDIENCE RELATIONSHIP

In less than a minute of stage time Beckett's characters in the excerpt above acknowledge the 'fourth wall', demolish it and then establish a completely different kind of relationship between themselves and their audience. Beckett brilliantly demonstrates how malleable this relationship can be.

Long before the realists turned the audience into voyeurs, theatre-makers had for centuries been exploring different ways of defining the relationship between the audience and the performers. In rituals such as those of the Australian Western Desert Arrernte people the 'audience' are joint participants, each with their own important role. In classical Greek drama the audience was represented on-stage by the chorus who spoke for the audience and negotiated their moral position through the drama. In mediaeval performance the audience were at different times both participants and spectators. And in Shakespearean drama the relationship was flexible enough for actors to talk directly to the audience (who presumably also responded). Even when the proscenium arch was constructed as a concrete physical barrier between the stage and the auditorium, actors would come *through* the proscenium arch, right to the edge of the stage to deliver their lines 'out front' or in the case of the court masques the action would flow out into the auditorium and include the audience in the spectacle.

There are many ways we can make the actor–audience relationship work, and it is worth thinking about *how* we want it to work, and how we as designers can help make it work the way we want it to.

WAITING FOR GODOT, **SET DESIGNER ROBERT COUSINS,
COSTUME DESIGNER TESS SCHOFIELD**

6.9–6.13
Tess Schofield's costume designs (6.9, 6.10), photographs of the art finishing process (6.11, 6.12), and production photograph (6.13) for *Waiting for Godot*. Tess used bold painterly effects on the costumes to communicate the characters' theatricality, and to distance them from 'reality', while drawing the audience into their humanity with carefully observed detail.

How passive or active do we want the audience to be? How intimate or shared should their experience be? Should the audience be emotionally, intellectually or imaginatively engaged (or all of these) all of the time? Theatre theoreticians have developed different ways of discussing the nature of the actor–audience engagement: suspension of disbelief, identification, alienation, [xvii] immersion, the fourth wall, and the 'hook' (➡ *Box, opposite*).

There are several factors that can influence how the actor–audience relationship works, and we need to understand how they will influence our design: the *production form, the production style* (which includes the acting style), *the venue* and *the design*.

The form of the production will influence the nature of the engagement: circus has a different actor–audience dynamic from contemporary dance, opera has a different dynamic from musicals, street theatre is different from cabaret. The audience understands that there is a different 'etiquette', or way of behaving, with each of these different forms of performance. In circus and cabaret it is okay to cheer and whistle, in drama and opera the audience will be in darkness and are expected to be silent; and in street theatre they may be invited to join in the performance. We can ask ourselves, 'How would the audience expect to "act" with our production? Do we want them to engage differently?'

The director's choice of production style also influences how the audience engages with the production: illusionism casts the audience as spectators entertained by the theatrical fantasy; realism invites the audience to become emotionally involved through identification and empathy; metaphorical productions inspire an imaginative engagement; dynamic productions provoke and challenge the audience to engage intellectually and become active interpreters in the work, or even active players in the production. The director might be choosing a particular production style because they want to engage with the audience in one way and not another (➡ *Chapter 5: Precedents of Production Style, page 60*).

The architecture of the performance venue has a big influence on how the audience engages with the performers. If the audience seating wraps around the stage, as in thrust or in-the-round, the audience will be very aware of each other and the production will feel like a communal event shared with the performers and the rest of the audience. If there is a proscenium arch this will separate the audience from the stage, while an apron extending from the front of the proscenium stage will reduce the effect of the proscenium barrier and help to link the audience and performers. When the performers have good eye contact with the audience the experience will feel more intimate. The scale of the venue will also influence how intimate the experience feels for the audience. As designers we can analyse the performance venue and think about how this physical space affects the audience's engagement, and then we can use the design to make it work *for* the production (➡ *Chapter 8, page 114*).

ENGAGING THE AUDIENCE

SUSPENSION OF DISBELIEF refers to the way an audience member is able to willingly suspend judgment of the plausibility of the events on stage—they effectively leave their world behind to imaginatively enter the world of the production.

THE FOURTH WALL: The realist theatre convention of the 'fourth wall' assumes that the actors perform as though the audience is not there, and that the audience has a privileged window into a framed slice of life through the invisible 'fourth wall'.

IDENTIFICATION is a psychological (Freudian) concept adapted by realist theatre-makers. It encourages the audience to put themselves in the shoes of the characters and to share their feelings (empathise) to such a degree that they experience what the characters experience.

ALIENATION is a Brechtian technique (*Verfremdungs-effekt*) that works in the opposite way to identification. It aims to distance the audience so that they become consciously aware that they are watching, and will therefore make decisions about what they are watching. Through this *active* interpretation Brecht believed that the audience became 'performers' in the event.

IMMERSION: This is an approach that uses all aspects of the production to totally overwhelm the audience's senses, so they completely 'lose themselves' in the production.

'THE HOOK' is a way of thinking that many directors and designers use when thinking about how to grab the audience's attention and draw them into the production. We will often use tantalising visual elements as 'bait' to initially excite the audience's attention and then devise a series of 'theatrical moments' that will keep them engaged (hooked).

The design, especially the set design, can do a lot to help create the kind of audience–stage relationship that will work for the production. We can choose to use the whole stage, or bring all of the action downstage up-close to the audience. We can make a formal theatre space feel friendlier by breaking it up and softening the edges (for example, I recoloured the house lights in a particularly unwelcoming venue with salmon lighting gels, and the effect was so successful the venue kept them set up like this). We can build the stage out into the auditorium or incorporate the audience onto the stage. We can make the audience physically move from location to location as the event unfolds. We can close off parts of the auditorium if the house is too big. We can costume the characters in contemporary clothing so the audience feel that they are 'like them'. We can play with the audience's expectations by keeping the stage hidden with a curtain or in darkness and reveal the world of the play magically, or we can stir their imaginations with a moodily lit space where they can't *quite* see everything. A strong opening image is a great way to 'hook' the audience. We can plan a whole sequence of little surprises that keeps them connected. Once we have taken on the challenge we will be able to find many other ways to build the right kind of actor–audience relationship—to engage the audience and keep them hooked. The best way to keep them engaged is to make great theatre.

There is no difference between high art and low art. I treat the back row of the NRL grand final in the same way I'd treat the front row at the theatre. Great theatre should be an event and great events are great theatre.

Tony Assness, events and theatre designer [xviii]

BLACK, DESIGNER ANNA TREGLOAN

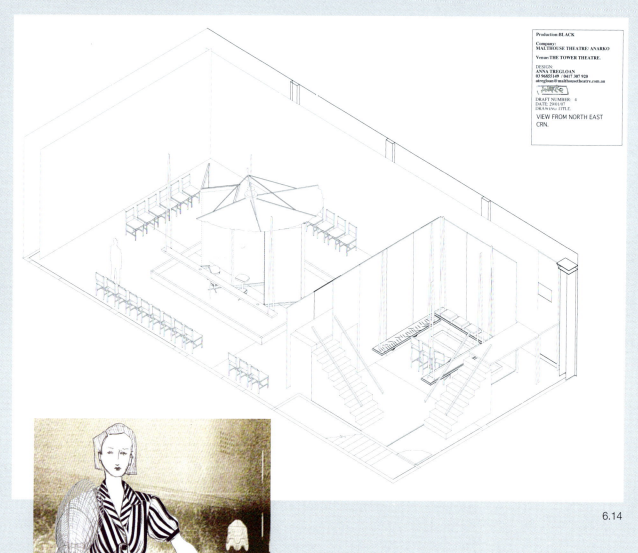

Production:BLACK

Company:
MALTHOUSE THEATRE/ ANARKO

Venue:THE TOWER THEATRE.

DESIGN:
ANNA TREGLOAN
03 96855149 / 0417 307 920
atregloan@malthousetheatre.com.au

DRAFT NUMBER: 4
DATE: 29/01/07
DRAWING TITLE.

VIEW FROM NORTH EAST
CRN.

6.14

6.15

6.14–6.17
Anna Tregloan's set drawings (6.14, 6.17), costume design drawing (6.15) and production image (6.16) for *Black*, a production she devised, directed and designed for Malthouse Theatre. Anna experimented with different ways of actively engaging her audience and playing with their connection to the work: taking them from one performance space to another, wrapping them around the performance area so they watched and were watched and viewing the performance through mirrored glass panels that gave each member of the audience a unique perspective.

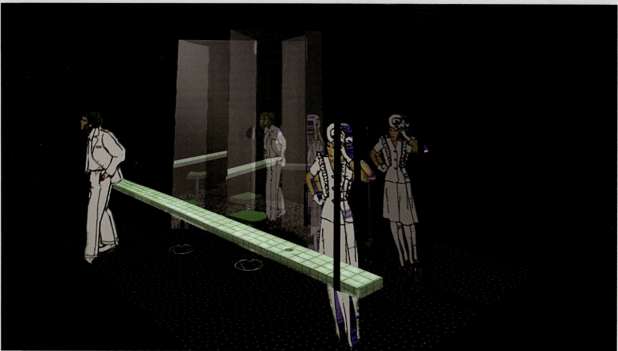

6.16, 6.17

EXPERIMENTING
WITH OUR IDEAS

Monstrous Body (Set Designer Joey Ruigrok van der Werven)

In this chapter we discover the joy of creatively playing around with our ideas and options to develop and refine the best design solutions.

ALSO IN THIS CHAPTER—FURTHER THINKING: The Design Toolbox, page 108

I've always let the fabric give me the ideas. All the things I could create with it! Strip it back, print over it to become something else, playing with it over the lines and contours of the body to accentuate the muscles…

Jennifer Irwin, designer

So far we have talked about analysis, discovery, interpretation—preparation. Well now it is time to play! Play in the way that children play—creatively, inventively, ambitiously, building up and knocking down and then building anew. Brecht, unfairly regarded as a rather earnest, theoretical theatre-maker, had a word for it (*'lustig'*): the actively pleasurable act of making theatre. He was often observed 'giggling with pleasure' when he and his key collaborator, set designer Otto Neher, hit on a good idea. [xix]

It's now time to literally throw open the lid of your paintbox, cover the floor of your workroom with cuts and off-cuts of cardboard, plastic and fabric, muck around with the size, shape and colour of everything, try this bit of photocopied texture in the model, or that bit of period detail in the costume sketch: experiment and play with all your design elements until you have the best solution. You might be familiar with the saying 'there's more than one way to skin a cat', well it's true, but this is more fun than skinning cats! What exactly are we playing *with*?

Playwrights experiment with ideas using words on the page, directors with words in conversation and in directions to the performers in the rehearsal room. Designers experiment with ideas by playing with *things*. We develop our ideas by experimenting with colour, texture, shape… all the visual qualities of concrete objects that will become elements in our design. We are playing around with different versions of degree (how strong the colour is… how sharp the shape…) and the relationship of one element to another element (is the floor rougher than the wall… is her shirt brighter than his jacket…?).

The objects that we are experimenting with are the elements that we have discovered or imagined through our script analysis, research and collaborative discussions. Let us imagine a production which centres around the idea of entrapment—the central character is caught, unable to move forward or back, unable to act freely. Our development work up to now might have revealed a number of images of this idea of entrapment: cages, bleak bare rooms, an island in an empty sea, a boxing ring, a fish in a goldfish bowl… there is no shortage of images to explore here. Let us now imagine that the director has identified the cage as the 'best fit' to the concept, but is unsure how subtle or strong the image should be. Our experimentation could now explore a whole range of possibilities, from a space with actual bars, to a simple raised square of tiled floor where the rigid grid of dark lines defining the tiles suggests an entrapping net, or the abstract use of shifting bars of light and shadow, or the more literal shape of light through the mullions of a window evoking prison bars. Our experiments could explore all of these possibilities, and many more (➡ Blackbird *Concepts to see how three designers have explored the theme of entrapment, pages 118, 120, 122*).

Imagine a different production where we are working around the idea of our central character becoming like a 'fish out of water'. We want all of the characters around her to reinforce the idea that she does not belong in their world. Our experimentation could explore possibilities of her starting the production dressed like the others and gradually transforming until she looks quite foreign and different, or that they are initially dressed like her and gradually transform, exposing her difference. Both versions express the same idea, but in very different ways and would be understood differently by the audience.

Once we have established what our design elements are we can open up our design toolbox and start fine-tuning the visual qualities, all the while remembering that the audience will see, interpret and understand based on the choices we make. An audience will understand a dark space differently from a light space; a character wearing a red costume will be interpreted differently from one in pink; a large object will create a different impression from a small one; angular shapes will affect the audience differently from fluid, organic ones, and all of these choices will be understood differently depending on the other visual elements around them. The audience's interpretation will ultimately be informed by each and every one of our design choices and how we use our design tools: shape/silhouette, form, line, scale, colour, tone, texture, pattern/rhythm, balance, contrast, unity/discord, detail, movement, transformation (➡ *Further Thinking, page 108*).

There are many theoretical texts that are available to art and design students that describe each design tool and how it works, but honestly I think the best way of learning how to use them is by experimentation. If you are not sure whether a dark space would be better than a lighter one—use your jumbo marker or paints to colour it in. Will a strong red costume work better than pink? Scan the drawing into your image-editing program (such as Adobe Photoshop) on your computer and try out each version. Is big better than small? Cut out a whole range of sizes and experiment with which one works best—and you can try out the angled versus fluid variations at the same time.

The formats that we are using to make these experiments will be different depending on whether we are designing sets or costumes. For the costume designer the *costume sketch* is our main format for experimentation. These

WORKING WITH THE SCALE MODEL

One of our most useful tools when we are designing the set is the model box. This is typically a version of the empty stage space built to scale. The scale most commonly used in Australia is 1:25mm as this allows us to see a useful amount of detail without the model box being too large and cumbersome. The model box will show the stage and the architectural elements that define the stage area. In a thrust or end-stage venue the model box might include all or part of the raked seating banks that define the edge of the stage, as well as the back wall and/or side walls if these enclose the stage. In a proscenium venue the model box will show the stage as a raised platform, the proscenium arch extending beyond the actual proscenium opening so that the venue wing space is also included and the back wall of the venue. The model box is usually painted black.

Model boxes can be quite time-consuming to make, and if we are using fly lines, revolves or lifts these also need to be built into the model box so that we can accurately explore and demonstrate our design intentions.

But we need to keep the workload in perspective. The process of building the model box is a good way to come to terms with the physicality of the space for which we will be designing, but it is the design that goes *into* the model box that is of most importance.

Include a scale figure of a performer in the model box so that every design idea is in scale to the human figure and to the performers whose space it will become.

Be careful to view your design in the model box as closely as possible to the audience eye-line.

sketches might be in any medium: ink, crayon, felt-tipped pens, paint, on the computer… They might be a precise line drawing or a loose collage of texture and colour. We might do a new drawing for each variation, or we could do multiple photocopies of the outline drawing and then play around with tone and colour without having to redraw it each time. We could tear colours and textures out of magazines and collage these pieces into the outline. We could scan the drawing into our image-editing program and explore colour, tone and texture simultaneously by playing with the various filters and effects. Mobile phones and tablets have similar, but more limited, editing capabilities. We can scale the design down to the same scale as the set model, and have a look at the costume design in the context of the set. Or we can do all of these (*Chapter 12, page 206*).

For the set designer there are two ways we can work: two- or three-dimensionally, and they each have their advantages (and disadvantages). Two-dimensional *sketches* and *renderings* can be a great way of playing around with mood and atmosphere, which is actually quite difficult to do in a model, and plans (either hand drawn or in CAD) are a good way of exploring how set elements fit together, especially if we are designing a set that has a number of moving parts. However, it is difficult to get a real sense of how the space will work three-dimensionally in a sketch or plan, so it is a good idea to start playing in a three-dimensional model form sooner rather than later, either in a sketch model or a 3D graphic/drafting program such as Vectorworks.

A three-dimensional scale model is a very tangible way of seeing and understanding every element of the set design. Spatial relationships and the visual relationship between design elements in particular are very clear. We can experiment with the placement of the performers within the space by moving scale costumed figures around in the model, and we can experiment with the way light works sculpturally in the space by playing with desk lamps and torches in our model. We may progress to a presentation scale model through a number of preliminary, or *sketch models* in which we play and experiment with design possibilities. The sketch model will be more or less to scale, and we may already be working in the scale model box for the venue. In the sketch model we can tear or cut up shapes from old supermarket cartons or art boards and tape, pin or staple them together trying out different combinations of scale, different uses of height, different blocks of tone and colour, sculpting the space by moving

GWEN IN PURGATORY, **COSTUME DESIGNER BRUCE McKINVEN**

7.1–7.6
Bruce McKinven uses costume drawings (7.1–7.3) and experimentation with the actor in the fitting room (7.4–7.6) to test and refine his design for the character of Daniel in *Gwen in Purgatory*.

7.7–7.12
A small selection of Tess Schofield's design development sketches (7.7–7.11), and the actor
in costume for the character of Lizard (7.12) in the musical *The Adventures of Snugglepot
and Cuddlepie*.

PORN.CAKE, **DESIGNER CHRISTINA SMITH**

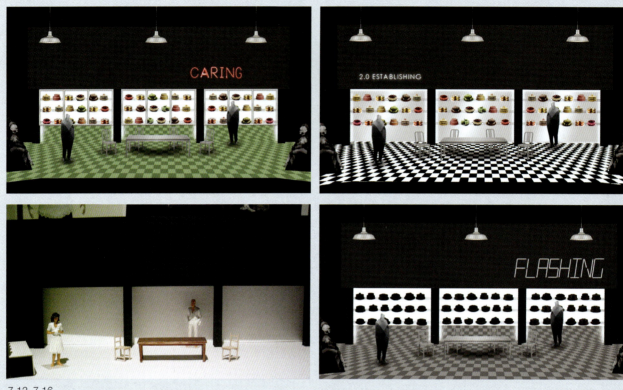

7.13–7.16
Christina Smith uses Adobe Photoshop to help her visualise different design possibilities for her set for *Porn.Cake* by photographing her preliminary model and using this as the basis for her experimentation.

the shapes around in relation to each other. We can quickly photocopy textures and architectural elements from art and architecture references (playing around with the tone and scale of the texture on the photocopier at the same time) and paste them into our sketch model, or use our computer and printer to do this. We can also photograph our sketch model, upload it into our image-editing program and start working on the image with our toolbox of design tools adjusting position, tone, contrast, colour saturation, scale and the way one element relates to another. A similar process of experimentation, trial and error and *play* can be done in virtual 3D in Vectorworks or AutoCAD (➡ *Chapter 11, page 190*).

Inevitably designers are increasingly using their computers as design tools. As designers become adept in using them they will become as natural a way of working creatively as the more traditional methods of sketching or model-making. Many designers who work digitally believe that their computer-based design work is enriched by their more traditional arts practice: they develop a deeper understanding of space and volume by working sculpturally

MADAGASCAR, DESIGNER JO BRISCOE

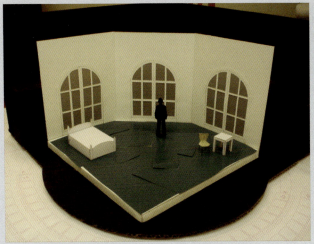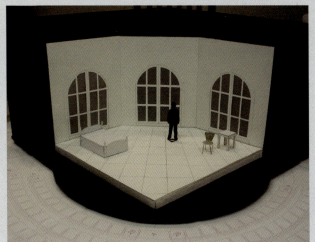

7.17 and 7.18

Jo Briscoe experiments with different versions of floor in her sketch model for *Madagascar*, positioning the model on a floorplan of the theatre to test sightlines.

in scale models, understand colour by mixing paint, or understand detail by painstakingly rendering this detail themselves. They will be less likely to simply cut and paste design elements imported from other design sources, and will understand that the precision of computer-generated designs can be deceptive— as early design ideas appear to be more resolved than they actually are. Many designers swap back and forth between manual and screen-based techniques, for example, scanning a hand-drawn sketch into Photoshop, working on the image in the computer, printing it out and continuing to work on the print with brush and paint. The most important point is that our method *helps* the flow, experimentation and development of our ideas.

Through this phase of experimentation the idea is to keep the design moving, growing, progressing: to play… experiment… consider the results… make some decisions ('actually dark *is* better than light, pink *does* work better than red, but it needs to be a rich, salmon pink')… and move ahead to the next step of the design. Each experiment will give us material to share with our director who will be able to see how the design is taking shape and give us feedback on the direction it is heading. This experimentation is enjoyable and profoundly creative. Our design will evolve before our very eyes. Anything is possible!

In this world of predictability, 'planability' and accountability, experimentation will often deliver the surprising, the strange and the beautiful. Breathtaking results will come if we make time for play and then allow our discoveries to inform the design and script. Joey Ruigrok van der Werven, designer

Case Study
Pygmalion — Stage 5:
Experimentation

Using tone, colour, scale, silhouette, balance, unity and contrast in the *Pygmalion* designs to create focus.

Using tone and colour to create focus

Experimenting with scale and position of key set elements

Exploring colour relationships and silhouette

I believe that EVERY part of a design should have meaning (if only to myself). The meaning in every detail helps me tell the story and also serves to remind me WHY I made particular design choices, as I negotiate the realisation of the designs with all the artisans who work with me.

Hugh Colman, designer

FURTHER THINKING
THE DESIGN TOOLBOX

The basic tools for any visual artist are *shape/silhouette, form, line, scale, colour, tone, texture, pattern/rhythm, balance, contrast, unity/discord* and *detail*. Because performance is kinetic we can also add *movement* to our design toolbox, and because performance involves time we should also add *change/transformation*.

We will each have our own personal way of using these tools: some of us will love working with colour, while others naturally express themselves through the structure and shape of things. These preferences become part of our personal style, and it is worth considering what your preferences are. But we can always extend our visual language by experimenting with all of the design tools, and we can learn the fine points of how to use them from the masters in other fields of the visual arts, such as painting, sculpture, couture fashion and architecture.

A very common approach is to start by establishing the shape and scale of a design element. And then go on to experiment with texture, colour, tone and pattern. The next step may be to put the developed element together with other parts of the design and begin experimenting with how they relate to each other by playing with balance, contrast, movement, transformation and unity. For most designers detail comes last, but it might be the very thing that *you* want to start with.

There is a range of variables within each design tool (shown opposite by ↔). Two elements that are at opposite ends of the range of variables will have high contrast: an angular shape will contrast with a rounded one, a dark shape will contrast with a light one. We can amplify the contrast by putting a number of variables together: for example, a large, dark, heavy, angular shape against a small, pale, light, rounded one will have extreme contrast, and will express our design ideas very strongly.

We tend to associate particular subjective qualities with many of the variables, (shown below by =). We can use these associations to consciously guide the audience's interpretation: for example, clothe a dominating character to appear heavy and hard, and the subject of their domination to appear light and fragile.

DESIGN TOOLS

SHAPE AND FORM can be two-dimensional (shape) or three-dimensional (form). In costume design shape may also be referred to as silhouette. The shape of something is usually determined by what it is (a hat, a door, a cloud). If the design is stylised the shape may *suggest* a particular object rather than literally describing it. If the design is wholly abstract the shape will be informed by aesthetic and expressive values: what it 'feels' like.

We can develop our appreciation of form by looking at sculpture and architecture, and learn by observation how to conceive our design sculpturally so that the space defined by the set works as a three-dimensional environment, and the costumes work from all angles as the performers move through the space.

Variables of shape and form include:

two-dimensional, 'flat'	↔	three-dimensional, sculptural
geometric (= order, man-made, masculine)	↔	organic (= free, natural, feminine)
angular (dynamic)	↔	rounded (gentle, fluid)
sharp (= precise)	↔	fuzzy/blurred (= ambiguous)
hard	↔	soft
heavy (= strong)	↔	light, fragile (= delicate)
simple	↔	complex
orderly, neat	↔	disorderly, tangled
vertical (= forceful, having stature)	↔	horizontal (= peaceful, landscape)

SCALE describes the relative size of elements. Scale is an important tool for communicating the significance of one element compared to another. We can also play with the scale of objects to communicate ideas, for example, a person sitting in a too-large chair will appear diminished.

large (= dominating, powerful	↔	small (= discrete, weak)

TONE describes how dark, mid-tone or light an element is. Dark tones recede, light tones advance, mid-tones appear neutral. Tone is a design tool that particularly involves the lighting designer who plays with tone by adjusting light levels. A study of the masters of black and white photography will extend our understanding of tone.

dark (= foreboding, death)   ↔   light (= hope, life)

COLOUR: There are a number of ways of describing colour (or hue). The primary colours are red, blue and yellow, secondary colours are purple, green and orange, tertiary colours are browns. Warm colours are red-purple, red, orange and yellow. Cool colours are blue, blue-purple and green. Warm colours advance, and cool colours recede. Complementary colours are opposite on the colour wheel and analogous (related) colours are grouped next to each other on the colour wheel. Colour is regarded as the design tool with the strongest emotional impact. It is also an important tool in the lighting designer's toolbox. Different cultures have particular meanings attached to specific colours (for example, in China red means good fortune; Westerners associate it with passion) but these meanings can be highly subjective and dependent on the context (for example, yellow can be the colour of sunlight or madness or danger!). Look to the colourists in painting to inspire your use of colour. The range of colours we use in a design may be referred to as a 'palette', and the way artists from the past or other cultures use colour can inspire the palette for our production.

intense, saturated, undiluted   ↔   pastel, unsaturated, diluted, neutral

tint, high value (mixed with white)   ↔   tone, low value (mixed with black)

warm (= emotion, happy, energetic)   ↔   cool (= intellect, sad, contemplative)

discordant, complementary, opposite   ↔   harmonious, analogous

TEXTURE: We have a great sensual pleasure in the feel of surfaces—their texture. But the audience is not close enough to feel our costumes and sets, so we might imply a texture using painterly techniques, or exaggerate the textures so the audience can 'read' it. The materials we use to make our sets and costumes will have particular textures that we can utilise to communicate the difference between one element and another: wool, frayed denim, roughcast cement or sparrow-picked stone on one hand; silk, fur, polished marble and glass on the other hand. Light can be used to reveal or eliminate texture: extreme high, low or side light casts shadows that reveal texture, and soft front light tends to wash it out.

smooth (= refined)   ↔   rough (= crude)

new, slick   ↔   coarse, distressed/broken down

even   ↔   uneven, crumpled

LINE/DIRECTION: Line might be used to define the shape of an object (an outline) or to define contours or structure within a shape. Line can also be usefully used to imply direction—to draw our eye from one point to another or to connect two elements.

straight ↔ curved

divergent (moving away from each other) ↔ convergent (moving towards a centre)

angled ↔ tangled

thick ↔ thin

PATTERN/RHYTHM: When a design element is repeated a pattern is established. The pattern might have a particular rhythm, where one part has more emphasis. The rhythm might be broken and the pattern interrupted for dramatic visual effect, or the pattern might vary from one part of the design to another. Types of patterns include stripes, spots, paisleys, florals, checks, plaids and animal prints.

plain ↔ patterned

geometric ↔ organic

regular ↔ irregular

BALANCE/HARMONY: When two design elements are more or less equal in scale, mass, tone, colour value or textural contrast they will appear to be balanced. Balanced elements appear harmonious. In theatre harmony is not considered dramatic, so we will often play with imbalance between design elements to create a sense of dramatic tension and potential.

balanced ↔ imbalanced

equal ↔ unequal

similar ↔ different

symmetrical ↔ asymmetrical

UNITY: Design elements that all fit together into a coherent whole will have visual unity. Contemporary aesthetics are much more elastic than in the past; modern audiences are happy to accept combinations of elements that even 20 years ago would have confused them. Even so audiences today might be irritated by a careless lack of unity in a production, whereas planned and considered disunity might usefully provoke, stimulate or challenge. We can consciously introduce discordant elements that break the unity of the production to create highly dramatic effects (➡ *Chapter 5: Post-Modernist productions, page 65*).

DETAIL: All of the design tools can be used in a big-picture way, or in a detailed way. How close or distant the audience are to or from the stage will determine how we use detail in our design. If the performance venue is a large one, most of the audience will only get the big picture, but enough detail still needs to be there for those who are close to the stage. We can think of it as being like the wide shot and close-up in film-making: the wide shot gives us the context, and the close-up gives us the detail. In theatre we don't cut between these two perspectives—the audience are always aware of the context even when they are concentrating on one part of the stage picture. Balancing the big picture with the detail is an important aesthetic juggling act for the designer.

MOVEMENT is intrinsic to performance. The director will spend hours with the cast in rehearsal choreographing when and how a character or group of characters moves, pauses, is still. Movement draws our eye, and a moving design element will always grab the audience's attention. It may be a twirling umbrella, a curtain moving gently in a breeze, or tracking a set element from one side of the stage to the other. Finding ways to dramatise our design elements through movement often links our work to the work of the performers who we can also think of as moving elements within the space.

TRANSFORMATION/CHANGE: The events of a theatrical performance happen over time, and within this passage of time characters, moods and situations change. These changes are usually a central part of the dramatic storytelling, and it can be a wonderful creative challenge to find ways to reflect, evoke or embody these changes within the design. Frequently a central character will change from one mental state to another, or their relationship to the world they inhabit might change, or we might want to transport the audience from one place to another, or shift the mood from one state to another.

These changes can all be expressed through our design by exploring how one element transforms into another. A change of costume can be a very effective way of using physical changes in our design to reflect psychological changes in a character. Lighting too is a very flexible tool for influencing changes in how the world feels to an audience. Physical changes in setting can be much more than shifts in location: they can express the themes and ideas in the script, and be a physical expression of the characters' journeys. Set and costume transitions can also be highly theatrical events that give the production an injection of visual energy that can stimulate and refresh the audience's imaginative engagement.

CONTRAST: Through all of these experiments we are really making judgments about the difference or contrast between each part of the design. Contrast tells the audience how to see things in relation to each other, and to understand these differences. We can use all of our design tools in a high- or low-contrast way. By playing with small degrees of contrast between elements the differences will be subtle, and the audience will read these elements as being similar or related (for example, a character dressed in charcoal and smooth textures in a sleek black set). Or we can employ extreme contrasts of scale, tone, texture or colour, and combinations of all of these and the audience will perceive these elements as being extremely, dramatically different (for example, the same character changes costume into a bright yellow woolly knitted top, within the same sleek black set).

FOCUS: Surely one of the most important roles of the design is to help direct the audience's attention to where we want them to look. Focus tells the audience what is more important or less important. We are 'directing' the audience's eyes, and by doing this we are communicating information that will influence their interpretation. The work of the actors and director during rehearsals will make the focus of each scene explicit to the audience, but the designer can also help to focus the audience's attention. We can provide a dynamic entrance, dress a character in a strongly contrasting costume, strip away distracting elements in the background or use levels or other devices to create well-focused places within the set for specific action. The lighting designer will also have an important role in shaping focus throughout the production.

We can use all of the design tools to focus a particular character, moment, object or quality. We can use focus subtly or boldly. Consider an evenly lit grey cement space where all of the characters are in neutral tones and colours—our eye will move around the space, giving each character equal attention… a character dressed in stark white enters… our attention will immediately shift to that character… one of the neutral characters removes a jacket to reveal a red shirt—there will be a contest for our attention between these two characters… we light one of them more intensely, or they move to a level on the set where they are higher than those around them and our focus shifts again. Seen in this way focus can be one of the designer's (and director's) most dynamic tools.

We will investigate the design toolbox, and especially focus, contrast, unity and transformation in more detail in following chapters (➡ *Chapter 11, page 190 and Chapter 12, page 206*).

When I was a student my tutor told me I was good with colour, I think he was desperately thinking of something nice to say, but I have hung on to that compliment for my entire career. It seems I often work with large amounts of saturated colour. Recently on **Carmen**, *one of the costume-makers commented, 'well you can't be accused of shying away from colour'. I will take that as another compliment, just 30 years down the track.*

Julie Lynch, designer

USING SPACE AS A DESIGN TOOL

Journal of a Plague Year (Set Designer Anna Tregloan, Costume Designer Fiona Crombie)

This chapter investigates a number of different ways the designer can think about space and use space visually to shape the performance.

ALSO IN THIS CHAPTER—FURTHER THINKING: Theatre Spaces and How They Shape

The simple choice of deciding if the audience are in the room *of the drama, or in a black void* looking into the room *of the drama is one I consciously make. Simple examples of this are choosing whether to place the performers on a raised stage or have them play on the floor level, or choosing to light the space, or to have design elements behind or only visible within the peripheral vision of the audience.*

Dale Ferguson, designer

We inhabit space: it shapes everything we do, and the performance space is no different. It can be intimate or vast, constrained or open, changing or static... These and many other variables have the potential to shape the performance and in turn shape the audience's experience. It is our role as performance designers to realise this potential.

There are several ways we can think about space as performance designers. Before we get stuck into the task of designing the set we need to get our heads around all the ways that space can work:

- *The physical stage space*: thrust, arena, end-stage, proscenium, traverse, in-the-round, found spaces, formal/informal space, focus, eye-line, scale and atmosphere.
- *Actor–audience relationship*: engagement, alienation and immersion.
- *Space and place*: identifying space with character and use, whose space is it, when and where?
- *Space for performers*: space for action, sculptural space.
- *The visual space*: pictorial/illusionistic, realistic, metaphoric, dynamic, imaginative space, invented space.
- *The changing space*: transforming the space to make meaning.
- *Practical, working space*: control, equipment, off-stage space, transformations.

Whatever we are doing with space as performance designers, space is never empty; it is always *doing* something and *meaning* something. By understanding how space works we can make it work for us, and for the production.

THE PHYSICAL STAGE SPACE

The architecture of the venue defines the stage space. This architecture has evolved over thousands of years as theatre-makers have continued to experiment with the best way of setting up the space for the performers (*the stage*) and the space for the audience (*the auditorium*). The stage will often be a defined, raised area, and the auditorium will usually be arranged in raked tiers of seating.

The basic types of stage space are: *thrust, arena, in-the-round, end-stage, proscenium* and *traverse,* and in Western theatre practice they evolved in approximately that sequence. (The historical development of these staging formats, and how they shape performance is investigated in depth in the next section (➡ *Further Thinking, page 128*).

In the thrust stage format the audience surrounds the stage on three sides as in a Greek amphitheatre; in the arena and in-the-round the audience completely surrounds the stage as in a sports arena; the end-stage audience directly faces the stage from one side only as in a cinema; the traverse audience is split in half with the audience facing each other across the stage; and the proscenium is a frame that clearly separates the audience from the stage.

Each of these different staging formats places the audience in a different relationship to each other and to the stage, and these different relationships give the audience a different experience. This experience might be more or less *communal* (where the audience strongly feel they are sharing the space and their experience with the rest of the audience), and more or less *intimate*. In communal spaces the audience will be very aware of each other and will tend to experience the production as part of a shared human context—an extension of the world we all share. Thrust, arena and traverse formats are all spaces in which the audience strongly feels part of a communal experience. End-stage and proscenium spaces are usually more isolating, especially when the audience are sitting in straight, parallel rows where they cannot see the rest of the audience around them. While we cannot change the intimacy or shared nature of the theatre space, we can take it into account in our design approach, and work with or rebalance the effect of the venue.

The *scale* and *atmosphere* of the venue will influence the audience too. Large venues will be less intimate than small ones; formal venues with rigid, symmetrical architectural lines and corporate textures and lighting will be less inviting than informal venues in which asymmetry and a less rigid interior design will make the audience feel more relaxed. The mood of the space will influence how the audience feels when audience members settle into their seats. Sometimes as designers we need to consider 're-tuning' the mood of the space, as for example designing a comedy for a very cold, formal venue might benefit from some design initiatives such as atmospheric lighting, an enticing pre-show image or a bold reveal to set the audience in the right frame of mind.

Different stage formats will also *focus* the audience's attention in different ways. Each venue will have an area on the stage that is especially well focused. This area of the stage might be thought of as a 'zone of command'[xx]—it is a strong position from which an actor will feel they have control over the whole audience. The best way to get a feel for the extent of this area of natural strong focus is to stand on the stage and experiment with moves to the side and up and downstage while looking out into the auditorium. Placing set elements

WHO, WHAT, WHERE, WHEN AND HOW?

When we are designing our set we are shaping the personality of the performance space so that the audience understands the context for the production. Even when we are working in a stylised or abstract style we still need to answer important questions about the characters and the space they inhabit.

WHO: *Whose space is it?* Is it a personal space? If so, what is their personality, and how would they express this in their surroundings? Think about their age, gender, status and occupation. How would these aspects influence the appearance of the space? If it is a public space or workspace how would the personality of the 'owner' of this space be expressed in the appearance of the space, and how would the personality(ies) of the principal character(s) fit with this? Are they in conflict or harmony with their space?

WHAT: *What is the space used for?* How is the function of the space expressed in how it looks? Is it a work or a leisure space, a meeting space, or a private retreat? And how will the physical actions of the performers influence this function? Think about the energy of their movements within the space, and their entrances, exits and resting places.

WHERE: *Where is the space?* What is the national, social and cultural context of the space? Is it a specific location? Is it part of a natural or man-made environment?

WHEN: What is the timeframe of the production? What is the period? Season? Time of day or night?

HOW: Once you have worked out the answers to these questions go back to your research and the concept and work out the best way to visually communicate this information with your design.

such as furniture, levels or entrances within the zone will provide potential for very strong, focused moves for the performers. Areas of the stage outside the zone will feel marginal, less focused and less powerful.

The *eye-line* of the performer in relation to their audience is also a key factor in how the theatre space works. Usually the performer will be on a raised stage so that those at the back of the audience can clearly see the performer. If the performer is too high above the audience they will appear somewhat alienated and superior to the audience. Conversely, if the stage is too low (as in venues where there is no raised stage) and most of the audience is looking down on the performer, the performer will appear diminished and 'lose status'. The ideal eye-line is where about half the audience are below the performer's eye level, and about half are above it. We can introduce raised stages or levels, ramps or treads as set elements to help rebalance the venue's eye-line.

Each theatre format will naturally work better for some forms of theatre than for others. Intimate spaces tend to work better for intense or immediate, highly focused productions with smaller casts where the audience is able to see every nuance of the actor's performance. Larger-scale venues are better for spectacle and illusion and highly physical works with large casts, epic and 'big picture' productions where the audience takes in a whole pictorial world. As designers we can use our designs to work with the strengths and minimise the limitations of our venue. The first step is to be aware, and to analyse the venue's format, scale and atmosphere, and then respond to these by considering design choices such as colour, audience lighting or extending the stage or performance into the auditorium.

THREE *BLACKBIRD* PRODUCTIONS: COMPARE AND CONTRAST

Three designers and their directors, in three different productions of *Blackbird* use space in different ways to communicate the raw themes of David Harrower's intense realist drama: entrapment, sexual abuse and the complex interplay of love and loathing, hope and desperation. Set in the present day in an impersonal office staff room the bleak, prosaic environment expresses the play's desolation, while acting as an ironic visual counterpoint to the characters' search for love.

COMPARE THREE PRODUCTIONS OF *BLACKBIRD*
BLACKBIRD #1 DIRECTOR MELISSA CANTWELL, DESIGNER CLAUDE MARCOS, LIGHTING DESIGNER MATTHEW MARSHALL, PERTH THEATRE COMPANY, 2012

Production image

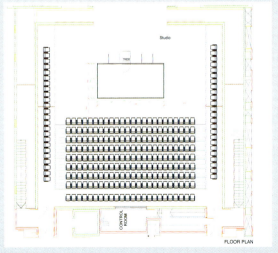

Plan

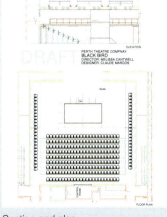

Section and plan

8.1–8.3
Claude's set design for an intimate end-stage venue keeps the audience close, but sharply separates them from the performers. The alienating glass box focuses action and is both an intensely atmospheric real room and a metaphorical prison. Choice of objects such as furniture gives us just enough information to understand whose space it is, where it is and what it is used for.

THE ACTOR–AUDIENCE RELATIONSHIP

The separation or closeness between actor and audience may be largely dictated by the venue in which the production will be presented. However, there is much a designer can do to draw the audience in or keep them removed, and it is important to reflect on how you want your audience to engage. Sometimes a director might want the audience to remain fully aware of who and where they are as they are watching the play, prompting them to think more objectively about what the play means to them and lead them to a specific understanding, as in the techniques of alienation. In this case, the designer will employ distancing techniques such as constructing a frame around the action, exaggerating the physical separation of actor and audience, using projected visual information or using text to proclaim the setting to emphasise the barrier between stage and audience. Alternatively the creative team might work to immerse the audience in the theatrical experience by blurring the boundary between stage and audience. Clothing the actors and the space they inhabit in ways that are familiar to the audience will make them feel more connected to the characters. Linking the stage and auditorium with lighting or set elements, seating the audience within the stage space, or providing actors' entrances through the audience will reduce the impact of physical barriers such as a proscenium arch. Seen in this way the design can be a psychological tool for shaping the audience's experience (➡ *Further Thinking, page 92*).

I am intrigued by the simplification of space and context. I truly believe removing superfluous elements and retaining the essence of a scene or environment allows an audience to engage with their own imagination, inspiring them to have a more involving theatrical experience.

Claude Marcos, designer

SPACE AND PLACE

A fundamental concept of space in performance is the way the space defines or reflects the character of the people who inhabit it. Just as in daily life spaces take on the character of their occupants, and also influence their occupants. This is why set designers need to think about character and costume designers need to think about space. For us as designers a big part of the function of the set design is to communicate the 'who, where, when and what'—whose space it is, where and when it is and what it is used for. Even abstract productions with non-realistic designs will be informed by this idea of space as used, personalised place.

When space becomes linked with people—who they are and what they do— it starts to become a specific *place*—a *lived* space, a location, and ultimately as part of the set design, a setting for the action of the production. Think about

COMPARE THREE PRODUCTIONS OF *BLACKBIRD*
BLACKBIRD #2 DIRECTOR PETER EVANS, DESIGNER CHRISTINA SMITH, LIGHTING DESIGNER MATTHEW SCOTT, MELBOURNE THEATRE COMPANY, 2008

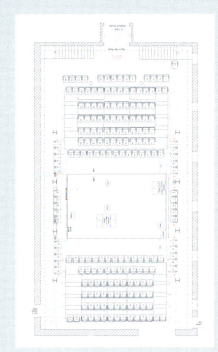

Plan

Concept visual

Production image

8.4–8.7
Christina's set design for an intimate traverse venue brings the audience into the room and makes them both spectator (watching others watching) and participants in the action. Her concept visual shows how the space transforms as lived space through the actions of the characters, transforming from pristine to chaotic. The two side walls are used to communicate specific architectural information that locates the action in a specific time and place.

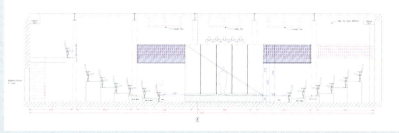

Section

the space you are in right now. Is it an interior or exterior space? Whose place is it? Is it your own personal place, or a shared place such as a family living room? Whose personality is reflected in the objects around the room, or the colour, textures and surfaces of the interior design? What is the function or use of the space? A bedroom will look different from a kitchen because they have different functions and are used in different ways. Is it a public place? Again, what is the use of the space, and how is the 'owner' of the space reflected in the architecture, scale, textures and details of the space? An office space will look different from a schoolroom; a police sergeant's office will look different from a corporate executive's office. We are very adept at reading even subtle visual clues in the world around us to understand the places we are in and what is happening in them: spotting the chocolate wrapper left on the bedroom floor, or morning light pouring through a window, or the pile of books left on the chair. We take in these details and interpret them to make sense of what is happening around us. Often in our first impressions we will have made a very sophisticated assessment of who, where and what. Our audience will also make the same kind of astute interpretation, based on the information we give them in our set and costume design, so we need to make sure that the information we give them is useful information.

Spaces reflect the character of their occupants, but frequently there is a dramatic tension between the personality of the principal characters and the places they occupy. In *Romeo and Juliet* the tender passion of the young lovers is set within a violent city in which the two most powerful families are at war; in *Pygmalion* Eliza, the young Covent Garden flower-seller, is like a 'fish out of water' in the privileged home of Professor Higgins when he takes her into his care. In *Blackbird* the ugly banality of the location acts as a counterpoint to the intense passion and vulnerability of the characters. Dramatic tensions between the characters and their environments is great 'visual food' for the audience's imagination, and when we express these tensions meaningfully in our design we really will be nourishing the dramatic life of the production.

Part of the location of the place/setting for the production is *when it is set*: the period, time of year (season) and time of day. When these are explicitly stated in the script we will identify this information in our script analysis. Often period and time are not explicit, and we can make our own interpretations which will inform how the audience interpret the production. For example, we could set *Romeo and Juliet* at any time in the past or any version of the present day that connected with the production concept. We are, however, told in the script that it is hot. The heat of summer, the sombre mood of winter, the brightness of daylight or the drama of night-time can all be powerful factors in our design thinking even when our production is not set in a particular period.

COMPARE THREE PRODUCTIONS OF *BLACKBIRD*
BLACKBIRD #3 DIRECTOR CATE BLANCHETT, DESIGNER RALPH MYERS, LIGHTING DESIGNER NICK SCHLIEPER, SYDNEY THEATRE COMPANY, 2007

Production image

Plan

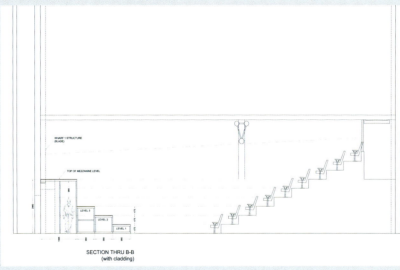

Section

8.8–8.10
Ralph's set design transforms a venue that is familiar to audiences as a thrust stage venue into an in-the-round venue, with the effect of initially disorienting them while immersing them in the action of the play. The steep eye-line down into the space and exposed steel railings suggest a sports arena such as a boxing ring and have an alienating effect that counterbalances the intimacy of in-the-round staging. The round table encourages action to keep moving around the performance area.

We identify the character and function of the space from our script analysis. From the script we learn the nationality, period, social context, age, occupation, gender and status of the owners or occupants of the script's locations. Our research will help us interpret this information through the design of the space. Our choices of architectural references, choice and placement of objects, choices of surfaces and textures, scale, atmosphere… every design element will help describe whose place it is and what it is used for. This is what we know of as the *setting* of the production. How realistic or stylised, minimalist or detailed the setting is will be influenced by the production style and visual style (➡ *Chapter 5: Precedents of Production Style, page 60; Further Thinking, page 74*).

SPACE FOR PERFORMERS

Spaces reflect what real people do, but the performance space is not a real place. It is a space for performers—actors, dancers, acrobats, musicians—to make a performance. We can see it as a 'play' ground—space for the performers to perform the play in—and literally a playground for their actions. Performers may be motivated by characterisation, frequently based on how real people behave, but their performances are also expressive, physical acts that use movement and gesture to dramatically communicate ideas. As designers we can consider a number of factors that influence how the performers will use the space: *scale, containment/openness, entrances and exits, resting places, levels/ hierarchy, sculptural space.*

Scale: A large space not only allows for expansive gestures and big movements, it invites them. A large space might also 'dwarf' the performer and make them feel isolated. A smaller space will contain and nurture the energy of the performer, and smaller, detailed gestures become more expressive. A very small space might also suppress or 'imprison' the performer.

Containment/Openness: A contained, walled space provides for clear demarcation of 'on' and 'off' stage. Entrances and acting areas are clearly defined, and the context of the action becomes more of an enclosed, complete 'world'. A more open, undefined space allows for a blurring of the boundary of when a performer is an active player in the scene or is part of the background to the scene. Entrance points will not be clearly defined, and will be more subtle and less dramatic. Performers might use the 'edges' of the space in interesting ways, observing the action or commenting on it.

Entrances and exits: The placement of entrance points for the performer will inform how dynamic (active) their entrances will be. Entrances in which the performer enters diagonally across the stage will be more energetic and dynamic than entrances that are made from the sides. Upstage entrances, particularly upstage centre entrances are more focused, formal and dramatic than downstage entrances, and correspondingly downstage entrances will be more intimate and subtle than upstage ones. Entrances down from raised levels are especially powerful, and entrances up from below stage level inherently subtle.

Resting places: In daily life we tend to gravitate towards a piece of furniture or an object in a space. How we gather around and interact with these objects can be a powerful expression of the dynamics of the individual or group. So it is in the performance space where the places performers rest, stay standing still or sit will be important focal points around which action will be choreographed. Designers and directors will often experiment with the placement of these resting places—pieces of furniture, or objects that work as furniture—so that action moves forward, away from and around these points in interesting and dynamic ways. The action may flow for example around a circular table, be divided between two objects, or gravitate to a central object.

Levels/hierarchy: A level performance space places all of the performers on an equal footing. By introducing levels such as platforms, ramps or treads (stairs) within the space the designer makes it possible for the director to make choices about the position of a performer higher or lower than another, by which the audience may read relative status or importance.

Sculptural space: Stage formats in which the audience wraps around the stage, such as thrust and arena give the performers more complex ways of positioning themselves within the space—the audience will read the variations of proximity as the performers move around each other. We think of these spaces as being more sculptural. End-stage and proscenium formats are more two-dimensional and less sculptural. In these formats the audience will read movements across the stage more strongly than movements up and downstage (➡ *Further Thinking, page 128*).

THE CHANGING SPACE

When the choreographer or director moves performers, or the lighting designer shifts the mood of the space with a lighting cue the space is transformed, and the audience reads and interprets these changes. As designers we can also look for opportunities to express meaningful dramatic changes by making physical changes to the space. These may be as subtle as moving a chair from dead centre where it is highly focused off to one side where it becomes less significant, or the spilling of a bottle of water over the floor making the prosaic surface reflective, slippery and dangerous. But changes to the space can also be bold and significant—communicating important changes in locale, time, mood or meaning. We can literally take the audience to a new place by transforming the space using any of the mechanical techniques—such as flies, automation, revolves—or by utilising the performers or lighting to effect change (➡ *Chapter 11: Set Transformations, page 200*).

THE VISUAL SPACE

Our set design is fundamentally a 'pretend' space—a fabricated, invented space conjured up by the designer. One of the thrills for the audience is that each time they come into the theatre venue they will see the stage transformed by the designer in a new way and will be transported to a unique imagined world.

We have seen how production style and visual style informs the kind of space, or 'world' of the production. The space might be more or less metaphoric, realistic, illusionistic or dynamic. It might be more or less abstract, more or less stylised, more or less fantastical, or more or less romantic or classical. All of these design choices will influence how the audience interprets the space. We can think of the visual space in terms of how literally descriptive it is (pictorial space), or how much it encourages the audience to use their own imaginations to fill in the gaps (imaginative space) (➡ *Chapter 5: Precedents of Production Style, page 60 and Further Thinking, page 74*).

PRACTICAL WORKING SPACE

We have looked at how well the performance space works for the audience and for the performers, but how well does it work for the designer? Each venue will have its own set of technical capabilities that will determine how well it works as a machine for getting the performance on—such as fly systems (hand or automated lines), revolves, lifts, lighting gantries, movable seating units and off-stage service space. Quite basic venues might function well despite a lack of technical facilities purely because there is enough service space around the stage to make working the production easy. Modern venues may be able to offer an amazing array of the latest technical resources for moving scenery and running the show, but new is not necessarily better—a hand-operated fly line operated by a skilled technician will probably result in a more sensitive cue and a better 'theatrical moment' in the production than an automated system that has been insensitively programmed by a less experienced technician. As set designers the venue's facilities and the technicians who operate them become part of our design toolbox—tools that we can use as an effective part of our design to enable us to transform the space during the production. Like any tools, we can develop a greater degree of control by learning how the venue's technical elements work and by carefully considering how they will work within our design (➡ *Chapter 11, page 190*).

Case Study
Pygmalion — Stage 6: Working with Space

The set model for Act 3 (and overhead view of the model overlaid over the floorplan), CAD floorplan and section show how the set design developed as a response to the theatre space: opening up the proscenium to give a pictorial scale, installing a raked stage to help make the stage more dynamic (and to conceal the furniture tracking system), bringing the action as close to the audience as possible by using only the front third of the stage, using a minimum of sculptural furniture elements to communicate place, character and period.

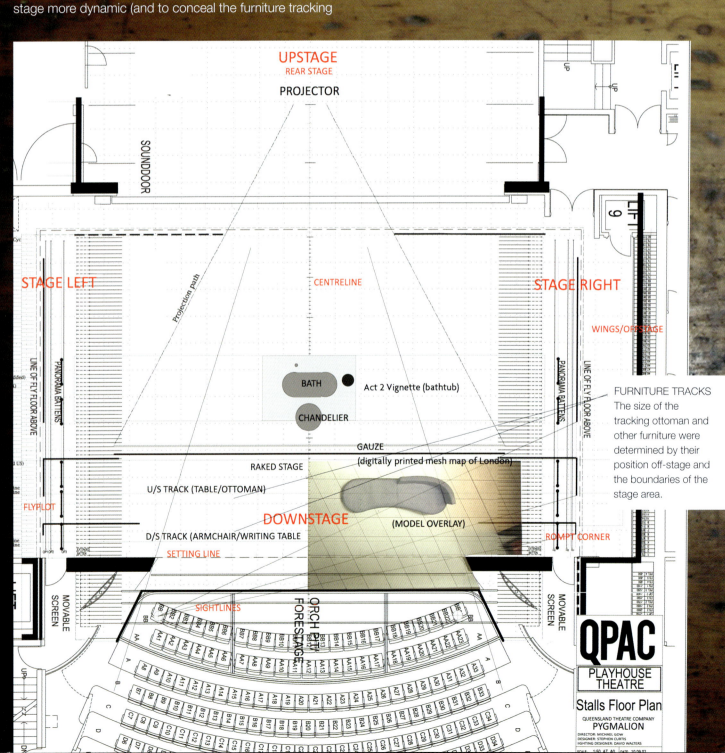

UPSTAGE
REAR STAGE
PROJECTOR

SOUNDDOOR

STAGE LEFT

CENTRELINE

STAGE RIGHT

WINGS/OFFSTAGE

LINE OF FLY FLOOR ABOVE

PANORAMA BATTENS

BATH

Act 2 Vignette (bathtub)

CHANDELIER

PANORAMA BATTENS

LINE OF FLY FLOOR ABOVE

GAUZE
(digitally printed mesh map of London)

RAKED STAGE

U/S TRACK (TABLE/OTTOMAN)

Projection path

FLYPLOT

DOWNSTAGE

(MODEL OVERLAY)

FURNITURE TRACKS
The size of the tracking ottoman and other furniture were determined by their position off-stage and the boundaries of the stage area.

D/S TRACK (ARMCHAIR/WRITING TABLE

SETTING LINE

PROMPT CORNER

SIGHTLINES

MOVABLE SCREEN

ORCH PIT/FORESTAGE

MOVABLE SCREEN

QPAC
PLAYHOUSE THEATRE

Stalls Floor Plan
QUEENSLAND THEATRE COMPANY
PYGMALION
DIRECTOR: MICHAEL GOW
DESIGNER: STEPHEN CURTIS
LIGHTING DESIGNER: DAVID WALTERS
SCALE 1:50 AT A0 DATE 10.09.02

Act 2 transition model, showing the bathtub set behind the digitally printed gauze map of London. With rebalancing of lighting these transition scenes could be set and revealed upstage of the gauze.

PYGMALION
SECTION
PLAYHOUSE   1:100 @ A3
Drawn by D. Walters

I long to break the proscenium to achieve greater audience contact, to deny the fourth wall and proclaim the innate theatricality, the sense of sharing, sense of community, of play, of intimacy that was achieved by the Elizabethan stage. There is no attempt to kid you that anything is real. You're there to share a space and an emotional experience.

John Bell, director

THEATRE SPACES AND HOW THEY SHAPE PERFORMANCE

In essence theatre consists of two elements: the performer and the audience. Wherever a performer has a 'show' to show us—a story to tell, a song to sing or acts of physical skill to demonstrate—people will gather around to watch. The most natural way for them to do this is to form a semicircle around the performer, allowing a small group of twenty or thirty people to see and hear the performers and engage with the performance—we are familiar with this arrangement when we watch a busker or street performance. When the audience expands the semicircle needs increase, so that the audience is never more than two or three people deep, and those at the back can still see and hear. As the semicircle expands the viewers are pushed further and further away. When the audience becomes too large this simple arrangement is less effective—the limits are dictated by everyone being able to see and hear satisfactorily.

The evolution of the performance space can be seen as an ongoing process of experimentation with how to solve this problem—how best to set up the physical relationship between the performers and their audience, and how to accommodate bigger and bigger audiences with good sightlines and acoustics.

To this end theatre-makers and theatre-builders have experimented with two factors: the arrangement of the performance space (*the stage*) and the arrangement of the audience space (*the auditorium*). This dual experimentation has resulted in many variations on several well-established forms of theatrical architecture:

- amphitheatre/thrust
- arena/in-the-round
- wagon stages
- end-stage and the hanamichi
- proscenium arch
- traverse
- the flexible space
- the found space
- cabaret.

In the following investigation we will review the historical precedents for each of these architectural theatre forms, and analyse the performance dynamics particular to each kind of space—how the spaces work and how as designers we can capitalise on their strengths and minimise their weaknesses. We will see how the shape of the spaces has influenced the way in which theatre is made, and how the desire for new theatrical forms has motivated the development of different kinds of theatre spaces.

THE AMPHITHEATRE/THRUST STAGE

Theatre spaces where the audience wraps 180° around the stage. Greek theatre and the modern thrust stage

The ancient Greeks understood that the most natural way for an audience to gather around a performer is in a semicircle, and the classical Greek stage developed and refined this layout to create the brilliantly successful open-air theatre spaces that can still be seen in many parts of the Mediterranean. Some of these spaces are so well preserved, and work so well as performance spaces they are still being used for theatre events today, 2500 years after their construction. In making their theatre spaces the Greeks sought a curving, conical slope or natural amphitheatre. They placed their performers at the bottom of the slope with the audience looking down on them from tiered seating levels cut into the slope. The tiers were later lined with timber bleachers, and still later with marble blocks, and it is these marble amphitheatres that we can still visit today in places such as Athens and Epidaurus in Greece and at Ephesus in Turkey.

When we sit in the marble tiers of these amphitheatres we are immediately aware of how good the sightlines are: every seat has a clear view to the stage, and every member of the audience's attention is focused to the centre of the playing space. The acoustics are also brilliant, with a spoken conversation on stage being clearly audible from the back of the auditorium.

It is easy to underestimate the achievement of the Greeks in shaping the auditorium in a way so successful that it remains the template for theatre architects today. Their raked (sloping), tiered auditorium is still the universal seating solution in theatres of every shape and size around the world. As well as providing excellent sightlines to the performers, this innovation brings the audience together as a unified, coherent whole, seated together to share in a special, collective experience. This congregational, communal space has a powerful connecting and bonding effect on the audience, which profoundly helps to reinforce the power of the performance event.

The sweeping 180° semicircular arc of the amphitheatre seating reinforces this effect. As we look around from our seat in the marble bleachers we are very aware of those seated around and with us. The space was designed to seat a whole community and it is a very communal space. This adds force to the sense of theatre as a shared, social activity. The curve of the tiered seating wraps around the stage, embracing the performance area, and we feel that the audience space and the performance space are strongly connected—two parts of a shared whole space. This factor, perhaps more than any other, characterises the amphitheatre and its close relative the *thrust stage*. The audience–performer relationship is defined by this very strong physical connection: the sense of shared space and shared experience.

As we look down from our seat at Epidaurus (built circa 300–400 BC) we will also feel the religious heritage of Classical Greek drama in the formal, symmetrical geometry of the space. The performance space here is circular, with an altar in the centre used by priests officiating at ceremonies celebrating the god Dionysus. These ceremonies later developed into dramatic festivals in which the chorus of fifty to sixty performers acted out tales of gods and heroes in dance, song and ritualised movement. Playwrights such as Sophocles and Aeschylus were engaged to write scripts for these performances, and as their interest shifted to the actions and motivations of individual characters actors were engaged to play these roles, and the theatre space adapted to this new use. A raised platform stage ('*logeion*') was added upstage of the *orchestra* to help focus the audience's attention on these performers and to give the actors greater command of the auditorium by elevating them somewhat in relation to the audience. (When you stand on a raised stage and look out into the auditorium you will immediately understand the power of the stage platform.) Over time as the role of the chorus diminished and their number was reduced, their space on stage was also reduced. The circular *orchestra* was reduced to a semicircle, which enabled the now more important *logeion* to be brought downstage, bringing the principal actors closer to the audience. These features are preserved in the theatre at Palmyra in Syria (opposite).

A wall with a number of openings and a higher platform level was added behind the *logeion*. This worked as an acoustic sounding board for the actors, as well as providing them with entrance and exit points and off-stage space for costume changes. It also functioned to conceal some of the stage machinery.

LEARNING FROM GREEK AND EARLY ROMAN THEATRE

THE THEATRE SPACE: Semicircular amphitheatre, unified, communal auditorium, raked tiered seating, excellent sightlines, focus and acoustics; raised stage helps focus actors, rear wall provides focused entry points for actors, huge venues seating up to 25,000.

DESIGN TECHNOLOGY: Masks, elevated shoes, *deus ex machina* (literally 'god machine'—a crane used for lowering characters of the gods from behind the *skene*), *periaktoi* (triangular units of scenery which were rotated to reveal a different scene represented on each face), *ekkylema* (stage trucks).

PLAYS AND PLAYWRIGHTS: Drama: comedy and tragedy. Sophocles, Aeschylus, Euripides, Aristophanes, Menander, Plautus, Terence.

CONVENTIONS: Plays written in verse; chorus (*khoros*: band of dancers or singers) provides social commentary and guides the audience's interpretation; dramatic conflict and the protagonist (*heroare*) are central dramatic elements; gods have human personalities.

DESIGN RESPONSES TO THE AMPHITHEATRE/THRUST SPACE: Capitalise on the intimacy in smaller venues and try to build intimacy in the larger ones; strengthen the link between the stage and audience; explore the potential of the floor surface; use levels, ramps or lifts to make the floor more dynamic and assist the flow of action; place furniture or other objects strategically within the space to help motivate action; use detail as an important design tool; explore imaginative rather than literal or pictorial solutions.

AMPHITHEATRES/THRUST

skene
logeion
theatron
orchestra

8.11 The theatre at Palmyra, Syria, was built by the Romans in the 1st century AD over an earlier Greek theatre. The distinctive features of a Hellenistic Greek theatre are still well preserved: the *logeion*, *skene* and the raked curved auditorium (*theatron*).

Further Thinking **131**

Initially this wall (*skene*) was a simple wooden structure, and later under the Romans become an elaborate architectural background to the performance space.

We cannot leave Epidaurus or Ephesus without remarking on the massive scale of these theatre spaces. There are two Greek Theatres at Ephesus: the Great Theatre seating an audience of 25,000 in 66 rows, and the Odeon seating 1500 in 22 rows. By modern standards even the Odeon would be regarded as a large theatre, and the name of the Great Theatre feels like a massive understatement. If we are sitting towards the back of one of these grand amphitheatres we are very conscious that the performers are a long way (perhaps 60 metres) below us. Ancient Greek theatre-makers developed a performance style in response to their large theatre spaces: stylised and exaggerated gestures, the formalised group work of the chorus, elevated platform shoes, brightly coloured costumes and the use of very graphic masks indicating the age, sex, standing and dominant emotion of the characters all helped to give the performers stature and focus, and these techniques are still used by designers today for large-scale *arena productions*. Innovative stage machinery was also employed to provide storytelling imagery that could be read right from the back row: from behind the *skene* a crane ('*deus ex machina*') could lower the characters of gods in from the heavens, platforms on wheels ('*ekkylema*') were used as trucks to bring in visions of the result of unseen action, such as the bodies of those killed in a war, and rotating triangular prisms ('*periaktoi*') were used to present pictorial changes of scene by revolving them from one face to the next. These design innovations continue to be used by theatre designers today.

We can now see, at this very early stage of the development of the theatre space, four of its most basic architectural elements are established: the raked, tiered auditorium, the audience wrapping around the performance space, the elevated stage, and the scenic wall providing focused actor entrance points. Following generations of theatre-builders and architects would go on to develop these elements into the thrust theatres we recognise today.

THE MODERN THRUST STAGE: DESIGN RESPONSES

In the amphitheatre the audience wraps around the stage; with the thrust stage the stage projects ('thrusts') into the auditorium. The terminology implies a difference, but the dynamic of the two spaces is almost identical. The only real difference is that today amphitheatres are usually thought of as large, open-air performance spaces, and thrust theatres as more intimate, indoor venues.

There are many examples of thrust stages in daily use today wherever theatre is being made because they work so well as performance spaces and work particularly well for drama. There are many variations on the layout of these spaces, and they all have their own quirks and challenges for the designer, but in all of them the audience surrounds the stage on three sides, or approximately 180°, and in all of them there is a close physical relationship between the audience and the performer.

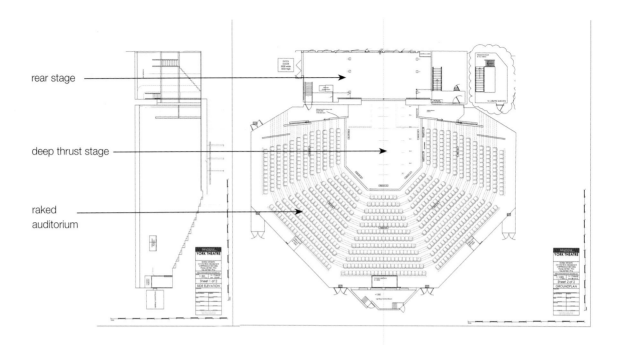

rear stage

deep thrust stage

raked
auditorium

8.12 Floorplan and section for the York Theatre, Seymour Centre—a large thrust stage venue (seating capacity 788) with a deep U stage. The stage is only slightly raised, with performers' eye-line to the bottom third of the raked auditorium.

For designers, directors and actors key features of the thrust stage include:

Intimacy: The close proximity of the audience to the performers, and the shared nature of the space help to produce a strong feeling that the audience are part of the theatre event and part of the social world being portrayed on stage. Directors and designers may strengthen this connection by placing action in the auditorium or by blurring the line between stage and audience, for example, by continuing the set into the auditorium. Some thrust venues are so large that they no longer function as intimate spaces.

Sculptural space: The audience are looking at the performers from three angles and will be very aware of the position of each performer in relation to each other on the stage. The audience will 'read' or derive meaning from the position of performers—how near or far they are from each other, who is in the foreground (downstage) and who is the background (upstage). On a practical level directors will need to find ways to keep their performers moving so that they do not mask the view to each other for any audience member for too long. Designers will need to help the director to find ways to keep the action moving, by thinking about the flow of movement through the set. Breaking the space up into fixed, defined areas can inhibit this flow. The placement of furniture or other objects downstage will help to motivate movement from upstage to downstage. Providing entrances through the auditorium, either down audience aisles, or through entrance tunnels known as '*vomitoria*' will also help to keep the action moving within the space.

THE TRIAL, SET DESIGNER CLAUDE MARCOS, COSTUME DESIGNER ALICE BABIDGE

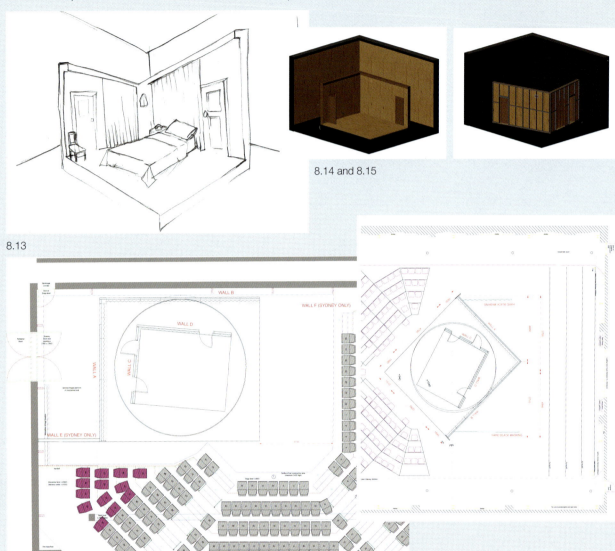

8.13

8.14 and 8.15

8.16 and 8.17

8.18

Claude Marcos's early set design sketch (8.13), 3D models (8.14, 8.15) and floorplans (8.16, 8.17) for two different thrust venues for an adaptation of Kafka's claustrophobic nightmare bureaucracy in *The Trial*. Claude's focused sculptural set extends the auditorium shape into the play space, and the revolving room-within-a-room juxtaposes a human-scaled intimacy within the imprisoning outer walls.

Detail: The audience are close. They will see everything. This allows designers to use detail such as the subtlety of texture or breaking down (aging) of costumes to communicate important information to the audience. It also means that there needs to be a very high level of design attention to how every detailed element of the design is finished. Actors' makeup will often be as subtle as street makeup. Lighting levels may be reduced as the audience are close enough to see clearly in low levels.

Eye-line: Many thrust stages are at floor level, with the performers' eye-line level with about the third row of the auditorium. Audience members sitting further back will to varying degrees be looking down on the performers. To improve this dynamic and to give the cast a greater command of the space, designers can introduce levels—platforms, ramps and treads (stairs). These will also help to make the space more sculptural and may assist the placement of actors and the flow of movement. Because the audience are looking down into the space, floor surfaces will be a very important visual element in the set design.

Limited pictorial potential: It is possible to 'paint a stage picture' on a thrust stage, and to create the illusion of a complete world on stage, but because the audience will always (to some extent) be aware that they are part of the picture, we are working against the grain when we try to do this. A design approach that encourages the audience to imagine what they cannot see rather than showing every literal ingredient works well in the thrust space.

Limited potential for illusion: The audience are close, and they are able to see the detail of how things work. Theatre as illusionistic magic works best when the audience is separated from the stage and their view to the stage is highly controlled, as in a proscenium arch space. If you are designing a thrust stage production that requires illusion it may be necessary to use the design to control the audience's view, or alternatively letting them simply enjoy the theatricality of seeing how it works.

ARENA THEATRE/THEATRE-IN-THE-ROUND

Theatre spaces where the audience surrounds the stage on all sides: Roman arenas, modern sporting arenas, entertainment centres, circus and theatre-in-the-round

When the Roman Empire expanded through Greece it absorbed the achievements of Greek theatre and copied and adapted their plays, performance styles and amphitheatres. As the Roman taste for spectacle and sporting contests overtook their interest in drama they developed a new architectural model for their performances: the arena—a massive in-the-round entertainment venue.

The tiered audience seating of a Roman arena surrounds the performance space on all sides, in a 360° elliptical format that is very familiar to us today from our large sports arenas or stadiums. The arenas were massive, designed for presenting extravagant events to huge audiences. Roman arenas were of a comparable size to our own: the Arena di Verona seated 30,000 spectators, the Coliseum in Rome seated 80,000 spectators, while a modern Olympic stadium seats around 100,000. The performers entered the arena through entrance tunnels (*vomitoria*) from beneath the seats, just as a sports team will do today. The Coliseum was also served by an elaborate network of underground tunnels and traps that allowed performers, wild animals and scenery to be raised by pulley-driven elevators into the arena, bringing them up into the centre of the action at various points. The performances were spectacular staged competitions, simulated battles and animal hunts, as well as ritualised executions, staged for the mass appeal of the Roman audience.

The arena space is the perfect solution for these kinds of events: the excitement of a big crowd gathered together, the swirl of constant movement, the audience always watching the 'big picture' while also able to see every moment of individual brilliance. Today when these arenas are co-opted for staging theatrical events such as pre-game shows, ceremonies and rock concerts the scale and shape of the space influences the shape these events take. They have forged their own unique production style—the 'arena spectacular'—to describe shows that combine action and spectacle for the mass audience.

vomitorium

harena

8.19 Arena di Verona, Verona, Italy, Roman arena built 30 AD. In ancient times 30,000 spectators filled the arena (derived from the Latin '*harena*', which means 'sand', which was used to absorb the contestants' blood) for the *ludi*, or public sporting contests and entertainments. Today the arena is still used for mass-appeal entertainments such as operatic and rock concerts.

LEARNING FROM THE ROMAN ARENA

THE THEATRE SPACE: Audience surround the stage/arena on all sides; performers enter via tunnels through the audience—*vomitoria*; huge venues seating 80,000 spectators; seating divided by class—the wealthier patrons closer to the front. Modern versions: the sports stadium, circus, in-the-round theatre spaces.

EVENTS: Spectaculars staged for the mass audience in honour of the emperor—mock battles and sea battles, sporting contests, executions. Today: sports events, rock concerts, arena spectaculars, circus, theatre-in-the-round.

TECHNOLOGY: Traps with pulley-operated elevators (lifts) to bring scenery and performers to stage (arena) level.

CONVENTIONS: Keep it moving!

DESIGN RESPONSES TO THE ARENA/THEATRE-IN-THE-ROUND: Strengthen the connection between stage and audience or consider the stage as a trap/island; place entrances or set objects in line with audience aisles or to promote flow of action; movable sculptural set/prop pieces; focus on costumes to provide important visual information; consider featured floor treatment; consider levels; consider ceiling elements; all design elements to be seen from all sides; use detail in intimate venues and scale up the designs graphically in large venues; consider using the arena floor as a projection surface.

The performances staged in these venues—sports matches, arena spectaculars and circus—all have one thing in common: constant movement. The audience are able to sit all around the performers because they are constantly moving; no section of the audience is blocked for too long from seeing the action in any part of the ring, arena or stage. This factor is integral to theatre-in-the-round, and we need to apply the rule in reverse when we are designing for these venues: *because* the audience is sitting all the way around the stage we need to keep the action moving.

Theatre-in-the-round is not a common format for drama. Although it is very actor-focused it is a challenging format to stage complex dramatic scenes. For designers many of the features of the arena/in-the-round performance space work in a similar way to the amphitheatre/thrust (sightlines and eye-line, social experience).

Intimacy: The in-the-round setup has the potential to be very intimate. In small-scale venues it is the *most* intimate of all staging formats, so the audience will automatically feel involved and 'connected to' the characters and design energy can go into fulfilling other needs. The in-the-round space can also be seen as a kind of 'trap' or island—the audience surrounds the stage and isolates the characters.

Movement: Even more than with the thrust stage continual movement and flow of action is essential so that sightlines to one performer are never masked for too long by another performer. The designer can help the director and actors to keep it moving by providing reasons to move from one place to another: the placement of entrance points or key furniture positions, the use of levels, and the control of light are some of the ways that the designers can help motivate action, or by inventing activities that keep characters moving. Diagonal lines of access and movement will help create a dynamic choreography of action. Fixed

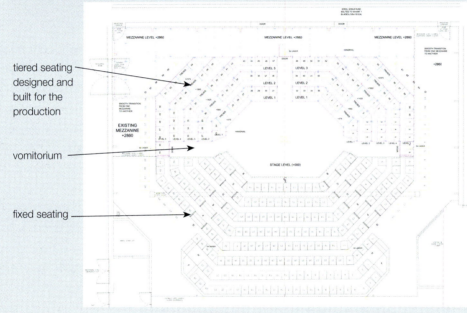

tiered seating designed and built for the production

vomitorium

fixed seating

8.20 and 8.21 Looking down into the performance arena and ceremonial entry ramp for the 2006 Commonwealth Games opening ceremony, and Dan Potra's pre-visualisation for part of the ceremony in which a tram 'flew' over the stadium roof and into the arena.

8.22 Floorplan for Wharf 1, Sydney Theatre Company, a thrust stage venue which set designer Ralph Myers converted into an in-the-round space for his production of *Blackbird* (➡ page 122 for more on this production). Compare this use of Wharf 1 with 8.16, page 134.

set items or furniture will be less of a sightline issue if they are positioned in line with the audience aisles.

Sculptural space: Conceiving every element of the design to be seen from every angle is vital—the back of a character's costume will be seen as much as the front; furniture or set elements should be thought of as like sculptures that look good from every angle.

Scenic potential: It is almost impossible to paint a stage picture with the in-the-round stage. The floor surfaces will be the set designer's principal means of communicating place, so a great deal of design energy will go into resolving the floor and making it as expressive as possible. Ceiling elements may also be possible, and may be integrated into the lighting design, for example, skylights and ceiling panels that filter or texture light in an expressive way.

Character-driven: Because scenic potential is limited the costumes will be even more important than usual. Most of the information about where and when the production is set, as well as the genre, style and themes of the production will be expressed through the costumes. Costume choices may need to be more graphic and bolder than usual to separate them from the visual background of the audience.

WAGON STAGE/PROCESSIONS

Temporary stages and theatre where the stage travels to the audience: mediaeval processions, modern festival floats, street theatre, simultaneous settings, commedia dell'arte

When the Roman Empire collapsed in 476 AD and the Middle Ages (often called the Dark Ages) began, the pagan excess of the arena performance disappeared, and theatre returned to its religious and ceremonial roots in the form of the Catholic liturgy. The Catholic Mass was at first a secret, modest celebration of the Christian story but over time became more and more theatrical: coloured light pouring from stained-glass windows into heavenly inspired buildings in which the opulent vestments of the clergy and the use of symbolic objects combined with music and ritualised movement in a highly theatrical event. Here we can see the theatre design elements of stage lighting, set, costumes and props at work. The aesthetics of the High Church Mass has had a huge effect on all of the Western arts, and has in fact defined what we now think of as 'theatrical'—sumptuous surfaces, impressive scale, artificial and exaggerated imagery. It is a style constantly referenced by designers in their work and in the past defined certain theatre forms such as opera and ballet.

The altar was the focal point of these festival-time performances (passion plays), and additional stages, or 'houses', were set up with simple sets around the church to portray locations used in the acting out of the bible stories: heaven, hell and the tomb of the Resurrection were all represented using simple, symbolic and representational objects that would be understood by the audience/congregation. These settings became progressively more complex with traps, cranes and elaborate mechanisms—early designers increasingly striving for more spectacular effects that would engage the audience with the story in new ways.

Over a period of several centuries these religious dramas became less sacred, and more about entertainment. The designs became more elaborate and the amateur performers were replaced by actors. The plays moved out of the churches and were performed outdoors as part of religious community festivals. In the largely agrarian villages the tray of an oxcart became a natural platform stage for a performance, and paintings and illustrations from the period show how wagons were set up as temporary stages for the performance of episodes from the life of Jesus, the lives of the saints or the telling of Old Testament stories. These pageant wagons or wagon stages could be set up in a line or in a circle (in-the-round) or be towed ('proceed') from one place to the next. The audience would watch one self-contained episode and then wait for the next wagon to arrive to perform the next part of the drama. This new form of performance is now very familiar to us from our own community festivals, where the wagon stage has become the present-day float. These will often be highly decorated elaborate stages where celebratory themes of popular culture will be represented pictorially using symbols and representational devices that are understood by young and old. We may find a similar set of elements in street theatre, where the temporary stage and bold vernacular visual style are common features.

ELIZABETHAN THEATRE

A hybrid thrust performance space with layered audience that has become a model for contemporary theatre

Up to the late 16th century touring acting troupes of fifteen or more actors were performing throughout Europe on temporary stages set up in the village square or in ready-made playing spaces such as inn yards. The paved courtyard of the inn yard provided space for an audience standing around a temporary platform stage, and the balconies ('*galleries*') surrounding the courtyard on three or four sides provided good sightlines down to the stage for audience members above. This format was the basis for the first permanent theatre spaces in London, of which Shakespeare's Globe Theatre is the most famous. It is an architectural form that has had a profound effect on theatre as we know it today. Its effectiveness as a performance space has been carried into the plays of Shakespeare whose works have been so influential on the way the theatre of English-speaking cultures has developed.

There is debate among theatre historians about the exact shape of the Elizabethan stage, and the many attempted replicas that have been built around the world are all different. However, we can see in the only surviving drawing of the interior of an Elizabethan theatre (*page 141 (8.23)*) that there are several distinct elements. It is an open-air space, with a raised platform stage surrounded on three sides by the audience in a format familiar to us as the thrust space. At the back of the stage there is a house-like structure known as the '*tiring* [or retiring] *house*' (reminding us of the *house* of the mediaeval simultaneous set) with two doorways, a gallery over and a roof supported by two columns. The doors were used for upstage entrances and were also used as hiding places and to reveal unexpected elements. The gallery may have been used by musicians and was almost certainly used for specific action, such as Juliet's balcony in *Romeo and Juliet*.

Unlike the thrust space of the Greek amphitheatre where the audience is a single, democratic body in a shared, unified auditorium, here the audience

LEARNING FROM MEDIAEVAL THEATRE

THE THEATRE SPACE: Wagon stages move in procession to the audience as with today's festival floats; temporary platform stages; simultaneous settings.

SIMULTANEOUS SETTINGS: These were an important innovation of mediaeval theatre, whereby a number of settings ('*houses*' such as Paradise, Limbo or Hell) would be set up side by side so that the audience could see all of them at the same time. The space in front of the houses (*platea*)—was a neutral acting area that could be used for any of the locations.

Simultaneous settings, also now known as composite or multiple sets were reinvented in the 1960s–1970s, and have been a common set design strategy until recent times. A number of fixed locations could be represented on stage at the same time and action could move seamlessly from one location to the next without breaking the dramatic tension of the production with scene changes. Simultaneous settings prescribe where a performer has to be on stage for each scene and for this reason may now be seen to limit the dramatic potential of the stage space.

PLAYS: Passion plays, mystery plays, morality plays, religious play cycles; comic character types led to the development of *commedia dell'arte*; today's street theatre, processions and public events.

CONVENTIONS: The *platea*, or neutral acting space; locations represented by '*houses*'; simultaneous settings; heaven is always on stage right/hell on stage left.

TECHNOLOGY: Pageant wagon stages; inventive use of stage machinery and effects. For one mystery play a hell's mouth machine opened and closed giant jaws, breathed fire and smoke and needed 17 mechanists to operate it.

DESIGN RESPONSES TO THE WAGON STAGE/ FLOAT: Minimal scenery, so props and costumes carry most of the visual information; the use of symbolic or representational design elements that are easily understood by a popular 'GP' (general public) audience; mechanisms such as traps, lifts, revolves used to create simple illusions; use of bold, graphic visual style as part of the festival/celebratory event.

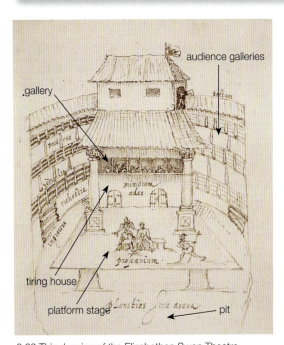

gallery
audience galleries
tiring house
platform stage
pit

8.23 This drawing of the Elizabethan Swan Theatre (c. 1596), copied from a sketch made by an eye-witness has formed the basis of many interpretations and reconstructions of Shakespeare's stage.

is divided into two distinct zones: the standing space immediately surrounding the stage, and the balconies on three levels around the periphery of the circular building ('this wooden O' described by Shakespeare in *Henry V*). About 1000 patrons would pay one penny to watch the play as '*groundlings*' standing at very close quarters around the stage platform in the area known as the '*pit*'. About 2000 wealthier patrons would pay two pennies each to sit in the galleries, or three pennies to sit with a cushion. Although theatre spaces had sometimes previously been divided into different class zones this was the first time that the theatre architecture divided the space so clearly.

The architecture is reflected in the way Shakespeare's plays work. His plays are actually shaped by the kind of theatre space he was acting in and writing for. Many of his plays contain a very strong element of comic, physical performance evolved from the traditions of *commedia dell'arte* (➡ *Box, page 163*). We can imagine that the uneducated groundlings would have particularly responded to this physical aspect of the performance. The open stage space could serve as any place at any time and is derived from the mediaeval *'platea'* —a simple prop or piece of scenery, or just a brief description at the beginning of a scene would be enough to tell the audience where the scene is set. It is an imaginative rather than a literal space. Shakespeare's plays contain rich poetic images that help to feed our imaginative response. His plays are also filled with complex allegories, metaphors and poetic allusions, and we can imagine that he was playing to his more educated audience seated in the galleries when writing in this way. We can think of Shakespeare's plays as culturally 'layered' just as the theatre building is culturally layered.

Many features of the Elizabethan stage are identical to the thrust stage: intimate, social, sculptural, character-driven spaces with limited pictorial and illusionistic potential. Although we are unlikely to be called upon to design for an Elizabethan-styled venue the plays of Shakespeare bring into focus two design considerations which we can apply to our work as designers.

The imaginative space: Audiences do not need much visual information to be able to imagine where the action is taking place. With one line at the start of each scene (from *Romeo and Juliet*) Shakespeare's 'acoustic scenery'[xxi] gives us all the information we need about where and when we are:

II/i BENVOLIO: He ran this way, and leap'd this orchard wall:

II/ii ROMEO: But soft! What light through yonder window breaks?

III/i FRIAR L: The grey ey'd morn smiles on the frowning night…

If the production excites the audience's imagination from the outset they will have no trouble imagining the missing detail. Shakespeare's conception of the stage space being an 'empty' flexible space that can transform from, say, palace to forest in a blink of the eye without the need for literal scenery is at the heart of many theatre-makers' practice today. As designers we may be tempted to visually describe the locations and characters of the play in great detail. The Elizabethan stage reminds us to ask ourselves: how much information does the audience really need? This will help us avoid designs that are too descriptive, or too specific and that limit the imaginative involvement of the audience.

Flow of action from scene to scene: Because Elizabethan plays were written for minimal scenery the action is not interrupted by scene changes and can therefore move quickly from scene to scene with an intense, dramatic pace. For designers, our challenge is how to achieve this kind of unbroken dramatic flow while also serving other aspects of the design challenge, such as building an atmosphere or creating a visual world for the story. We can apply this thinking to any production in which the story unfolds over many scenes. Stage machinery such as revolves, trucks and flies may help us solve this challenge, but the rule of 'less is more' generally applies.

END-STAGE

Theatre where the stage is at one end of the audience space. Court masques; kabuki and the hanamichi; the contemporary end-stage space

Towards the late 1500s theatre became an established form of entertainment, rather than the occasional result of a religious festival or a touring troupe of actors arriving to put on a play. Theatre audiences wanted to see productions unbothered by rain and short winter days. Theatre-makers began experimenting with putting on productions in indoor spaces. They began by co-opting existing spaces large enough to be converted into theatres. The Blackfriars Theatre (1597) was a conversion of the dining hall of a former priory, the ceremonial hall and the Banqueting House at the Palace of Whitehall were used for the presentation of theatrical court entertainments known as 'court masques', and an indoor tennis court became the Théâtre du Marais in France. These buildings were inevitably the property of the aristocracy whose theatrical tastes had a huge influence on the shape of theatre to come.

Many of these converted spaces had galleries around the sides of the room, similar to the Elizabethan theatre, but instead of a platform stage thrusting into the main auditorium the stage was set up at one end of the space, with most of the audience either standing or sitting on bleachers directly facing the stage. This is a format familiar to us today in lecture theatres, cinemas and concert halls, and was the prototype for what we now call the end-stage theatre.

In the end-stage format the audience shares the same 'room' as the performers. They are usually seated on raked seating that spans the width of the space, and directly face the stage at one end of the room. It is a much less dynamic relationship than the wrap-around audience of thrust and in-the-round theatres. It favours a more presentational or pictorial performance style, drawing less on the audience's imagination as they become spectators taking in the 'big picture'.

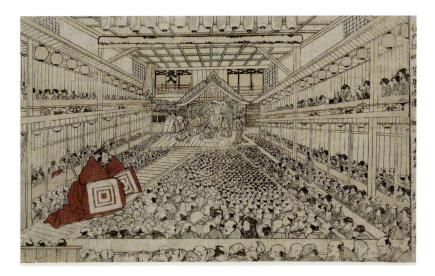

8.24 This 18th century woodcut by Utagawa Toyoharu shows a lively kabuki performance with an elaborately costumed and made-up actor making an entrance through the audience on the *hanamichi*.

8.25 The 16th century Corral de Comedias in Almagro, Spain, survives as a still-functioning example of the inn courtyard spaces co-opted by touring theatre troupes throughout Europe. Essentially an end-stage space with surrounding galleries, it is a format that was modified by Elizabethan theatre-builders and later applied to aristocratic halls to adapt them for use as English and French court theatres.

When theatre moved indoors it was no longer lit by daylight, but by candlelight. It is difficult to appreciate the effect this must have had on acting styles as performers adapted to the much dimmer lighting levels by moving to the front of the stage where they were closer to the audience and better lit, and presumably adjusted their facial and body gestures to meet the new demands. We also know from surviving playscripts written 'for candlelight' that themes of artificiality, illusion, magic and intrigue came to the fore. The theatre space and the theatre event continued to adapt and influence each other.

THE MODERN END-STAGE

Today the end-stage is the third most common format (after thrust and proscenium). The stage is usually an extension of the auditorium floor and is not raised, and there is often a fixed grid (no fly space above the stage). For designers characteristics of the end-stage include:

Formal space: The audience is seated in straight rows directly facing the stage and is therefore less communally aware and more self-contained. This formality suits some work where a degree of *alienation* is appropriate or where the audience are spectators rather than participants, or where movement is quite formally choreographed. End-stage spaces can work particularly well for dance.

LEARNING FROM END-STAGE AND KABUKI THEATRE

THE THEATRE SPACE: The first indoor theatre spaces; audience in a single block facing the stage; audience shares the same space as the stage; usually no side off-stage 'wing' space.

EVENTS: Shakespeare's later plays, Jacobean tragedies, court masques, *kabuki*. Today: dance, drama with a formal or choreographed quality.

CONVENTIONS: Pictorial, presentational style; *coup de théâtre*—the spectacular moment of visual triumph.

KABUKI: The *hanamichi*: a platform similar to a fashion catwalk/runway that extends out from the stage through the audience to the back of the auditorium, used for entrances and exits and may have a lift within it for surprise entrance of characters.

TECHNOLOGY: Candlelit; 'self-contained' scenic transformation techniques such as shutters, *periaktoi*, revolving and flipping panels, stage trucks; flown scenic cloud borders and *deus ex machina*; symmetrical stage picture. 16th century theatre had as many as 23 changes of scenery in a production. Over centuries of practice Japanese designers for *kabuki* have devised many ingenious ways to change scenery: break-apart panels; drop and drawn curtains; revolving or sliding panels; scenic panels could be flipped to reveal a whole new scene (the *gando gaeshi* technique).

DESIGN RESPONSES TO THE END-STAGE: Capitalise on the presentational pictorial format; consider stage levels that penetrate into the audience; provide entrance points at the sides of the stage with wings, legs or a false proscenium; use cross-stage lines of movement in the set design. Study the ingenuity of 16th century theatre and *kabuki* designers in creating theatrical illusion and spectacle.

Pictorial space: The audience face the stage as if looking at a large picture. The end-stage works well for presentational designs that conceive all of the visual elements—set, costumes, props and lighting—working together to produce a striking stage picture. Whether the aesthetic is lavish (as in the court masque) or graphic (as in kabuki), the image will be taken in as a whole picture by the audience who share a similar fixed point of view of the stage. In larger venues panoramic designs that emphasise the horizontals work well. Cross-stage movement (side to side) reads strongly to the audience.

THE HAM FUNERAL, SET DESIGNER ANNA TREGLOAN

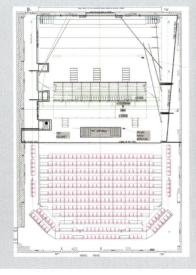
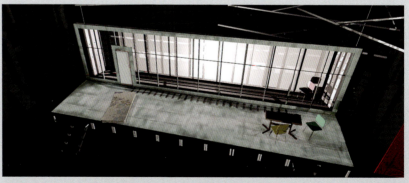

8.26 and 8.27 Anna Tregloan's 3D model and plan for *The Ham Funeral* in end-stage format at the Merlyn Theatre, Malthouse. Anna designed a movable raised platform stage to improve actors' eye-lines and to enable set transformations (➡ *page 33 for more on this production and page 134 (8.17) for a thrust format in this theatre*).

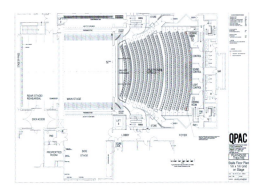

8.28 Modern proscenium arch theatre plan (*QPAC Playhouse* ➜ *page 126*)

8.29 Teatro Farnese Parma, Italy, built c. 1618. The horseshoe-shaped auditorium, seen here from the point of view of the Duke of Parma's seat, faces the raised stage which is framed by the proscenium arch. The auditorium floor area (*orchestra*) could be used to seat audience, to stage court ballets and was also flooded for a mock sea battle.

No wing space: In end-stage spaces the stage usually fills the whole width of the theatre with little or no wing space. Set designers may need to provide ways to provide actor entrances from the sides. Sometimes a 'false proscenium' will be installed to achieve this. Self-contained scene change techniques such as revolves and *periaktoi* are a solution to the lack of wing space.

PROSCENIUM ARCH THEATRES

Theatres where the audience is separated from the stage by the frame of the proscenium arch; the fourth wall

Theatre of the 16th century in Europe became more and more visual—as much about the design as the performers or the script. Theatre like all of the arts came under the overwhelming influence of the Italian Renaissance in ways that had a profound effect on the shape of theatre. The two great innovations of the Renaissance stage—*perspective scenery* and the *proscenium arch*—are closely connected.

The proscenium arch is an architectural frame that divides the stage from the audience. It allows for much greater control of the illusionism of the stage picture—lighting can be controlled so that the performers are brightly lit while the audience is in darkness, the stage mechanisms can be hidden and the scenic illusion of the set can be more precise. The frame makes the stage picture perfect.

The proscenium arch evolved in the courts of the Italian princes for their lavish theatrical celebrations ('*intermezzi*') and was firmly established in Italy by the late 16th century. In the oldest surviving proscenium arch theatre (the Teatro Farnese in Parma) we can see the architectural frame of the proscenium

LEARNING FROM THE PROSCENIUM ARCH THEATRE

THE THEATRE SPACE: The audience separated from the stage by an architectural frame (proscenium arch); raised platform stage; audience seated in raked seating in an arc facing the stage with a controlled point of view to the stage; often several levels to the audience—stalls, dress circle; audience in darkness, the stage in light; orchestra pit in front of the stage may be raised to stage level to form an apron; stage may be raked higher towards the back to accentuate perspective; wing space to the sides of the stage provides off-stage working space, fly tower over the stage provides for flown scenery.

EVENTS: Drama, opera, ballet, musicals, revues, burlesque.

CONVENTIONS: The fourth wall.

TECHNOLOGY: House curtain closes the stage off from view of the audience; perspective scenery: sliding shutters and wings using the pole and chariot system in grooves in the stage floor; wings and borders, flats and cloths; *periaktoi*, traps, revolving units (*machina versatilis*); flown scenery using complex diagonal flying rigs; tripped (flipped) scenery, especially used to change borders; trucks; painted light effects (*chiaroscuro*) on the scenery; manual or mechanical counterweight flying systems; hydraulic lifts; automated revolves.

Today's proscenium arch theatres are likely to be equipped with flies, house curtain and black legs and borders, and frequently have the option of an apron stage.

and the deeply curved (horseshoe) shaped auditorium which was a Renaissance interpretation of the classic amphitheatre. These were to become the template for proscenium arch theatres all over Europe for the next 300 years.

The invention of linear perspective in early Renaissance Italy was a breathtaking artistic innovation that allowed artists to represent three-dimensional space in a two-dimensional painting. When stage designers adopted this technique and painted their scenery in perspective to enhance the sense of depth it produced a magical effect. Textbooks of how to use perspective in 16th century theatre practice were widely studied by theatre designers, and audiences through Europe were entranced by their magnificent depictions of streets, palaces, and forest glades appearing to stretch to infinity.

For the next 300 years illusionistic painted perspective scenery in proscenium arch theatres was the prevailing theatrical form of Western theatre. Theatre scenery gradually became less symmetrical and more complex, more three-dimensional and more ambitious in its illusionism. It wasn't until the realist movement of Zola, Ibsen, Chekhov, Stanislavski and others at the end of the 19th century that the proscenium arch stage was used in a new way. Instead of just framing the stage picture the proscenium arch became a barrier that separated the stage from the auditorium and the convention of the 'fourth wall' separated the audience from the world of the characters. The audience became outsiders, looking in.

The line between the world on stage and that of the audience is now usually assumed to be more complex than the convention of the fourth wall suggests, and designers will often try to 'break down the fourth wall' to create a more direct relationship between the actors' performance and the audience.

8.30 The court theatre at Český Krumlov in the Czech Republic. Built c. 1680 it is a perfectly preserved example of the early Baroque proscenium theatre. The stage is an ingenious mechanical space designed for the magical transformation from one scene to another. It is set here for the forest scene, with a series of symmetrical perspective illusionistic sliding wings and flown borders. The still-operational stage machinery includes the kind of 'cloud machine' used to realise Inigo Jones's masque design (➡ *page 60 (5.1)*).

THE MODERN PROSCENIUM ARCH THEATRE

The proscenium arch theatre is still the dominant form of theatre architecture. It is very versatile and is used for a very wide range of theatre events: opera, ballet, drama, musicals, revues and burlesque, contemporary dance… whenever a production needs the armoury of technical devices for changing scenery that make the proscenium arch an enduring presence. The modern proscenium theatre will often have the addition of an *apron* stage, projecting through the proscenium into the auditorium to reduce the effect of the arch as a barrier, and to try to link the actors and audience. The apron may be on a lift, able to be lowered to below stage level to form an orchestra pit. A fly tower above the stage provides for flown scenery, and some theatres have built-in revolves installed in the stage floor.

DESIGN RESPONSES

A complete world: The 'prosc arch' frames the on-stage world created by the designer in such a way that the audience may be completely unaware of anything else beyond the frame. The audience is encouraged to imaginatively enter this world for the duration of the production and to completely suspend disbelief. The designer will need to decide whether to let the audience enter the world gradually by seeing the set before the show, or to reveal it magically at the start of the show. Set designers for productions that need a more dynamic audience–performer relationship might build the stage out through the proscenium arch or use their design to visually break down the impact of the proscenium as a barrier.

Sightlines: The set designer will need to check sightlines from the different points in the auditorium past the proscenium to make sure everyone can see everything important and nobody is distracted by seeing off-stage into the wings. (The end seats in the rows closest to the stage are particularly important ones to check.)

LEARNING FROM THE 16TH CENTURY SPECTACULAR

The court masque was a theatrical extravaganza staged in honour of the monarch in which courtiers and even the king would be ornately costumed to take part in exotic tableaux and choreographed allegorical fantasies. They were an early expression of what we now know as 'total theatre' with the audience totally immersed in the theatrical event. The masque was essentially staged propaganda: the intentional blurring of the line between reality and fantasy affirmed the idea of the divinity of the king. Because of their reliance on visual imagery famous artists such as Inigo Jones (in England) and the painters Raphael and Vasari (in Italy) were engaged to design these theatrical events.

THE THEATRE SPACE: Temporary (end-stage) performance spaces with a raised stage and decorative frame were set up in large royal rooms such as the Banqueting House at Whitehall.

CONVENTIONS: One-point perspective scenery designed to be seen from the royal seat; allegorical themes and motifs; 'dumbshow' (a mimed allegorical pantomime); combining music, ballet, recitation, drama: masked audience members participated as performers; the coup de théâtre—a brilliant show-stopping theatrical moment of spectacle.

TECHNOLOGY: Perspective scenery gave the illusion of infinite depth; the proscenium arch framed the spectacle, establishing the enduring partnership with the proscenium arch; all of the technology of the proscenium arch theatre was utilised.

Pictorial space: The picture frame of the proscenium evolved for designs that were pictorial, illustrative and 'theatrical'. Even when our designs are minimalistic the audience will tend to see them as a complete framed picture. However, it is possible for designs to subvert this pattern.

Controlled space: The proscenium allows for great control of light which helps designers to achieve theatrical illusion and focus. The audience's point of view is also very controlled and focused by the frame. We can design knowing precisely what the audience will see and how they will see it.

Theatrical toys: Every possible scene-changing mechanism may be at our disposal in a well-equipped proscenium theatre. The opportunities they afford can be seductive! If we are using any of the inbuilt 'house' systems we need to be very familiar with how they work—what they can do and their limitations. We need to consider carefully how the show should move and what is the best way to tell the story, and which scene-change method (if any) is right for the show.

20TH CENTURY EXPERIMENTATION

Traverse stage; found spaces; cabaret; the flexible theatre

In the 1960s and '70s theatre-makers became frustrated with the proscenium arch theatre and playwrights began writing plays that required a different kind of relationship with the audience. There was great exploration of new ways to set up the actor–audience relationship, and the thrust and in-the-round were revived. Theatre was also performed in *found spaces*, and in cafés and nightclubs in *cabaret format*. Theatre architects built *flexible spaces* that could transform from one seating format to another. The *traverse* stage is also a result of this experimentation.

TRAVERSE STAGE

Theatres where the audience sits on opposite sides of the stage

In the traverse stage the rectangular stage has audience on two sides, directly facing each other across the stage. For all audience members the main visual background will be the audience sitting opposite. There are very few permanent traverse stages and it is only occasionally used as a staging format, but it can be very effective in productions that have a strong sense of opposition or dichotomy. For designers it works somewhat like the thrust and in-the-round, except that all entrances and scenic opportunity are at the side walls.

TENDER NAPALM, **DESIGNER CLAUDE MARCOS**

8.31 and 8.32 Section drawing (8.32) for Claude Marcos' set design for *Tender Napalm,* utilising traverse staging. (➡) Blackbird *production #2, page 120*)

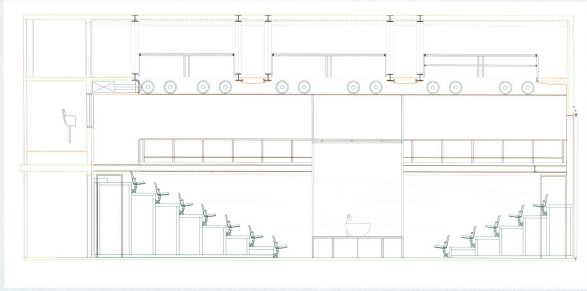

ADAPTED SITES

Site-specific theatre events shaped around non-theatre spaces

Staging a performance event in a special environment that is not a conventional theatre building can be an exciting experience for an audience. The real-life location may have a particular aesthetic quality, such as the poetic beauty of a sandstone quarry or the grungy dystopia of an underground car park. The space may have particular social or political significance that reinforces the themes of the production, or it might be part of a special festival experience. Some companies specialise in staging work in site-specific spaces, and for others it is a special one-off experience.

For designers it can be an inspiring exploration and a challenging experience. For the set designer the space often *is* the design, and the search for and selection of the space is pivotal. One of the designer's main tasks will be working with the producers to help resolve all of the regulatory issues around public spaces: safe and appropriate seating, emergency egress, installation of lighting towers, audience facilities, access to the site, etc.

CABARET

Where the audience sits at tables

Some performance genres work particularly well when the audience is in a relaxed, informal social setting with the audience members sitting at tables—cabaret, stand-up comedy, revue and burlesque all thrive with the very lively physical relationship between the performer and the audience that this format offers. Sometimes this will seem to be the perfect choice for a production we are designing. For example, a production of a *commedia* play using improvisation and knock-about humour may work well in cabaret mode. For designers, positioning the stage and making sure all of the audience can see enough of the action will be the main challenge.

THE FLEXIBLE SPACE

Theatre spaces that are designed to work in a number of different formats

The flexible space (also known as the *black box*) seemed to be the ideal architectural solution at the end of the 20th century for maximising flexibility in a small-to-medium-sized venue. These spaces are usually designed to work in end-stage, thrust and in-the-round formats, and also possibly traverse. The seating is broken up into movable units which can be positioned into the various formations, and the production team can select the format that best suits the production.

In practice, the labour costs of moving the seating units, the compromised audience and actor entry, and compromised focus and efficiency too often result in the flexible space becoming 'not-so-flexible' with the seating rarely moved or locked off in one format. If you are designing for a flexible space talk with the theatre's head mechanist or house manager early to find out what is and isn't possible, and the implications of this for any of the formats you are considering.

FIRE/WATER, SET DESIGNER JOEY RUIGROK VAN DER WERVEN

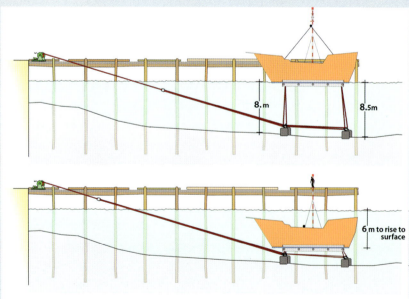

8.33 and 8.34 Director/designer Joey Ruigrok van der Werven devised an ingenious method to make his ghost ship rise from the waters of Sydney Harbour in this site-specific spectacular.

THREE DESIGNS FOR A FLEXIBLE SPACE, **DESIGNER ANDREW BAILEY**

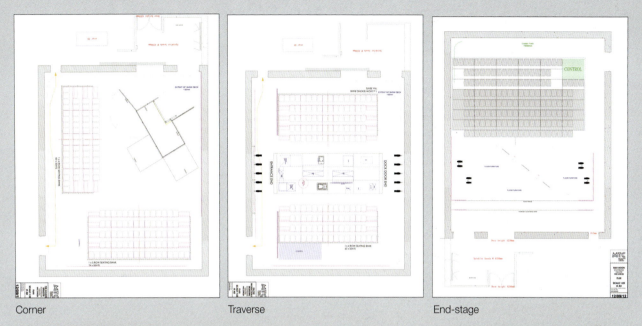

Corner   Traverse   End-stage

8.35–8.37 The Lawler Studio at Southbank Theatre is a flexible space offering corner (thrust), traverse and end-stage formats (seen here for *The Golden Dragon*, *On the Production of Monsters* and *Ruby Moon*, all designed by Andrew Bailey).

CONVERSIONS

New theatres are always being built in response to changing demands for different kinds of theatre experience. Frequently architects will adapt existing (often historical) buildings to use as theatres. They may convert the building to any format: proscenium, thrust or end-stage. The original character of the building often influences the performance space, resulting in some unique variations on the standard formats, which provide additional interest and challenges for designers.

Designers rarely get to choose the venues for the performance. However every venue has its own particular qualities. The challenge for the designer is to capitalise on the strengths and work around or minimise the limitations—to 'tune' the venue to the specific staging demands of the production, and tune the production to the opportunities presented by the venue.

USING CHARACTER AS A DESIGN TOOL

Diary of a Madman (Costume Designer Tess Schofield, Set Designer Catherine Martin)

In this chapter we see how a performer's character takes shape in the costume, and investigate the many factors that come into play in the interpretation and communication of character.

ALSO IN THIS CHAPTER—FURTHER THINKING: The Performer–Designer Relationship, page 172

I'm just amazed by the power of makeup and costume...
I see images as a wrapping. Why not?
It's something to play with, people take it far too seriously.

Annie Lennox, lead singer, Eurythmics[xxii]

Eurythmics lead singer Annie Lennox acknowledges the wonderful paradox of performance costume: it's magical power on one hand, and the playfulness of 'dressing up' on the other. Dressing up to take on the character of another being is at the very heart of performance. From the very earliest rituals participant 'players' have decorated their bodies with painted ochre designs, amazing feathered headdresses or fantastical body ornaments as a way of inhabiting the spirit of an archetypal character, and to perform in the character of this spirit in their ceremonies. The Ancient Greeks went on to develop masks in the character of tragic heroes, heroines and comic satyrs and performers dressed in platform shoes and exaggerated robes to portray gods. Paintings from the Middle Ages show amateur actors wearing elaborate costumes to portray Christ, the saints, and even the devil—dressed in a bearskin and grotesque animal mask—in their re-staging of the Bible stories. In the Renaissance touring troupes of actors developed character masks and costumes that over time became the 'uniform' of universal *commedia dell'arte* characters such as Arlecchino/Pulcinella the quick-witted comic servant, or Pantalone, the lean and slippered miserly old man who we can still find in cartoon and advertising character 'types'. Over the whole history of performance the putting on of costume, makeup and mask has been a kind of magical act of transformation. When we see a performer do this and 'slip into character' it is one of the great joys of theatre-making.

However, something fundamentally changed when in Stanislavski's realist productions actors started to wear street clothes for the first time. The idea of a photographic and psychological accuracy and 'realness' was introduced to performance costume, and with this realism some of the magic of transformation disappeared. Today there is once again a fashion for productions that dress the performers in 'real clothes', as close as possible to the clothes that real people are wearing on the street, and costume designers have tended to become stylists. This is a choice of production style that aims to show the audience how alike they are to the on-stage characters, to help them connect and identify. But the characters on stage are *not* real people; they are *characters in a performance*, and we need to remember the transformative, magical aspect of the costume, even when we want the production to feel 'true to life'.

THE PERFORMER'S COSTUME

The performer is at the centre of the performance. Obvious, but true. It is the actor, dancer, singer or acrobat who will create the drama and entertainment each night for the audience. Although we are the ones who imagine, design and create the costume it is nevertheless the *performer's* costume. Some performers will happily wear whatever we design, others will develop their whole sense of character from the costume, and others will want to have some or even a lot of input into how the costume develops. For us as designers keeping the performer at the centre of our thinking is fundamental—while negotiating all of the stylistic, practical and conceptual concerns that are part of our role. We can do this by conceiving the costume *through* the performer, so that at every stage of designing the costume we are imagining the performer within it, using it, investing it with their character. If we do this the performer will truly inhabit the costume, and the costume will be a true extension of their performance (➡ *Further Thinking, page 172*).

9.1

9.2

9.3

Jennifer Irwin's toile (9.1), costume drawing (9.2) and production photograph (9.3) for the 'sun-eclipse' costume for *Warumuk – In the Dark Night*. Jenny develops her costume designs with an intimate understanding of the symbiosis of dancer and designer, working closely together through rehearsals to make sure that the expressive potential of the costume is explored by the dancer and the dancer's expressive needs are met by the costume. 'Everything changes so much in the choreographic process—numbers of dancers, movement, music—everything changes right up to opening!' Jennifer Irwin, designer

COSTUME AND CHARACTER

We are very adept at reading any person's character from how they dress. We make instant judgments about their cultural background, age, income, gender, sexuality and peer group. We can also read how they feel about themselves and how they project their personality in the way they wear their clothes and how they dress. All of this information is there on the surface ready to be read and interpreted, and in the theatre all of this information is there in the costumes for the audience to interpret. However, people do not always reveal their personality in the way they dress. Sometimes a lot of effort goes into concealing the inner self. There are also many examples of 'uniforms'—such as the corporate suit—which have the express purpose of obscuring the wearer's personality. For us as performance designers this tension between what is revealed and what is concealed is a subtle and expressive tool. When we choose to reveal information that has previously been concealed we are exploring *character development*, which is a vital part of theatrical storytelling and a powerful tool in our costume design toolkit.

The factors that shape a character and their character development will be identified from our script analysis:

- age
- gender
- status/class
- occupation
- cultural background
- personality traits
- character development
- the function of the character in the storytelling—the values or themes they 'represent' or embody, whether they are a major or a minor player and their relationship to other characters.

Additional factors that will determine what they are wearing are:
- the performer playing the role, their actions and practical and personal issues
- the form or genre of the script
- their context—the space they are in
- season and time of day
- period
- fashion.

During our design process each of these variables will be analysed and 'weighed up' to work out how best to use this information in guiding the audience's interpretation. We also need to decide how subtle or overt our visual clues will be.

LA BOHÈME, COSTUME DESIGNER JULIE LYNCH

9.4

La Bohème
6 x Prostitutes in Coats [removable collars, 3 in hats 3 in head scarves + handbags]
Transition
www.julielynchdesign.com

9.5

La Bohème
Dressed Prostitute 1 & 2
Act 2 & adds Seller Costume for Transition
www.julielynchdesign.com

9.6

La Bohème
6 x Peasant Women selling wares
Act 3
www.julielynchdesign.com .

Julie Lynch's costume designs for the opera *La bohème* explore differences in class and occupation while remaining within a subdued palette and 1920s period silhouette. Costume props are included in her design vision to communicate important differences.

INTERPRETING CHARACTER

At this stage of our design process we are laying down the 'big picture' of our costume design interpretation. The amount of detail we have to deal with can be baffling unless we establish a secure conceptual framework. Start from the outside and work your way in:

- What is the world, society or culture?
- Are there groups of similar characters? What quality defines the groups?
- Who are the main players?
- Arrange the characters in groups of most alike, most unlike. What qualities link the characters who are alike? What are the strongest differences between the opposite/unlike characters?

- Are there character developments that are key to the storytelling? Define the character at the beginning and end of their development. Is the transition abrupt or gradual, dramatic or subtle?
- Think about the performers. Meet them, measure them, photograph them. How are they thinking about their character?
- Think about what the performers will be doing in their costumes—how physical they might be or how they might move.
- Think about how your costumes can do something unique and special. Not 'just clothes'—costumes!

AGE: *Young, middle-aged or old.* People tend dress according to their age, and different clothes suit an older or younger person. Sometimes people dress inappropriately (the teenage 'little old lady' or the elderly 'mutton dressed as lamb'). Often an older person will continue to dress in the fashion of their youth—they might wear their hair in a certain style because it suited them when they were younger. Establishing the age-range of the production will be a useful guide to how extreme the differences might be. Knowing how closely the performer matches their character's age is very important so we can decide if we need to use costume to age a performer up or down.

GENDER: *Female, male, transgender, homosexual, androgynous.* Ideas of masculinity and femininity have changed a lot over the centuries, and even in the current decade. Our ideas of masculinity and femininity, and how these ideas are expressed in clothing, have also changed radically (compare a man's suit from the 1920s to one from the 1950s). Some believe that we are each a balancing act of the two extremes of masculinity and femininity, and that we all contain some of each. Establishing the nature of the balance and how overtly a character projects their sexuality can be a useful differentiation between characters.

STATUS/CLASS: *High status or class—authority figure, boss, leader, aristocrat, wealthy. Lower status or class—servile, servant, worker, follower, blue-collar, poor.* In the past the differences in status and class were marked by clothing—especially by uniforms of rank. The cut and cloth of higher status and upper class clothes were refined while those of the lower class were more simple and coarse. Those of lower status often aspire to look like the privileged, and historically have adopted their style as soon as they were able, only to have the upper class adopt a new elitist look. With today's consumable fashions the differences are often less marked. A lower income person might dress in a cheap copy of a designer label ('gutter chic'), and a wealthy person might dress discreetly to downplay their wealth.

OCCUPATION: *Employment, defining activities.* A character might be dressed for their work—such as in a suit, overalls or dust coat. Some occupations have very distinctive uniforms or dress codes (such as the military and the religious) and it is important to research these thoroughly if we want to get the detail right. A character's clothes might be stained or showing signs of wear from their work. If we know the occupation of the character, this will also help determine their status or class.

CULTURAL BACKGROUND: *Nationality, ethnicity, cultural influences and cultural identity, religion, politics, cult or clique.* It is important to identify both the cultural background of a character, and how they identify culturally. A character may be from a second generation migrant background while trying to conform to the mainstream of their adopted nationality or to a particular gang or faction, and we might see these conflicting factors reflected in what they are wearing. Some religions (such as Sikh, Muslim or Amish) and gangs or sub-cults (such as bikers or Goths) have very particular dress codes. There are many informal cliques too, such as the group of young women we see out on a Friday night all wearing versions of the same micro mini and killer heels.

PERSONALITY TRAITS: There are a number of ways we can investigate character: psychology, astrology, fashion, religion and philosophy have all given us different ways of understanding, analysing or identifying different personalities. Essentially they are all tools for differentiating different character 'types'. These types will inevitably be a broad brush-stroke interpretation but they can be a great way to start to plot the individuality and differences between characters when we are starting to design costumes for our production. When a type is pushed to an extreme they become a caricature—an inherently more theatrical version of the type. We can see extremes like this in real life, such as the too-neat businessman in button-down collar, contrast collar and cuffs with a tightly furled umbrella over his arm, or the neo-punk who is sporting every possible cliché of the punk look.

Many tribal rituals dramatise character archetypes—the warrior, hunter, trickster, earth spirit, rain-maker or fertility figure—or characterise culturally important animal totems. These ancient archetypes have developed in many cultures into codified 'systems' of personality types which can be useful tools for identifying and communicating the differences between our characters. For example, ancient Roman and mediaeval medicine describes four character types (humours) that each correspond to an element: melancholic (earth), phlegmatic (water), sanguine (air) and choleric (fire). These four elements are the basis of the astrological 'star signs' which describe and define twelve character types. On the other hand the Eastern Taoist philosophy defines individuals as more or less masculine (yang) or feminine (yin).

Fashion has also defined different types, and these have changed as fashions have changed. (A 1920s department store advertised six different types of woman: romantic, statuesque, artistic, picturesque, modern and conventional. By 1945 an American self-help manual described the six types as: the exotic, outdoor, sophisticate, womanly woman, aristocrat and the gamin.)[xxiii] We think we now live in a very pluralistic society, with great personal freedom to dress how we want, but could we still identify six basic types today?

Psychology describes various extreme behavioural types such as, anxious, pathological, obsessive-compulsive, delusional, depressive or paranoid personalities. More usefully psychology has also identified the conscious (ego) and the unconscious (id). It is worth considering the degree to which a character is expressing who they *want us to think they are* (their projected selves) through their clothing or who they *actually are* (their inner selves), or actually using their clothing to *disguise their personality*.

Even for the sceptic the universality of these types indicates some usefulness in how the systems define personality, but really, whichever way you approach

THE 25TH ANNUAL PUTNAM COUNTY SPELLING BEE, **DESIGNER DALE FERGUSON**

9.7

9.8

9.9

Dale Ferguson's lively costume drawings for the musical *The 25th Annual Putnam County Spelling Bee* communicate a strong sense of the personality of the characters using colour, branding, detail and pattern as well as the characters' facial expressions and pose to portray their distinct types.

it, finding a way of identifying and describing the 'character' of your characters is useful. I even encountered one designer who was fond of dogs, and described the characters in terms of different dog breeds (one character did in fact end up looking a little poodle-ish!).

CHARACTER DEVELOPMENT: Dramatic storytelling is frequently built around how a character or group of characters change or develop over the course of the action—a kind of condensed life journey. There might be a physical aging, a subtle growth through experience, a fall from grace, a self-realisation or a triumph against all odds. We can plot the main steps in the character development through our script analysis, and then look for opportunities for the character's costume to change at these points. If there are scripted costume changes we can investigate these for their potential in revealing character development. Sometimes the fact that a character *doesn't* change, or is unable to change is significant, and this can also be reflected in costume and perhaps accentuated by having the characters around them change appearance while they remain physically unchanged.

SERVANT OF TWO MASTERS, DESIGNER STEPHEN CURTIS

9.10   9.11   9.12

Strong pattern unifies the author's costume designs for Carlo Goldoni's *Servant of Two Masters* in which the *commedia dell'arte* tradition is translated into a free mix of period styles—ranging from contemporary 'street' to 1950s and 19th century. These three characters reference Arlecchino, Pantalone and Lelio *commedia* types.

THE HERITAGE OF *COMMEDIA DELL'ARTE*

Over the 1000 years of the Middle Ages travelling troupes of itinerant actors kept alive the performance traditions that had developed from Greek drama. These actors took on the performing of comic roles in morality plays as these became less religious and more a form of public entertainment, performing on small temporary stages up-close to the audience. Tragic and especially comic character 'types' started to evolve and became the basis of the dramatic form which became known as *commedia dell'arte*. This actor-focused performance style was characterised by improvisation, dance, song, acrobatics, mime and brilliant physical comic routines (*lazzi*) and has had a huge influence on later dramatists from Shakespeare to Beckett. An understanding of the *commedia* tradition is important for actors, and it is important for designers too.

These stock *commedia* characters developed standard character traits, styles of movement and gesture, and standard costumes and half masks which have been very influential in the design of character costumes ever since. Versions of *commedia* types crop up today in circus clown costumes, and character costumes in TV commercials, sitcoms and in cartoons. *Commedia* characters and character types include:

- *Arlecchino*: the outlandishly rogueish acrobatic servant in patched clothes (e.g., Groucho Marx and the classic clown)
- *Il Capitano*: the cocky soldier with phallic nose and feathered military cap (e.g., Cyrano de Bergerac)
- *Pantalone*: the mean-spirited, greedy old man with a scrawny, hunched stance (eg Montgomery Burns in *The Simpsons*)
- *Lelio*: the motor-mouthed fop, dressed in the latest absurd fashion (e.g., Ruby Rhod, in *The Fifth Element*)

THE FUNCTION OF THE CHARACTER AND THEIR RELATIONSHIP TO OTHER CHARACTERS: Some characters are protagonists (the central character) others are antagonists (in conflict with the central character) and others will have supporting roles. They will all be important to the drama as a whole, but the audience needs to know where to focus their attention, and costume can help them do this. We can use any of our design tools (colour, texture, tone...) to help focus and differentiate a significant character in a particular scene.

Sometimes a character will embody a particular theme, image or idea in the script (for example, in Shakespeare's *Hamlet* the title character is connected to the idea of indecision), or there may be characters who represent opposite extremes of an idea, or a group of characters who together represent related aspects of a single idea or point of view. Costume can help define these differences visually and signal the information to the audience. It is important to think holistically about all of the characters, and when we make a choice about one character to follow that choice through to see how it influences the characters around them.

THE PERFORMER PLAYING THE ROLE: As we know, we cannot think about costume without thinking about the performer who will be wearing the costume. Their age, personality, skill and body type will have a profound influence on how we shape the design for their costume. There will be practical, personal and aesthetic considerations, such as the need for supportive footwear, pockets in particular parts of their costumes, knee-pads if they are doing a lot of floor work or sweat-guards if they are prone to heavy perspiration. We will need to know what the performer's actions are and accommodate these in the cut and fabric choices of the costumes. Performers are generally very conscious that they are

ROMEO AND JULIET, **DESIGNER STEPHEN CURTIS**

9.13–9.16
Costume drawings (9.13–9.15) and costume schematic (9.16) for a production of *Romeo and Juliet* designed by Stephen Curtis. Family groups and factions, and protagonists within these groups are identified using colour and tone.

'exposed' on stage with an entire audience looking at them, and it is important that they feel good about what they are wearing. Part of our job as costume designers is to help them look good and feel good while balancing all of the other costume, character and production style issues. Sometimes the production process can be set up so that the costumes are being designed and developed through rehearsals, in which case the design can be very responsive to the performers' input. Otherwise meeting the performers early in the design process and finding out their thoughts on their character is very helpful. This may not be possible within a conventional production process—our first opportunity to discuss the designs will most often be at the design presentation on the first day of rehearsal. In any case the end result will always be better when we establish an open and receptive dialogue with the performers as early as possible.

THE FORM OR GENRE OF THE SCRIPT: Traditionally form has had a big influence on costume style: ballet, circus, opera and burlesque all have costume conventions (respectively: the tutu, the body suit, the prima donna 'gown' and the spangled feather headdress). Some genres also have established costume conventions, such as visual exaggeration in musicals and melodrama, or the historic costumed archetypes of *commedia dell'arte*. These days the conventions may not be so prescriptive, and many creative teams set out to play against convention, or playfully combine conventions of different genres (➡ *Chapter 5: Post-Modernist productions, page 65*).

THE CONTEXT—THE SPACE THEY ARE IN: We have already seen how spaces take on the character of their occupants, and also influence their occupants. This is why costume designers need to think about space and set designers need to think about character. As costume designers we need to know the world of the characters and imagine the costumed characters within that world. This relationship might be explicit, for example, when the production is specifically set in the home or workplace of a particular character, or perhaps we simply identify it as 'their' space. In this case the set and costume designs will need to tell the same story, and communicate the same idea of the character. Even when there is no literal link between the characters and their space, the scale, textures, tone, colours… everything about the size, shape and look of the space will have an impact on the costumes, and vice versa. We might decide to make our characters stand out from the space, or for them to blend in; we might identify a particular element on stage that relates to a character and link their costume to that element; we might use colour or another design tool thematically to link the costumes and set; we might communicate important information with the costumes (for example, the period, or cultural setting) because this information is not communicated in the set design; we might think about how a character will look when they stand in a particular place on the set, or the impact a costume will make on a particular entrance. The more we conceive both costumes/character and set/space as a whole (rather than as separate parts) the better the result will be.

CABARET, **DESIGNER BILL HAYCOCK**

CABARET

SALLY
SHOW COSTUME
OVER BLACK DRESS

backlit
black
silk
velvet
lobes
cut motif

little
skimpy
black
dress

black sheer
stockings
+ shoes

9.17

CABARET

CHORUS

bandages

black
sheer
open net
sleeveless
tops
painted
(nude) with
opposite
breast on
each chest

bruises

bruises

short
fitted boy
leg pants

flappy
big
pants

MALE/
FEMALE

sheer black
stockings
shoes

9.18

Bill Haycock's costume drawings (9.17–9.19) for the musical *Cabaret* draw on the traditions of circus, the freak-show and burlesque in a conscious decision to sidestep the flashy values associated with the conventions of the American musical.

CABARET

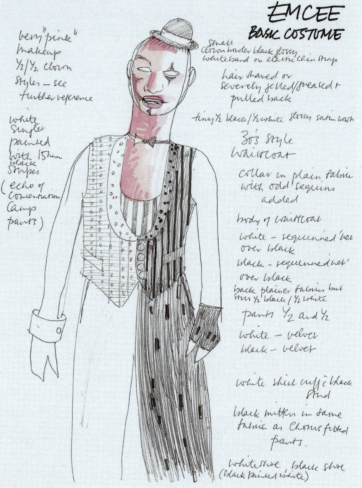

EMCEE
BASIC COSTUME

very "pink"
makeup
½/½ clown
styles — see
further reference

white
singlet
painted
with 15mm
black
stripes
(echo of
concentration
camp
pants)

small
clown bowler black glossy
white band on elastic chin strap

hair shaved or
severely jelled/spread +
pulled back

tiny ½ black/½ white glossy satin bowti

30's style
waistcoat

collar in plain fabric
with odd sequins
added

body of waistcoat

white – sequinned net
over black

black – sequinned net
over black

back plainer fabric but
front ½ black / ½ white

pants ½ and ½

white – velvet

black – velvet

white shirt cuff + black
stud

black mitten in same
fabric as Chorus fitted
pants.

white shoe, black shoe
(black painted white)

9.19

9.20

SEASON AND TIME OF DAY: The time of year and time of day may be explicitly stated in the script (and our script analysis will identify this information) in which case we will apply the logic of the clothing choices people make according to season and time of day or night. But we can also use seasonal choices to give the production a distinct mood. We might, for example, choose to set a bleak story in winter so we can use the darker, sombre tones of winter clothing for an emotional effect, or conversely use the high key tropical colours and sensuality of summer clothing for a bright comedy of manners. Lighting intensity and colour associated with season and time of day will also come into play, and we will want to work together with the lighting designer to achieve a consistent palette for the production (➡ *Chapter 10, page 177*).

PERIOD: The year the production is set might be specified in the script, or the director might choose to reset the production in a different time as part of their production style and concept, or to mix periods or to leave the time open and unspecified. Research will help us get the period details right, but we need to keep it in perspective. Period 'accuracy' can become something of a fetish, partly because of the way it is used in film and television where the close-up shot capitalises on period detail. Slavish use of period research and period detail is not a substitute for communicating character, for good storytelling or for creating a strong theatrical event for the audience to enjoy. In my experience audiences have a very selective sense of period accuracy, particularly when it comes to periods of the recent past which they themselves have experienced: they can find fault with an item of costume that is a photographic reproduction of a true-to-period costume because it is not 'how they remember it', while accepting bold and off-beat adaptations of period style. We actually have tremendous licence to use period as best suits the production. We are creating a performance, not recreating life—this is the difference between costume and clothing. If it is useful to the integrity of the production to painstakingly apply period accuracy (and this is especially the case with military uniforms and documentary-style productions) then our specific research will be a great, shared resource for everyone working on the production.

FASHION: What people wear, how they wear it and when they wear it constantly changes with the year, the season and the day. A huge industry has grown up around the constantly changing fashion cycle. We tend to think of ourselves as more able to dress as individuals and less subject to the whims of fashion than our forebears, but the influence of fashion on clothing is still both strong and subtle. For us as costume designers we can learn a lot from fashion about the way clothes reflect society and the individual within it. We have already looked at some of the social factors of fashion and costume (class, status, economics, occupation, age, gender, cultural background and personality). Let us now investigate some broader factors that we can explore and use as performance designers.

FASHION IS NOT UNIFORM: If you look around you now you will see a wonderful mix of fashion and 'un-fashion'. You will see people who are *in* fashion (wearing the most up-to-date look) and those who are *out of* fashion. Fashion is closely linked with youth culture, and it will be the icons of youth culture who will become the fashion leaders and set the fashion agenda (Ezra Pound stated

GWEN IN PURGATORY, **COSTUME DESIGNER BRUCE McKINVEN**

9.21

9.22

9.23

Bruce McKinven's preliminary designs (9.21–9.22) and final costume design (9.23) for *Gwen in Purgatory* conceive the lead character, Gwen, as a lurid bombshell within the soulless beige blandness of her new home.

that culture is made by twelve people). You will see some people who get the fashion look 'right' as worn in the magazines, and others who miss slightly or try 'too hard' (the 'fashion victim') or consciously adapt fashion to their own tastes or subculture. You will see a rich mix of fashions as people combine new 'fashionable' garments with items they have owned for a number of years, while others carry on dressing in styles from their past. By thoughtfully mixing fashion in this way we can develop a costume design that will feel more convincing.

We know that today's fashion magazines do not represent what people are actually wearing. Fashion references from the past are no different—they tend to only document the most fashionable clothing worn by the elite. These references can be useful if we remember how narrow their focus is, and extend our research with photographic collections and images from art and other sources.

There will be those who conform to fashion with the aim of fitting in and achieving a kind of anonymity (think about the way fashion creates a pool of clones) and there will also be the non-conformists who choose to declare their individualism or radicalism through their clothing. Our fashion choices can blend in or stand out. We can look respectable or disreputable. Counter-cultural dress that rejects fashion is quickly taken up by mainstream fashion, as with the 1950s hipsters, the 1960s hippies, the Rastafarians, new romantics and punks of the 1980s whose off-beat looks were soon absorbed into conventional dress. Fashion fads often define a period and stick in our collective memory—an item like leg-warmers instantly screams '80s, although not everyone actually wore them!

There is high fashion (*haute couture*) and low (street) fashion. The difference between high and low used to correspond to a class difference. Today everyone can aspire to the look of privilege, with fashion magazines running regular segments on how we can recreate the high fashion look on a budget, and cheap knock-offs of couturier designer labels. This has had a levelling-out effect on high and low fashion; we would need to be inventive to create a convincing contemporary look of privilege on stage today.

Fashion continues to play (yes, it is a game) with degrees of naturalness and artificiality, degrees of masculinity and femininity, and degrees of romanticism and asceticism.

A study of fashion provides rich food for thought for us as designers, and we can explore any or all of these factors, as well as age, gender, status, class, occupation, cultural background, personality traits, character development, the function of the character in the storytelling, the performer playing the role, the form or genre of the script, season and time of day, their context and the period. That's a lot to be working with! On any production just one or two of these factors may guide us in shaping our 'big picture' costume interpretation. As we get down to the detail the other factors might also come in to play (➥ *Chapter 12, page 206*).

Case Study
Pygmalion — Stage 7:
Defining Character

A different kind of character definition is seen in these designs (below and opposite, top) and fittings (opposite, bottom)

Pygmalion character definition and character development. In this sequence of costume designs and fitting and backstage photographs we see the steps in Eliza's development from Covent Garden flower-seller to toast of London society conveyed through costume design choices. Every possible scripted opportunity is explored and exploited, guided by 1950s documentary photographs and couture references. Her act 3 costume (seen here in calico

toile) was conceived as an almost-vulgar extreme of high fashion where she (and the men in the play who have dressed her) has not got it quite right.

A different kind of character definition is seen in these designs (below) and fitting photographs for three characters portrayed by the same actor (character 'doubling'). Here the task was to use silhouette, colour, tone and texture to make the differences as clear as possible.

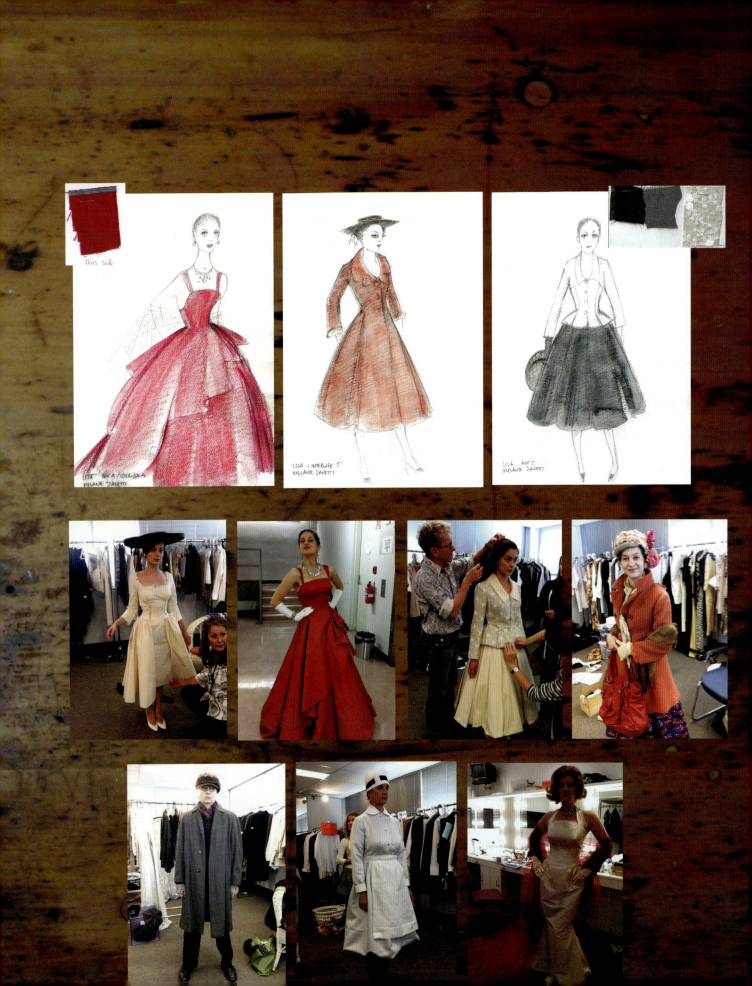

For me a costume is the top-to-toe external mask of a character — not a mask for hiding but a mask for revealing. It is an exo-skeletal projection of a character's inner life. It will establish a figure in a landscape. It will dictate a character's centre of gravity, their movement, the contradictions, their ornamentations, how they command or retreat from the given space… Geoffrey Rush, actor, director

FURTHER THINKING
THE PERFORMER–DESIGNER RELATIONSHIP

It is hard to imagine two creative processes more different than the performers' and ours as designers: we are among the first members of the team to start work and have already done much of our creative work and the designs will be usually quite resolved and 'complete' before the performers begin their first day of rehearsal. We essentially work alone, coming together with the director and other members of the creative team from time-to-time to share ideas and develop the work, whereas performers work together as a close-knit company. While the performers are rehearsing together in the rehearsal room we are all over the place: in costume and set workshops, paint floors, props stores and departments, in production meetings, out in the stores buying… and when we have time we will be in the rehearsal room watching from 'out front' to see how the performances are developing. The performers are with the show right up to the last performance, while the designers have completed their work by opening night. The performers' work is ephemeral, conjured anew nightly for the audience, and subtly grows and changes over the run of the show, whereas our work is concrete, physical and predetermined, and can only change in response to new conditions if items are redesigned, re-made or altered.

When we do come together in production week, when all of the elements of the show are brought together for the first time in the theatre, we are still separated, both by the architecture of the space, with the performers on-stage and us out in the auditorium and by the creative roles we are each fulfilling. You could almost think of us as in parallel universes.

Yet the performer is at the heart of what we do because the performer is at the heart of the performance event. It will be the unique life they portray on stage as actors, singers, dancers or acrobats that engages the audience, entertains them, moves and inspires them. It is our job to support that process. We can do this by thinking about the performer at every stage of our design process, so that our designs develop from an understanding and sensitivity to what they will bring to the process. This kind of 'performer-centred' thinking develops over time as we come to appreciate the performer's process of preparation, their needs and vulnerabilities, how they use space and inhabit a costume and the way a performance is shaped through them by the director or choreographer in the rehearsal room. Spending time in the rehearsal room and talking to the performers about what they are doing benefits all of us—we learn more about how they work and about their performance and they learn more about how we work and about our design ideas. Our aim is to do whatever we can to make the two elements mesh. Finding these opportunities is especially important for the set designer who is not also designing the costumes, because the regular coming together of the performer and the costume designer in the costume fitting provides a normal practical way for the two creative processes to interconnect that is not available to the set designer. Production styles such as those of Brook, Grotowski and Kantor (➡ *Chapter 5: Dynamic productions, page 63*) were developed to provide a work environment that would actively combine the processes of the performers and the rest of the creative team. Some directors will set up such a process—in which the design is improvised and developed through rehearsal along with other elements of the production.

Having a performer-centred design process does not mean we need to lose focus of our specific role as designer, but that we factor the performer into our thinking *while* we are designing. We can literally imagine the dancer or actor into the costume we are creating—how they will move, project character and relate to the other performers around them. We can imagine the performer in the space we are shaping—how they will enter, how free or constrained their movement will be, how motivated they will be to move through the space and how groups of performers might occupy the set.

This imaginative visualisation can start from the very beginning of our design process—when the director casts the show. Every performer is a unique 'package' of qualities that the director or choreographer tunes into when they are casting a production. They will be thinking about the performer's physical qualities: their age, gender, physique, vocal qualities and nationality (though increasingly directors are adopting colour-blind casting—where they cast a performer of any ethnicity in roles that don't require a specific nationality). They will be considering their skills and experience, their depth of feeling and their personality—both in terms of the character they might play and how they will work with the rest of the company. And there is also often some other difficult-to-identify quality that makes one performer ideal for the role. We can talk with the director about their casting choices as these choices are often a strong early indication of the performance style and production style of the production.

When we are designing the set we can think about all of the elements of the set from the performers' point of view: whether the scale of the venue will mean the performers will need to work hard and push hard to get their performance across to the back row, or whether in a more intimate venue their performance can be more nuanced and laid-back; how the eye-line of the audience (looking up or down on the performers) will give them more or less contact with the performers; how the size and shape of the space will be scaled to the kind of performance they will give; whether an entrance or a special position on stage will give them absolute command of the space; and whether the space will work as a kind of playground for them to find physical ways of expressing their character.

When we are designing the costumes it is easier to keep the performer in mind, but even so we can specifically think about how a particular character interpretation will fit with the relevant performer; whether the design will suit the performer's colouring and build; how demanding a costume might be to wear; how a costume might constrain or provide for freedom of movement; how the fabrics we are considering will feel on their skin and respond to what the performer will be doing; and how the costumes for the whole cast will work together. During rehearsals we need to make sure we keep track of how each performer's role is developing, and integrate any changes of interpretation into our designs to ensure that the costume designs are a real expression of the performer's characterisation.

When we present our designs to the cast, usually at the beginning of rehearsal, this is a great opportunity to explain our ideas and get them on board with our concept. It is important that they hear this in our own words as well as from the director so they understand the whole picture and how they will become part of it. It is an important early step in building trust and understanding.

Performers, and particularly actors, tend to work from a position of finding an inner 'truth' to their performance. This might be based on their understanding of real people's behaviour or what feels natural with their co-performers or just what instinctively feels right to them. A non-naturalistic, theatrical stylisation will typically be built up from this base, and the performers will actively use all of the stylistic clues available to them. Our designs are important clues—a powerful visual way for them to see what the style of the show is going to be.

It's all about good communication: the actors share their often intensely focused insights into their character while I help them see themselves as part of the big picture—the whole world and the whole concept. Together we arrive at a point where there is a beautiful melding of the costume and the performer.

Tess Schofield, designer

Like us, actors begin their process with a detailed study of the script and a systematic weighing up of the scripted information about their character and the script as a whole. Many directors begin rehearsal with a detailed line by line discussion of what the script means and how it works, and the rehearsal process will continue to develop these insights. Throughout this process performers develop very carefully considered responses, and when our relationship is at its most productive these insights will complement our own. It makes sense for us to set up a relationship of mutual exchange and respect in which their work as performers informs our designs and our work as designers informs their performance.

During rehearsals as their performances are taking shape we will be offering up costumes, furniture and properties for the performers to use. This process can be quite straightforward, but frequently these items need to be adapted to the particular way the performer is using them. It is helpful for us to get items into rehearsal early so their process of exploration can begin. When adaptations are required it is best to work directly with the performers themselves to resolve any problems. Finding out the context of why, how and what they are doing is a good start to creating a solution.

Over the four or so weeks of rehearsal the performers will have developed a real rapport with each other and with the director or choreographer. The rehearsal room will have become a safe place for exploration, experimentation and shaping their performance. When a show moves into the theatre this is a big shift for the performers. They will be looking forward to it with a degree of nervous anticipation. The move is made even more difficult for the cast as they may 'lose' the director for several days during the lighting sessions. It is easy for us to forget about their needs as we are in the thick of getting everything ready for the technical rehearsals. We can make this transition easier for them by making sure that everything they need to use on stage is ready for them. If the technical team is running behind schedule (and this is not exceptional) try to prioritise any part of the design that is used by the performers so that they are secure in what they are doing when they come on-stage for the technical rehearsals.

DIARY OF A MADMAN, COSTUME DESIGNER TESS SCHOFIELD, SET DESIGNER CATHERINE MARTIN

9.24

9.25

9.26

9.27

9.28

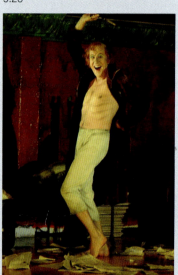

9.29

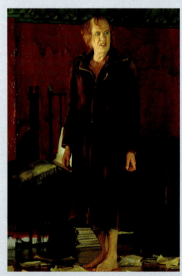

9.30

Tess Schofield's costume designs (9.24–9.26), art finishing (9.27), fitting photograph (9.28) and production photographs (9.29–9.30) of Geoffrey Rush in the role of Poprishchin in *Diary of a Madman*. Tess's strong visualisation of the character is communicated in her drawings and becomes a key component around which the character is shaped. Through costume fittings Geoffrey will 'play' with the costume and becomes an active factor in how the design evolves to become 'his own'.

CHAPTER 10

USING LIGHT AS A DESIGN TOOL

Romeo and Juliet (Designer Pip Runciman)

In this chapter we investigate the design potential of light and how we can get
the best from our creative partnership with the lighting designer

The key to a successful partnership between designer and lighting designer is finding a shared sympathy for the desired outcome. If the designer and lighting designer are speaking the same creative language the technical issues seem to solve themselves.

Matt Scott, lighting designer

Our work as designers shapes *what* the audience sees. Our co-creative team member—the lighting designer—shapes *how* the audience sees it. It will be their work that determines how brightly lit, how warm or cool, how subtle or bold, how comic or tragic our designs will appear to the audience and ultimately how the audience will interpret the whole production.

Clearly their work is fundamental to what we do, and it is important for us to develop an understanding and awareness of the lighting designer's process and contribution, and to engage with the expressive qualities of light (and darkness). In this chapter we will explore these issues from our perspective as costume and set designers. It is not my intention to overlap with the many, many books on lighting design for performance. Unlike our fields of performance design, lighting design is an area very well served by publications dealing with the aesthetics and technical aspects of the craft, and I encourage you to read further. My intention here is to relate their work to our own so that we can build a productive relationship in which the physical design and the lighting designs mesh perfectly.

We are all designers: lighting, costume and set designers. We have a lot in common. Many of the design tools we use, many aspects of our process, the way we see and the way we talk about what we do link us all as creative visual artists. There are important differences too. Ours is one of the first layers of visual information to take shape, whereas the lighting designer's work is one of the last layers to be added to the production; we work with concrete things, they work with non-material light; theirs is a highly technical area determined by the capability of equipment and programming of the lighting cues as reliably predictable events while our designs are shaped through a somewhat unpredictable, visceral process using 'messy' tactile materials such as paint, steel, fabrics and glue; their work can be readily modified in response to the performance by keying numbers into a lighting console, while any changes to the physical design require rebuilding, repainting, unpicking seams or some form of physical reworking; our design takes shape over many weeks of physical construction while the lighting designer will bring their vision to completion within just the last few days of the production period.

LIGHT AS A DESIGN TOOL

Because light is the final visual component to be added to the production it might be tempting to think of light as 'just the final brush-strokes that complete the stage picture'. Think again! Light was there in those first dramatic events when painted bodies, sacred objects and ritualised spaces were illuminated by flame, and it has been one of the great expressive tools of performance ever since. To be able to reveal and conceal and literally direct the audience's eyes with light is a very large part of the magic of the performance event.

The more we are able to think of light as *part of* what we are designing, right from the very beginning of our visualisation process, the stronger our designs will be. A large part of it is just keeping our eyes open and seeing how light shapes everything around us, and will in turn shape everything we design. We can see the way a shadow may be twice our size and fearsomely grotesque; we can see light falling softly through lace curtains onto someone's face, or slashing boldly through venetian blinds—splitting a room into fragments; we can see light reflecting off a red wall making a child's yellow T-shirt orange; we can see how the strong light of summer makes high key colours jump, and how the same colours look dead in the soft, low light of winter; we can see how the diffuse fluorescent light in an office washes out any sense of excitement in the space, and we can see from the street which offices have 'warm' and which have 'cool' fluorescent fittings; we can watch a shadow cast by a passing car's headlight move along a wall, how the single light of an opened refrigerator door captures a whole moment and how the moment vanishes when the door is closed; or how the low golden light of sunset creates the magic of 'magic hour'. When we are seeing light in this way, we are observing the lighting designer's tools at work: the angle, intensity, colour, movement, shape and focus of light, and the way these tools are used to reveal or conceal things, to shape them, to create mood and to show us where to look.

We can extend this awareness into our design process and actually think about what we are designing *as if it is lit*. We might imagine a set that is composed of layers where the lighting reveals someone behind one of the layers, or a sequined braid sparkling against the richness of a velvet, or light funnelling into the space from an opening such as a window, or a backlight turning a wig of teased hair into an aura, or the subtle shift of organza over the sheen of satin… if we imagine light as part of our design from the very beginning we will be able to share this awareness with the lighting designer and build a coherent lighting concept together.

For the lighting designer the lighting instruments (which may also be known as lights, lanterns, fixtures or luminaires—yes there is a lot of jargon in this field!) and control systems (dimmers) are like our repertoire of paints, surfaces and textured materials. Each kind of instrument (spotlights, floodlights, fluorescents, LEDs, projectors...) has particular qualities which the lighting designer will consider when creating their lighting design. The designer will be thinking about the expressive potential of the instruments and also their technical capabilities with an aim of combining control, flexibility and expressiveness. They are likely to choose a different combination of equipment for each lighting design, as the stylistic and technical needs of each production will inspire different choices. Their design thinking will include:

LIGHT ANGLE which is determined by the position of the instrument in relation to the performers and is a very powerful tool for the lighting designer. We can think of the angle as high/low and front/side/back light. Extreme high or low angle from any direction creates strong shadows and an inherently dramatic effect, and reveals textures in sets and costumes. Extreme side-light comes from a low angle directly from the side of the stage and is a great sculpting light; extreme (high) top light creates a powerful melodramatic effect, and extreme low-angle light (footlights) may create a more comic or grotesque theatrical effect. A medium angle from the front (ideally at around a 45° angle) is good for conventional visibility and shaping while a flatter front angle closer to level with the performer tends to flatten out the space and everything in it. Backlight will often be used to help define the shape of the performer with edge-light and lift them out from their background. Light angle may also be used to imply time of day in a realist production (high angle corresponding to midday, low angles to dawn or dusk) or may be determined by the realistic logic of the positioning of windows in a set.

LIGHT FOCUS: Focus has both a general and specific meaning for the lighting designer. In general terms, like us, they will use their whole lighting design to help focus and direct the audience's attention to the most important elements on stage at any moment in the performance.

They will also select and adjust the specific focus of each instrument during the lighting focus session: the instrument will be pointed to a specific part of the stage and the light beam will be shaped to the appropriate size (spot or flood), with a soft or hard edge, which will be made square, round or shaped by the use of shutters (or 'barn doors'). A sharply focused light will produce sharper shadows and cleaner definition and at its most extreme can produce a dynamic or harsh effect, while a softer focus will blur, blend and unify the stage picture. Flat soft light tends to 'wash out' or eliminate texture and for this reason is useful for lighting scenic elements such as cycloramas or conventional flats that have an imperfect surface. Lighting designers will generally use a mix of instruments with different qualities of light focus to create different effects: wide-angled floodlights for general, even illumination, and narrow-angled spotlights for tightly controlled areas of light. Hard-edged shapes of light may be used as strong graphic visual elements in the lighting design, and these shapes can complement strong architectural angles in a set design.

WHAT LIGHTING DOES

Visibility: Reveals and conceals.

Modelling: Shapes and sculpts.

Mood: Creates an atmosphere and an emotional response.

Focus: Shows us where to look and aids in composition.

Transitions: Takes us from one moment to the next.

LIGHTING EQUIPMENT

Spotlight: These give a controlled narrow beam, e.g., profile spots, fresnels (softer-edged), followspots (manually operated, very powerful, tight beam used to follow individual performers).

Floodlight: Wide-angled, even light source, e.g., cyclorama or groundrow fixtures.

LED (light-emitting diode): A very bright, long-lasting light source that can mix colour digitally without the need for lighting gel.

Moving lights: These new automated lighting instruments are able to pan, tilt, spot in or flood out, shutter in and out, and colour-mix—it's all controlled from the lighting desk. Many also have a digital 'library' of textures and effects.

Projector: A specialised fixture that is able to project still or moving images from either digital or slide sources. Projection systems may use front or rear projection.

Gobo: A metal plate inserted into a profile spot to create textured light (also referred to as a decal).

Lighting desk/console: The computerised interface that controls the level of each fixture. The lighting design is plotted into the desk during the plotting session and operated by the lighting operator.

INTENSITY describes how bright or dim (high or low level) the lighting state is. Intensity is determined by the number of instruments, by the power of the lamp in the instrument and by the control of the light with the dimmers. Most importantly, intensity for the human eye is relative: after a period of sustained darkness, the light from a candle can seem bright in a dark space, and conversely we may see little difference when a powerful spotlight is added to an already very bright scene. The lighting designer will sculpt the stage with light by subtly adjusting the light intensity of individual instruments and groups of instruments during the light plotting session. Bright light is conventionally thought to work well for comedy and for when the audience is required to understand complex language (if we struggle to see we struggle to understand). Low level light is more atmospheric, contemplative and dramatic. It is interesting to observe how people instinctively tend to move forward into light or hold back in the shadows depending on their motivations. We tend to associate the presence of light with goodness and its absence with the unsettling and the unknown.

COLOUR: Like us the lighting designer will use colour as a powerful expressive tool. The colour of the light is a major factor in the emotional impact of a scene, its mood and atmosphere, and the interplay of coloured light on a coloured set and costume surfaces offers endless creative opportunities. The lighting designer will also use colour to shape and sculpt the performers and other physical elements in the space. Typically this is done by using cool light from one direction and warm light from the opposite side and balancing the level of these from one moment (lighting cue) to the next. The use of colour in this way adds extra three-dimensionality to the stage picture. In white light productions (in which no coloured gels are used and every instrument is in 'open white') sculpting with colour is more subtle, with lights at low level registering as warmer from one side and lights at a brighter level appearing cooler on the other.

The relationship of the lighting designer's colour palette to our own is crucial; coloured light can either enhance or impair the colours we are using in the costumes

THE BABEL PROJECT, **DESIGNER JOEY RUIGROK VAN DER WERVEN**

10.1–10.4
Joey Ruigrok van der Werven's design drawings (10.1, 10.4) and production photographs (10.2, 10.3) for *The Babel Project*. Co-deviser and designer Joey collaborated with director Alan Schacher, lighting designer Sydney Bouhaniche and video artist Sean Bacon to shape a distinct language of light for this physical theatre performance, incorporating projection, wall-mounted fluorescent fittings and moving lights on performer-operated cranes.

HOW LIGHTING WORKS

Rig: All the lights for the production as 'rigged' on-stage and in the auditorium or front-of-house (FOH), on lighting bars, booms, ladders and other rigging points.

Focus: Each fixture is aimed to a particular part of the stage, the beam is spotted in or opened out, the light edge is made soft or hard and the beam is shuttered to a specific shape.

Plot: In the plotting session the lighting designer sets (plots) each state and the cues for the whole production. These are recorded in the lighting console (desk).

State: A single moment in stage lighting when a number of fixtures are set to specific levels.

Cue: A shift from one lighting state to another over a specific period of time (usually a number of seconds for up and down times). The cue points are recorded by the stage manager, who will 'call' each cue at the appropriate time in the production.

Level: The degree of intensity (brightness) of a fixture at any moment in the production. High level = bright, low level = dim.

Fade: Reduce the level of a fixture or group of fixtures—to become darker.

Cross-fade: Reduce the level of one group of fixtures while increasing the level of another group.

Blackout: Simultaneously taking the level on all of the lighting fixtures to zero. This usually marks a dramatic end of action.

Preset: The pre-show lighting state. This will often aim to set the scene and add an air of expectation.

and set. This is particularly the case when strong saturated lighting colours are used. For example, a strong blue light that has some green in it (such as a teal) will harmonise and complement blue-greens in our design but will 'kill' purple-blues (such as ultramarine or indigo). The advent of new ways of producing coloured light (dichroic gels, colour-mixing LEDs, etc.) greatly enhances the lighting designer's palette but also adds a new dimension of complexity. If we are planning to use colour in a definite way it makes sense to discuss our colour scheme early with the lighting designer and do lighting tests of set and costume materials if necessary.

TEXTURE in light is made by fitting a gobo into a profile spot to break the light beam up into areas of light and shadow, or by using the standard textures that are part of the library of effects in a moving light. These may give the impression of a natural effect such as light through leaves or water ripples, or may be abstract slashes or strips of light. Special gobos can be made to the shape of architectural openings such as windows in the set design, to give the effect of light coming through the opening. Textured light can be used to add visual interest to untextured surfaces and an element of mystique to textured surfaces, making it hard to read exactly what they are, but this can equally work against the design by confusing and obscuring textures that we may have worked hard to achieve.

MOVEMENT in light is created by using manually operated followspots, automated moving lights or effects projectors. Movement can be a very dynamic element in the lighting design, particularly when a strongly stylised feel is desired, such as with dance, spectaculars and music theatre. 'Natural' moving light effects such as moving clouds, flame and rippling water can be achieved, but these usually require the building up of a number of layers to achieve a convincing natural effect. An impression of movement can also be achieved by slowly or rapidly changing the intensity, colour or focus of the lighting. This can be as subtle as the slow changes during a sunset or as confronting as the rapid flashes of a stroboscope. A very dynamic sense of movement can come from visibly moving light sources such as hand-held practicals or flares.

WORKING TOGETHER

Ideally the director will have brought the whole creative team together in the first meetings to discuss the production in general terms, and to get everyone 'on the same page' from the start. Ideas about the script's meaning, how to work with the venue, the casting, early ideas of the production concept and style will all be exchanged and developed through this collaboration. Key references and research images will be shared as a way of initiating the development of the production's visual style. The lighting designer will analyse the script, concentrating on mood, atmosphere, time (season, time of day or night), the passage of time and scripted references to light. It is most important that we develop a common understanding of the visual style at this stage: how abstract, stylised, fantastical or real it is; and what the overall stylistic quality is: hard-edge contemporary, romantic, bright and cheerful, melancholy, garish, melodramatic…

The lighting designer may continue to work closely with the set and costume designers through the whole of their design development, making light an intrinsic part of the design thinking. Lighting ideas might be tested in this development phase, and fabrics and set colours might be tested for light. As the visual language of the production takes shape through the costume and set designs the lighting designer will respond with considerations of colour, texture and angle, special lighting positions within the set, the different feel of light from different kinds of equipment, visual style and atmosphere.

Despite the obvious advantages of beginning a collaboration early, the lighting designer may be brought into the creative process much later—at the design delivery—when the set and costume designs are quite resolved. In this case the physical design will be an important statement about the production's creative direction, and the lighting designer will understand the production style, visual style and concept through how they are expressed in the costume and set designs. In these circumstances part of our role is to make sure that the lighting designer is brought into the creative conversation promptly and that any practical issues concerning light in the design are discussed and resolved early.

During rehearsals the lighting designer will attend production meetings with us, and will attend rehearsals to see how the production is taking shape—where particular moments are played, the energy of entrances and exits, the timings on crucial scenes and the groupings of characters from one moment to the next. This will influence early choices of lighting equipment and position, and these choices will ultimately feed into the development of their lighting plan. The lighting plan is a scale plan, showing key elements of the set floorplan, and also the venue's lighting bars or rigging positions. The plan maps the position of each lighting instrument and diagrammatically records the type of instrument, its focus, colour, filters and the grouping of instruments into channels. Combined with a section, the lighting plan is the lighting designer's key document and will be used by the entire lighting team to order equipment and get the stage ready for the lighting sessions (➡ *Case Study* Pygmalion – *Stage 8 for one version of a lighting plan, pages 188–189*).

During production week the lights are rigged one by one, patched (plugged into grouped circuits), coloured and focused. This is often staged around the set bump-in, but the lighting designer will need to have the set in to complete the focus (and it is very frustrating for them when the set build and bump-in run behind schedule). During the plotting session the lighting designer works with the director, stage manager and lighting operator to plot light states for each cue, and this is an important time for us as designers to be part of the shaping of the production with light. If we have developed a close working relationship with the lighting designer in pre-production this will invariably flow into a productive involvement in the plot. If we have created the design with light in mind this will be our opportunity to contribute to how this is expressed. This is the lighting designer's key creative moment in which they are bringing their vision of the use of light as an expressive element in the production to fruition. They have very limited time to do this and the plotting is a time of intense concentration for them. Our involvement will be a subtle process of representing our own interests in the set and costume design while being sensitive to the creative voice of the lighting designer.

LIGHTING CHALLENGES

Each production and each design will pose particular new challenges for the creative team to resolve. Early discussion of our design proposals with the lighting designer will normally allow time for solutions to be developed. Some specific challenges are discussed here.

Reflective and very light toned surfaces in our design (especially white or highly reflective floors) may create focus issues of bounce or reflected light which will illuminate the space in a way that is difficult to control. Very low angle side-light that lights the performers but keeps direct light off the floor may be a solution. Mirrors on the set or mirrored surfaces are a challenge for a lighting designer that will often require specific solutions.

Sets that are enclosed with very high walls and/or ceilings will limit the rigging options and lighting angles for the lighting designer. This may present problems for the lighting designer but may also encourage new, unconventional lighting positions such as footlights, single-source lighting, use of practicals or lighting through openings in the set.

Sets and costumes that are closely related in tone make it more important for the lighting designer to use backlight and side-light to model the performers and separate them from the background.

Projected scenic imagery requires extensive development with the whole design team. It is important that the technical constraints are clearly understood and worked within from the outset: projection is expensive and will usually define how the budget is allocated; the size of the projection image is constrained by beam throw (the distance of the projector to the screen) and projector lens; ambient light needs to be very carefully controlled so that the image is not washed out; and the delineation of roles in the selection and editing of the projected imagery (content or media) needs to be clearly defined. On productions which use projected imagery as a big component of the show a specialist audio-visual (AV) designer may be engaged to work with both the set and lighting designers.

Practical light sources ('pracs') are working light fittings that are part of the set design. They may be such things as a ceiling light fitting or a desk lamp, a real or electric candle, a flame effect in a fireplace, the illuminated display of a prop radio or a lit computer screen. These may be used by the lighting designer to 'motivate' light so it feels to the audience that the scene is being lit from the practical source. Pracs need to be wired safely for stage use and will often be modified by the lighting designer to achieve better results.

Masking ('blacks') is a vital area of collaboration between the designer and lighting designer. Conventionally legs and borders have been used to mask the on-stage lighting positions from the audience when the concept of 'invisible' light sources is desired. Ideally this masking should be flat (that is, not gathered). The positioning of the masking is critical to determining off-stage lighting positions and heights of lighting bars and often requires a careful balancing of the need to provide clear and useful lighting 'shots' with the need for a 'full mask' where no audience members can see between the masking into the off-stage areas. Alternatively an exposed lighting rig can form a strong visual ingredient in the design. We are familiar with this approach from rock concerts, and the right dramatic and stylistic concept might also make it a valid choice for our production (➡ The Secret River *images, pages 1 and 3*).

Black areas on-stage are conventionally understood to be neutral 'no-space', outside or beyond the world of the performance zone. If the audience is aware of the texture of the black masking this illusion will be undermined. The lighting designer and set designer will need to collaborate carefully to resolve the position, texture and quality of the 'blacks', and to control light spill so that the 'blacks' stay black.

Colour is chiefly about the conjunction and context of every design element, and is entirely dependent upon light. Find your ideal collaborative lighting designer and bind them to you with love, bribery or threats. Whatever it takes!

Hugh Colman, designer

SWAN LAKE, DESIGNER HUGH COLMAN

10.5–10.9
Hugh Colman's set model (10.5), photograph of a scenic cloth being painted (10.6) and costume drawings (10.7–10.9) for *Swan Lake*. 'We experimented with the use of atmospheric mist, but interestingly, in the context of the "traditional" painted scenery, with its illusionistic misty lake backdrop, the painted mist seemed more "real"! Much of this was due to the skill of the lighting designer, Rachel Burke, and yet I felt it also relied on that willing suspension of disbelief unique to theatre, that audiences find spell-binding…'

Case Study
Pygmalion — Stage 8:
Lighting Design

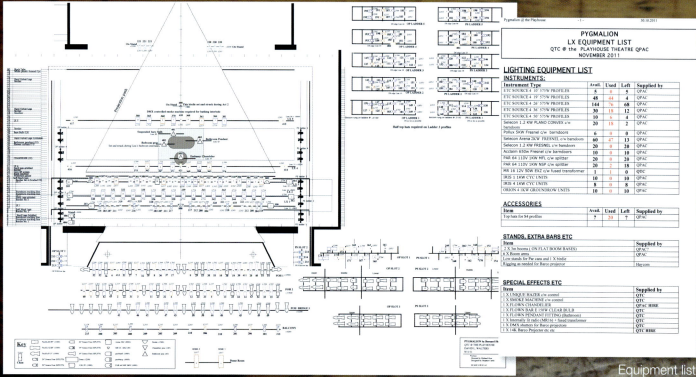

Lighting plan

Equipment list

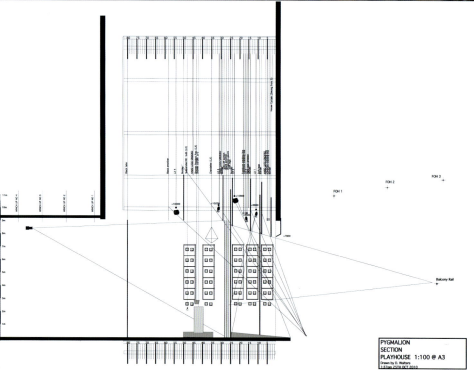

Section

Cue sheet

Lighting designer David Walters' lighting plan, section, equipment list and cue sheet for his lighting design for *Pygmalion*. Seen here in the set model and artwork, the set design used very large format light and shadow window shapes that described the principal locations of the play's action. Rear projection on the gauze map was used to realise this scenic element. Extensive discussion between the lighting designer, production manager and designer during the design of the set was necessary to explore and resolve this element.

RESOLVING THE SET DESIGN

The Trial (Set Designer Claude Marcos, Costume Designer Alice Babidge)

In this chapter we explore ways of creating dramatic set transformations, and follow the step by step process of detailing and documenting the set design ready for design delivery.

The scale model is a great communication device. It allows you to see your idea exactly, and see if it works.

Jacob Nash, designer

We are by now well advanced on our set design journey. We have developed a clear visual interpretation of the world of the script through our script interpretation, research, concept development and experimentation. We will have considered the performer and character, the performance space, the actor–audience relationship, light and visual style. Our set might be metaphoric, illusionistic, dynamic, realistic or a mix of styles. It may be quite abstract, stylised or represent an actual location. It may be a fixed, permanent set or a space that changes over the course of the production. We will have developed our set design concepts and communicated these to our director using sketches, renderings, plans or sketch models. We are now ready to develop the design detail and bring our designs to completion, ready for presentation.

Many different people will be referring to our designs as part of their work on the production and our designs need to provide the information they need in different ways. Everyone from the director, cast and other designers, right through to the set- and props-makers and scene-painters and the marketing team will want to see what the production will look like, and visualisation tools such as the scale presentation model, storyboards or set renderings are perfect for this job. The production manager, lighting designer and construction team will also need the design information in precise, measured formats that they can use to plan, budget and build, and this is where our scaled plans, sections, working drawings and props drawings come into their own. Lists, such as props lists, scenic elements lists or lists describing scene by scene variations will also be useful to the stage manager and production manager.

But the model and drawings are not just for the use of others: they are first and foremost tools for ourselves to work out and resolve the detail of our design—the way each part of the set fits together, the way a particular moment on stage will happen, the transition from one scene to the next, the detail of every element of the design and how it performs as part of the whole design— what it looks like and how it works.

WORKING IN SCALE

It is technically possible to execute a set design without using scale models or scale drawings, as sometimes happens when a visual artist from another field creates a design for theatre. But working to scale allows us to design with a high degree of accuracy—every part of the design can be measured, dimensioned and built precisely and correctly.

For a designer just starting to work with scale it can initially be a bit of a mystery. The first step to understanding and working with scale is to acquire a scale ruler that includes useful theatrical scales. In Australian theatre the most-used scales are 1:50, 1:25 and 1:10. The metric system makes using scale quite easy. A standard metric ruler which is divided into millimetres and centimetres allows us to measure to a scale of 1:1 (that is actual size). In scale 1:10 each millimetre on the ruler = 10 millimetres in actual size, and each centimetre = 100 millimetres. We can use the metric system to keep expanding on this logic, so in scale 1:100 each millimetre on the ruler = 100 millimetres in actual size.

Different scales are useful for communicating different kinds of design information. A floorplan showing the stage and auditorium is likely to be at 1:50 (English Imperial/USA customary ¼" = 1'), a floorplan showing just the stage will be at 1:25 (½" = 1'), and this is also the scale most commonly used for the scale model and construction drawings as it allows for a useful amount of detail in a manageable-sized format. The scale 1:10 (1" = 1') will be used for construction details and furniture drawings, and occasionally a designer will draw a specific detail up in full scale (1:1) so that the construction team can copy it exactly.

It is most important to use scale consistently over the whole design. It is very easy to accidentally flip the scale ruler over and measure an element in the wrong scale. When we are starting the best way to make sure we are working with scale consistently is to scale everything in relation to the human figure. The first thing we should make is a scaled figure of the performer, and we should use this constantly as a point of reference, so we can check that every part of the set design is proportioned correctly to the human figure.

THE SCALE MODEL

As part of our early process of getting to know the performance venue for our production we will have made a scale model box of the venue (➡ *Box, page 101*). We will have experimented with the size, shape, texture and colour of various set elements in the model box with our preliminary or sketch models. We may have used pieces of cheap craft board, photocopied textures, scraps of packaging foam, plastic or metal taped, stapled, glued or pinned together just long enough to test and explore different design proposals—levels, walls, ceilings, ramps, openings, elements that rotate or truck or fly. When we have resolved the overall size, shape, proportion, architectural form, colour and texture of the set design elements we will be ready to move into our presentation model. The right time to do this will vary from designer to designer and production to production. Some directors have trouble visualising the set until the model is in a relatively

THE SET DESIGN DELIVERY 'PACKAGE'

Sketch model: There may be a number of these rough, preliminary models that explore various design possibilities. They will be broadly to scale, and work within the model box for the production venue. They allow us to experiment with and refine our design solutions.

Presentation model: A precise, coloured, scaled model that accurately represents our final set design proposal. This is a key visual aid to everyone involved in the production. It will be a specific reference for set construction and scenic art.

Floorplan: A precise, scaled drawing of the footprint of the set overlaid onto the plan of the performance venue. It is a crucial document used by the teams in construction, stage management and lighting, and others in the production team.

Section: A precise scaled drawing showing a side view of the set.

Construction drawings: Precise scaled drawings of all constructed set elements showing all measurements and information required for their construction.

Set plot: A list of all scenic elements in the sequence in which they are used in the production.

Storyboard: A sequence of pictorial representations of variations and transformations in the appearance of the set from one dramatic moment to the next.

Set rendering: A pictorial representation of the set indicating lighting and mood.

Props and prop drawings: Properties (*props*) include hand props used by the performers, furniture, costume props (such as a walking stick or backpack that are designed as part of the costume) and *set dressing* (prop elements used to detail the set for character, period or style). Prop drawings are precise drawings that detail all of the information required for the construction of the props and will be annotated and in scale as necessary.

Props list: A list of all property elements that are intended to be part of the production, indicating the scene (or page number of the script) in which they are used.

finished form; some designers like to keep things loose and adaptable until quite late in the process while others like to move quickly into precise and accurate measurements. Often the production manager will do an initial costing of the set design based on the preliminary/sketch model.

The presentation model will show the entire set design accurately to scale. The dimension of every element, its texture and colour treatment, its position on stage and in relation to every other part of the set design will be rendered accurately. We should aim for a tolerance, or variation from accuracy, of 1mm (in a scale of 1:25 this would be a tolerance of 25mm in actual size). To make the model we will use more refined materials such as art boards and textured art papers, sheet plastic, sheet aluminium ('shim') or foam core board to render the thickness and dimension of set elements accurately. Over time we develop an 'eye' for scale so that when we are in hardware, hobbyist and bargain shops we will be able to spot useful items that can represent part of our design to scale in the model. Small objects such as beads, jewellery and supplies sold for model railway or aircraft hobbyists can be very useful as components for furniture or other model pieces. Wire (especially brass wire which can be soldered) and strips of balsa wood sold in hardware or hobby suppliers are also indispensable.

YING TONG—A WALK WITH THE GOONS, DESIGNER MICHAEL SCOTT-MITCHELL

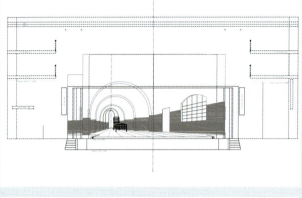

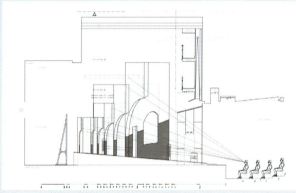

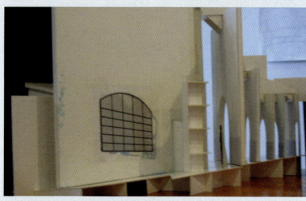

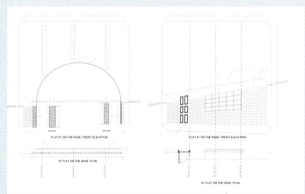

11.1–11.3
The above sequence of images details Michael Scott-Mitchell's set design and model-making process for *Ying Tong—A Walk with the Goons*. Michael uses the illusionistic device of forced or false perspective (seen here in a front elevation) (11.1) to create the vast, surreal and nightmarish ward of a psychiatric hospital.

11.4–11.6
Here we see the egg-crating to strengthen a wall section (11.4), model pieces and floor made in false perspective (11.5) and the assembled 'white card' model prior to painting (11.6).

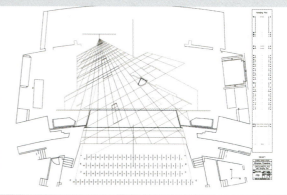

11.7–11.9
The model is painted in base coat (11.7) and then all surfaces are 'broken down' or aged to add character to the set (11.8). The model is lit to help visualise how the set will look under light (11.11). All of the details of the model are realised in the completed set on stage.

11.10–11.12
Michael's *Ying Tong* plan (11.10) and section (11.2) test sightlines, determine the geometry of the false perspective and communicate information to the whole production team on the layout of the set on-stage.

MODEL MAKING TECHNIQUES

Essential equipment:

- scale ruler
- pasteboard
- foam core board (white and black)
- textured art boards and papers
- cutting mat
- steel straightedge (such as a steel ruler, for cutting against)
- cutting knife (such as a disposable blade craft knife)
- PVA (white) glue
- clear fast-drying model-making glue
- spray contact glue
- masking tape
- pins, bulldog clips and clamps
- acrylic paints and paint brushes.

Measure and mark all model pieces accurately and check the measurements before cutting. Always cut on the cutting mat using the steel edge. Keep the straightedge in position until the blade has cut right through the board (this might take several strokes). Swivel-blade cutting knives make cutting tight curves easier. Tape or pin model pieces together for a trial assembly in the model box before gluing. Use PVA to glue cardboard and balsa. Use clear model-making glue to glue metal, plastic, beads or other components. Use glue-sticks or spray glue to glue paper or thin board to thicker boards. Always coat both faces of the model piece with glue to achieve a strong bond. With spray glue read the instructions and use in a well-ventilated place. When using unfamiliar materials test glues on sample materials before using on your model pieces.

Walls, model box stage floors and levels such as treads and rostra are usually made from pasteboard, which retains its rigidity and has a very tough, smooth, polished surface. To keep model pieces rigid struts of pasteboard or balsa are glued to the reverse side using PVA glue, with the model piece held flat with weights such as books while the glue dries (ideally overnight). Stage floors and elements such as the proscenium arch are often 'egg-crated' to achieve maximum rigidity. This involves gluing a grid of struts to the back of the model piece and weighting the piece until the glue dries.

High gloss stage floors can be created by (spray) painting the back of a sheet of clear acetate with the desired colour, or laying acetate over the model floor.

To make gathered curtains arrange spray-glued folds of crepe or tissue paper over a spray-glued base board, then shape the folds with the end of a paint brush.

BASIC ELEMENTS OF SCENERY

Flats: A flat unit of scenery, timber- or steel-framed and usually clad in canvas or ply and may be textured and painted. A *run* of flats is a series of flats joined together to make a whole scenic element or set.

Return: A narrow flat that is added to the edge of a flat to give the illusion of wall thickness.

'Built scenery': Three-dimensional, sculptural scenic elements. These may be constructed of a timber or steel frame with carved polystyrene or other textured layers.

Level: A raised unit of scenery such as a rostrum (platform).

Treads: Units of steps or stairs.

Rake: A sloping set floor.

Floorcloth: A painted canvas scenic floor that is stretched over the theatre floor.

Show floor: The floor surface that is part of the set design—may be a floorcloth, a hard floor of masonite or ply sheets or a showdeck (a raised timber- or steel-framed floor that may contain automated set elements such as a revolve or tracking system).

Soft scenery: Includes cloths and gauzes: Cloth: An unframed canvas unit of scenery. A *cut cloth* has a shaped edge. Gauze: An open weave cloth such as sharkstooth or scenic gauze, that appears solid when front-lit and transparent when backlit.

Cyclorama (cyc): A stretched, battened backcloth which may be front or backlit.

Masking: Usually black scenic elements used to frame the set and limit sightlines into off-stage areas. Masking typically consists of *legs* (vertical units framing the set at the sides) and horizontal *borders* (framing overhead). Masking may be *soft* cloth (such as wool or velveteen) which is flat or gathered, or *hard* (such as framed ply).

Staging machinery: May be hand operated or automated (driven by motors or hydraulics), and includes *revolves*, *flies*, *trucks* and *lifts*.

Steel structures such as scaffolding or metal trusses are made from brass wire which is cut to size, the components taped into position on a base board and then carefully soldered together (this takes practice). Epoxy glue can also be used, although the bond is not as clean or strong.

Brick wall surfaces are made by scoring the grout lines into pasteboard with two fine cuts very close together and peeling a fine layer of cardboard out of the grout line. A more free-form style of brickwork can be made by gluing brick-sized paper rectangles onto the model piece using measured grout lines as guidelines. Note brick-textured papers sold in hobby shops are seldom in 1:25 scale.

Computers have made scale model-making much easier as surfaces such as brick walls, floorboards, timber panelling, carpets, stained-glass windows, patterned lino or ceramic tiles can be scanned from photographs, art-worked in Adobe Photoshop or other image-editing program and printed out on appropriately-textured paper, photographic board or clear acetate. The textures can be scaled to the appropriate scale arithmetically, or by scanning in the outline of the model piece and laying the appropriate texture over this outline; when it is printed out it will be the correct size and scale. Computer-generated model artwork has made the designer's job easier, but it has also led to a generation of designers who can't paint their own models, and consequently don't know how to talk with a scenic artist about the painting techniques and colour-mixing that will be used to realise their designs. I encourage you to look at the painterly effects of all artists and to explore the expressive potential of paint in your own work. Unless your design specifically calls for realistic reproduction of real surfaces the visual world we create in our design is only limited by our imaginations.

Everyone loves a model. The director will be able to see the whole stage picture and get a real idea of how the space will work. The lighting designer will be able to plan lighting angles and positions, the costume designer will be able to see how the colours and textures of the environment will relate to the costumes, and the cast and everyone else involved in the production will be able to visualise the production. However models are time-consuming to make, and we need to balance the need for accuracy and detail with the amount of time we have. A sketchier model accompanied by very detailed construction drawings may work just as well. A beautiful model is not a substitute for a resolved design. There is no point progressing to an obsessively finished model if the design has not been fully tested, developed and resolved with the director, and the thinking has not been done to make the set elements work practically and creatively.

PLANS, SECTIONS/ELEVATIONS

The measured drawings of our set design will be used by the construction team to plan, build and bump in the set. The lighting designer will also work with our floorplan, and the stage manager will use it to mark up the rehearsal room floor for rehearsals. All of our scaled drawings need to be precise and accurate. Where measurements are shown they need to show the measurement of each part of an element, and the measurements need to reliably add up to the total overall measurements. It is a good idea to measure each element of the model (even photocopying these if they are flat pieces) *before* finally assembling the model as it is much more difficult to make these measurements when the model is assembled. The drawings can be made by hand on tracing paper with drafting pens or pencils, or using a computer-aided drafting program. In either case line thicknesses or colour variations are used to make each part of the drawing easy to differentiate, and standard symbols are used to show flats, overhead set elements, borders and legs, cloths and gauzes, and other scenic elements. Drawings are often produced at conveniently copyable sizes (A3 and A4).

FLOORPLANS

The floorplan will include the outline of the stage area, showing at least the front row of seating, to allow sightlines to be checked. Most floorplans will also show a centre-line (C/L) and a setting line (S/L). It is extremely important to show these lines in their correct position as they are used to position the set accurately on the stage. If there are fly lines overhead the floorplan will also show the fly plot on the same side of the stage as the fly counterweights (usually on stage left). The fly plot identifies and numbers each fly line that will have an element of scenery, masking or lighting fixtures rigged on it, and names the item. The set design will be drawn over the stage outline. The extent of the show floor (for example, masonite, ply, tarquet or stagecloth) will be shown as a fine line and the edge labelled. Levels such as rostra, treads or raked stages will have the height shown (for example, as + 250mm) at key points. All set elements that are set on stage level will be shown as solid lines, and overhead elements as broken lines. Set items such as trucks that are stored off-stage for part of the production will be shown in both their on- and off-stage positions. A production with multiple set changes may require multiple floorplans.

SIDE ELEVATION/SECTION

The side elevation, or side section, shows a side view (through the stage and set) along the centre-line. The section will usually be a view to stage left. Any set element that cuts across the setting line will be shown as a solid line, and a lighter-weight line is used for set elements that are positioned further back from the centre-line. The section is an important drawing, especially for the lighting designer as it will show any overhead elements, including lighting bars and borders in relation to the height of the scenic elements. Sightlines from the front row seats determine the height that the borders are positioned, and this can be shown very clearly in the section.

WORKING DRAWINGS

Each scenic element is drawn up as a front elevation, and usually as a side elevation. These drawings have measurements clearly shown. Small degree measurements are shown next to the object, larger measurements further out, and the overall dimensions of the object are the outside measurements. When drawing the construction drawing we need to be asking ourselves, 'What information would the set- or prop-builder need to build this *exactly* how I want it?' Every detail of the set element will be shown, dimensioned and annotated to make our design intention very clear.

Cut-out areas in a flat, as for a door or window are labelled *void*.

The finish of all surfaces is annotated, for example: *canvas-covered ply, primed and painted*; *stained timber (care to be taken with filling and sanding)*; *surface prepared for high gloss paint finish*. A *run* of flats, such as might make up a set in the shape of a room, will be shown as an *extended elevation* as though all of the flats are laid out in order next to each other. The flat on extreme stage right of the set is shown on the left of the page, and then each flat in sequence around to the most stage left flat as if viewed from the auditorium. All flats, including returns are shown in the extended elevation. Each flat is identified by a number on the floorplan and construction drawings.

Cloths are also drawn as measured front elevations, and the seams, pocket (for the foot pipe that keeps the cloth rigid) and the ties at the top (for tying off to the fly batten) are shown.

SET RENDERINGS, STORYBOARDS, OTHER DRAWINGS

Set renderings are an excellent way to communicate the way the set will look under light. If we are using light as a powerful element in our design this might be the best way to communicate our intentions. Renderings can be hand painted or rendered on the computer. A useful technique is to photograph the preliminary or presentation model, scan these images into the computer and render textures, tones and light effects into the image using an image-editing program. For productions that have multiple set variations we can use storyboards to illustrate the sequence of staging events. A storyboard is essentially a series of pictorial representations, frame by frame of what the production will look like. The storyboards might be sketched or they might be a series of photographs of the model set up in a scene by scene sequence, or they might be produced as computer renderings (➡ *Storyboards for* Pygmalion, *pages 72–73; for* Romeo and Juliet, *pages 86–91 and for* Troupers, *page 202*).

As we are supervising the designs through manufacture we will often be asked for more detail, or we will find ourselves in conversation with the set-builders discussing different approaches to detailing the set. It is always helpful to be able to draw what we are describing—it allows everyone to see what is being proposed, and the drawing becomes a record of the conversation and the agreed plan of action. It can be a wonderful collaborative experience when our sketch gets passed around, added to, changed and perfected through these discussions.

LISTS

Our final design package is likely to include lists that itemise elements of the design. The designer will provide a list of all furniture and props. We may also provide a list of set elements if there are a lot of these, so nothing is overlooked in the planning process. A show with multiple scene changes might also need a scene change plot which lists and describes the sequence of changes (➡ *Props list for* Pygmalion, *page 205*).

SET TRANSFORMATIONS

One of the great delights for an audience is to watch a magical transformation in which the set dissolves from one state, and before their eyes becomes something wonderfully new. A production cannot always do this—often a permanent set (fixed or *unit set*) is the strongest solution, but when we decide that a change of location, or of atmosphere or a change of symbolic or psychological state is an important dramatic ingredient in the production we can use our scenic invention to physically represent this change. In thinking about set changes we will need to make sure that our design does not interrupt the flow of the play. Long scene changes are death to writers such as Shakespeare, whereas a play such as *Death of a Salesman* presents opportunities for subtle, but telling variations on the single location from one act to the next. Changes between scenes can be

RICHARD III, **SET DESIGNER SHAUN GURTON**

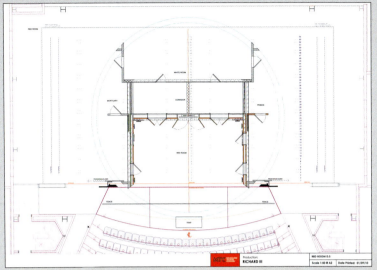

11.13–11.15
Shaun Gurton's plan (11.13) and scale model (11.14–11.15) for *Richard III*. Shaun's design divides the revolve into four rooms which each have a distinct architectural character evoking the corridors of power in the White House. The set design was conceived for a continuous movement of action from one room to the next through connecting doors as the revolve rotated (*page 67 for more on this production*).

an exciting component of the production, particularly if they happen in view of the audience, and give the designer an opportunity to express a conceptual point of view. There are two different approaches to the set transformation: the *reveal*, in which a new element is magically brought to light, and the *progressive change* in which the audience watches the transformation unfold before their eyes. Techniques for creating a scenic transformation include:

A REVOLVE is a motorised rotating disc installed as part of the stage floor or built as a scenic element. Revolves can be small, or as large as the stage itself. The revolve can be used very simply as a great moving shape that energises the production. The circular movement is particularly suited to a sweep of events that keeps taking us on and on. Performers can step onto the moving revolve upstage and be brought around to the front, and objects such as furniture can be repositioned on the stage in the same way. The revolve can also be divided into segments (halves, thirds or quarters) with a different set in each segment, and the rotation of the revolve will take us from one set to the next.

TRUCKS (or wagons) are moving platforms on castors that are either set on tracks or free-moving. They may be moved by the stage crew (mechanists) or driven by motors (automated) and they will often be guided by tracks in the set floor. A truck can be small or large, and may have a complete and quite complex set built onto it which can then be *trucked* into position. Alternatively trucks can be re-dressed off-stage with new scenic elements and reintroduced to provide a continuously changing scenic effect. Multiple trucks moving in different directions at the same time, or coming together from different directions can produce a stunning effect. Trucks are usually a minimum of + 250mm high, to allow for the castors; however much higher than this they become more difficult for the performers to step on and off them to the stage floor level. Provision needs to be made off-stage for the storage and movement of the trucks.

LIFTS are platforms that rise from the stage floor. The introduction of a new level in the set can be an exciting change to the dynamics of the space. Lifts are limited by under-floor access, and the cost of removing a stage floor to install a lift can be astronomical.

FLIES are a very common set-change technology available in most proscenium arch theatres and also in many other venues. The fly system may use hand-operated lines or automated lines operated from a control desk, or a combination of both. Each line has a bar to which scenic elements can be attached to enable it to fly in (down to stage level) or out (to the grid). The fly lines are usually about 300mm apart, and there may be 30–70 of these. Each line will be rated to be

TROUPERS, DESIGNER CHRISTINA SMITH

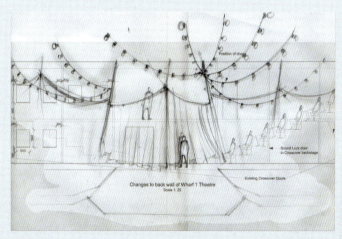

11.16–11.18
Christina Smith uses a combination of hand drawings (11.16) and computer rendering techniques (11.17–11.18) to storyboard her sequence of set transitions for *Troupers*, using curtains to reveal scenic storytelling elements and lighting to evoke a shifting atmosphere from one scene to the next.

able to take up to a certain weight, and each line is counterweighted, so that the weight of the scenic element is balanced by an almost equal weight at the other end of the line to make it easy to fly heavy items in and out. Flown scenery is conventionally quite flat (cloths, gauzes and flats) so that multiple scenic items can fly past each other, but three-dimensional scenery can also be flown using a number of lines which will be *brailed* together to all operate as one.

GAUZES are made from a fine see-through mesh, and appear solid when front-lit, and become transparent when backlit. (They operate in the same way as the advertising mesh that is used on bus windows, and this product can also be used as a theatrical gauze, with a photographically printed image as in *Pygmalion*.) The gauze will be a single seamless piece of mesh that may be painted with dyes, and may be *sharkstooth*, which is quite coarse and strong, or *scenic gauze* which is very fine. Gauzes allow us to create a wonderfully romantic theatrical transition by using light to dissolve through to a stage picture upstage of the gauze, or to create a very ambiguous, ethereal stage environment.

PROJECTION is a form of lighting which allows still or moving images to be used as a scenic element. Projection may be front or rear projection and is determined by the power, position, lenses and throw of the projector. It is important to consult with the lighting designer if we are planning to use projection. Projection works best when it is more poetic or metaphoric. Realistic pictorial projected images can be less sustaining as their texture and scale somehow diminish the power of the live performer, as though we are attempting to put them into a movie.

CURTAINS can fly in or out, track (french action) or butterfly open and closed. Brecht introduced the half curtain that is pulled by hand across the stage on a wire stretched above head height from one side of the stage to the other. Curtains can be a very dynamic element in a reveal, and are the classic theatrical device when used in this way. Curtains and gauzes are often referred to as *soft scenery*. When we are designing with curtains the fabric is crucial (wool, canvas, velvet, molton, silk or gauze) and we also need to specify the fullness of the drape (how much the fabric is gathered). Theatre drapes are usually at 100 per cent fullness, and like all scenic items are fireproofed before being rigged in the theatre.

Many hours will be devoted to finalising our set design. Through the process of model-making and drafting it is important that we keep our eye on the main game—the design as a visual expression of dramatic ideas which we are communicating to our audience. Each decision we make as we detail and dimension the design should confirm our design vision. These final steps in our process are procedural, but they must always also be creative.

Set transformations are always more satisfying when they advance the drama through movement rather than being just a location-changing device. Dale Ferguson, designer

Case Study
Pygmalion — Stage 9:
Set and Property (Prop) realisation

Construction drawing

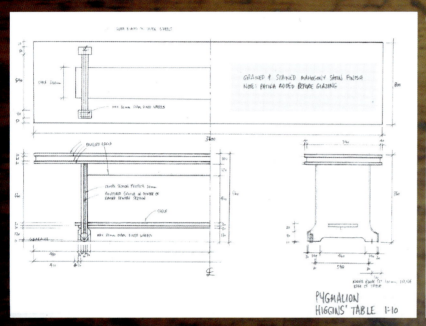

Prop reference sketches

Model

Set construction

Act 2 is set in Professor Higgins' study. The central scenic element around which all of the action moves is a large Arts and Crafts–inspired table, which is laden with curios drawn from the professor's eclectic interests. The table trucks on- and off-stage, guided by tracks in the raked floor (we can see the guides set into the underside of the table legs). Prop reference sketches, construction drawing, model, prop lists and references are all part of the detailing and realisation of this set element.

PYGMALION DRAFT PROPS & FURNITURE LIST
PERIOD: MID 1950s

Each scene has a strong colour accent, picked up where possible in the props and furniture.

ACT 1 (COVENT GARDEN) COLOUR STEEL GREY
- Higgins' notebook and pencil
- 3 x black umbrellas, wooden handles, each different
- Eliza's flowerbasket (an old cane bassinet) containing bunches of violets x 20
- coins

INTERLUDE 1
- broken coat rack
- wire birdcage
- broken wooden chair or armchair
- bare lightbulb

ACT 2 (WIMPOLE STREET) COLOUR OXBLOOD
- red leather club chair, '50s styling
- large arts and crafts table (make)
- set of encyclopaedia
- box files
- files in manila folders
- 1950s reel to reel tape-recorder
- microphone on table stand
- 1950s telephone
- London phone book or referdex
- 1950s typewriter
- globe
- medical models of face
- bust of Bernard Shaw
- stuffed animal
- set of Japanese swords on stand
- African mask or figurine
- human skull
- silver tiered dessert dish containing fruit and chocolates
- Higgins' silk handkerchief
- Higgins' penknife
- bell
- English 5 pound notes
- wire rubbish bin

INTERLUDE 2
- claw-foot bath
- shower curtain
- curved shower curtain rail (flown)
- tubular chrome chair
- long-handled scrubbing brush
- 1950s pendant light fitting

INTERLUDE 3
- dressing screen
- dressing table and stool
- 1950s table lamp

ACT 3 (CHELSEA) COLOUR: DELFT BLUE
- writing table (make)
- slipper chair
- ottoman (make)
- set of writing paper, envelopes, fountain pen
- bell
- coins and keys (Higgins' pocket)

INTERLUDE 4
- large chandelier

ACT 4 (WIMPOLE STREET) AS ABOVE
- Higgins' slippers
- letters

INTERLUDE 5
- wardrobe with mirrored door
- women's clothes on wooden hangers

ACT 5 (CHELSEA) AS ABOVE
- book or magazine

RESOLVING THE COSTUME DESIGN

Gwen in Purgatory (Costume Designer Bruce McKinven, Set Designer Stephen Curtis)

This chapter explores costume design strategies such as designing with fabric, approaches to costume making and detailing and documenting the costume design ready for design delivery.

The costume sketches are, for me, my own search for the character within the page. You could never make the costume from that information alone, but the drawing also contains information for the director and actors. If I can find the character with a simple stance or a quick scrape of thick paint, it can distil the mush of research that is spinning around in my head. I also provide the wardrobe staff with working drawings and/or pictorial references but they appreciate a character sketch that doesn't just give the technical information.

Dale Ferguson, designer

Our costume designs are by now very well advanced. The processes of script interpretation, costume research, concept development and experimentation have resulted in a clear visual interpretation—which we will have shared and developed with our director through several drafts of costume sketches. Our characters might be based on actual people, true-to-life characters, universal types or caricatured stereotypes. Our designs might be highly stylised or quite real, they may be based on a particular period silhouette, or an invented combination of period and fashion references. We will have considered character, the performance space, the actor–audience relationship and light. We will have explored the potential of different visual styles such as stark formal minimalism, romantic decadence or earthy natural textures, and shaped our designs to the production style and concept. We are now ready to develop the costume design detail and bring our designs to completion, ready for presentation.

THE COSTUME DRAWING

The best way for us to present our costume design vision is through costume drawings. There is no specific format for these, but they do need to communicate our design vision to our director, performers and the production team clearly. Some designers create quite loose and expressive drawings that require a degree of creative interpretation and would require the designer to be very involved in that interpretation, while other designers create very precise drawings that include every seam and button. Personally, I try to strike the middle ground—enough clear information, and room for the costume-maker to contribute creatively.

Drawings should be in colour. They may include notes to explain our intentions and may also include fabric swatches, reference images and construction detail sketches (though all of this information could be included in separate parts of the design package). A useful technique is to photocopy the costume drawing (ideally as a line drawing before we have rendered it in colour) and to include notes, references and construction details on this copy. Photocopies can also help with characters that have multiple costume changes as we can draw the variations over the photocopied base outline rather than creating a new drawing each time. I believe that it is important to communicate something of the production style in our designs, so the whole production team get a feel for the kind of show it is—comic/tragic, formal/informal, bold/subtle… It is also helpful to try to communicate the essence of the character in the drawing with an expressive pose and facial detail. Our drawings are, after all, a device for communicating not just the functional detail, but the creative spirit of the production. Our costume drawings need to include:

- the name of the character
- the scene/s in which the costume will be worn
- the name of the performer
- any variations on how the costume is worn.

There are many different techniques for rendering our costume designs. It is not essential to be a good drawer, but it makes our work so much easier if we are! We can simply pick up a pencil and sketch what we mean when we are in discussion with our director, co-designers or production team. Drawing is a basic skill for a designer, and if our collaborators can put in the time learning the basic skills of their craft (voice and movement technique for performers, budgeting and time/people managing for production managers, technical facility with lighting instruments for lighting designers), we can put in the time practising our drawing skills.

There are many media at our disposal, and they each have their own qualities that may suit our personal style or creative vision. Pencils and pens give a fine precise line; inks, pastels, watercolours and gouache give us expressive colour; felt-tipped pens give us a very graphic way of applying strong colour choices. Computer drawing programs have been developed for fashion designers, and like any tool can also be used expressively and subtly with enough practice. An effective way of using the computer as a costume design tool is to scan in our sketch and use the image-editing software to apply texture, colour and tone.

Our costume design presentation package will also include:

- construction details/working drawings, which may include a back view of the costume
- design notes
- costume references
- references for costume accessories (wigs/hair, makeup, millinery, shoes, gloves, handbags/wallets, jewellery, costume props such as umbrellas, walking sticks, etc.)
- costume plot
- fabric swatches
- schematic costume overviews.

COSTUME ESSENTIALS

COSTUME DRAWING: A finished, coloured drawing that shows all aspects of the costume for each character or each performer in the production. These drawings are the principal costume design communication tool, and will be used by the costume department, stage management and many others in the production team.

COSTUME PLOT: A scene by scene breakdown of what each performer is wearing at each stage of the production. Character doubling (when a performer plays more than one role) and quick changes (when a performer has limited time to change from one costume to another) are clearly indicated.

CONSTRUCTION DRAWING: A line drawing showing important construction detail for the garment, such as seams, fastenings, paddings, trim.

FABRIC SELECTION: Cuttings or swatches of the fabrics selected by the designer will form part of the costume design package. Fabric choices will influence the budget and how the costume is made.

TOILE: A preliminary version of the costume, usually made from a cheaper fabric and used to determine the exact cut of the garment before proceeding into the actual fabrics.

COSTUME FITTING: An important event in which the costume is fitted onto the performer to test all aspects of how the costume fits and is worn. There will usually be a number of fittings for each costume for each performer, with the costume progressing to completion in the final fitting, at which time all elements of the costume including shoes, accessories and wigs should be approved for performance.

ART FINISHING: All of the processes of detailing the costume using paint, dye, texturing and abrasives. This process is often referred to as *breaking down* the costume when it applies to making the costume look more lived-in, but these techniques may also be used to give the costume a highly individual or stylised look.

CONSTRUCTION DRAWINGS, REFERENCES AND NOTES

Regardless of whether our costume is going to be made, bought or adapted from stock our costume production team will need to understand our intentions. If we have included a lot of detail in our costume drawing, then the drawing alone might communicate everything, but usually there are design elements that require more detail. We can provide this detail as notes on the design that, for example, explain the number and size of buttons, where seams are top-stitched, heel-height of shoes, hair styling… Often the detail can be explained with the aid of photographic references. We can create a file of references for the production, character by character and present these in digital format or as a folder of hard copies which will be a valuable resource for the costume supervisor and buyer, milliner, wig-maker, costume-cutters and -makers. Alternatively, they can be included with each individual design. When a costume is to be made we may need to provide construction drawings for the whole garment. These will show front and back views of the costume indicating relevant details such as seams, hems, fastenings, linings, trims and foundations. These drawings are best as clean, clear line drawings. We are not expected to be expert cutters ourselves and to know everything about how the costume is to be made, but we can record what we do know. I have found that my construction drawings usually become the

COSTUME RENDERING TECHNIQUES

12.1–12.6
Five different designers show how different rendering materials, techniques and personal rendering styles can be used to communicate their design ideas.
Costume drawings by Tess Schofield (*Love for Love* (12.1), **collage**), Christina Smith (*The Turn of the Screw* (12.2), **pastel**), Dale Ferguson (*Great Expectations* (12.3), **acrylic impasto**), Jo Briscoe and Genevieve Dugard (*La Traviata* (12.4–12.5), **gouache**) and Dan Potra (*How To Train Your Dragon* (12.6), **gouache**).

start of a conversation with the cutter, and we might add or change construction lines and details as we talk through the best way to construct the costume. The revised construction drawing becomes a record of what we have agreed to do.

COSTUME PLOT

If our production is a complex one involving multiple costume changes as part of a performer's character development or *character doubling* then we may want to document exactly how this will work by presenting a costume plot. The plot is a table that lists all of the performers and their characters on one axis, and all of the production's scenes on the alternate axis. We can show when a character is in a scene by checking the appropriate box, and it is also a good idea to mark when a performer has a *quick-change*.

SCHEMATIC DRAWINGS

When a show is very large and contains groups of characters that need to relate to each other from scene to scene, as with a chorus in a musical or full-scale production of a Shakespeare play it may be useful to show this relationship with schematic drawings that present a line-up of the whole group of characters (often drawn in miniature with minimal detail) as they appear in each scene. A production that has complex character development with multiple characters changing costume over the production may also benefit from a schematic for each performer or character that shows all of their costumes in sequence, scene by scene.

12.7
Esther Marie Hayes' costume designs for the drama *All About My Mother* show all the characters for each scene together in a schematic overview. We can see at a glance how strong and subtle choices of contemporary fashion clothing individualise the characters within her highly controlled colour scheme.

DESIGNING WITH FABRIC

A garment will be shaped by the fabric it is made from. The weight, texture and drape of the fabric will determine how structural, fluid, soft, tailored, earthy or sophisticated, subtle or flashy the costume and therefore the character will appear. For us as costume designers knowing and understanding the qualities of different fabrics is an important design skill, and we can develop it by consciously taking note of what clothing is made from and what it looks and feels like. Retail sources for buying fabric are becoming scarcer as fewer people make their own clothes, and we may need to become adept at ordering fabrics on-line from sample cards, which makes it even more important to know the difference between chiffon and georgette, tweed and flannel.

NARRATIVE OF NOTHING,
COSTUME DESIGNER JENNIFER IRWIN

12.8 and 12.9   12.10
Jennifer Irwin created individual graphic designs for her costumes
for *Narrative of Nothing*, which were digitally printed (12.8–12.9)
prior to being made up into the costumes (12.10).

There are two main categories of fabric: natural and synthetic. There are many grades of fineness/weight, stiffness/drape, texture/weave and finish (matte, pile or shiny) available in all of these fibres.

Weaves can be broadly divided into plain, brocade, pile, satin, knit, felt or lace, and include: broadcloth, flannel, herringbone, drill, gabardine, bouclé, jacquard, damask, plaid, burnout, jersey, velvet, chiffon, georgette, voile, satin, habutae, taffeta, crepe, tulle, shot. Get out and feel the difference! (Fabrics.net offers a detailed description and photographic references for many of these fabrics.)

Natural fabrics tailor and shape well, dye and art-finish beautifully and are pleasant to wear as they are breathable. They might require regular ironing and may not be colour-fast. Natural fibres include fur, leather, wool, cotton, silk, linen, bamboo, hemp and hessian (jute).

Fur: sheepskin, fox, rabbit, mink. Leather: pigskin, cow hide, snakeskin, alligator, ostrich. Wool (sheep, angora, cashmere, mohair): flannel, broadcloth, felt, tweed, gabardine, jersey, challis, crepe, tartan. Cotton: denim, poplin, swiss cotton, flannel, flannelette, organdie, voile, gingham, lawn, polished cotton, oilcloth, sateen, percale, muslin, terry-towelling, velveteen. Silk: dupion, see also weaves, above.

Synthetic fabrics are usually cheaper, durable, colour-fast and often require less ironing. They may be difficult to dye and art-finish and might be less comfortable to wear. Synthetic fibres include: rayon, acetate, polyester, acrylic, nylon, spandex/lycra, sequin, lamé, lurex, vinyl, faux fur. Each fibre may be woven into a number of the weaves as above. Synthetics mixed with a natural fibre will often combine the benefits of both fibres.

Trims include braid, ribbon (satin, petersham, grosgrain), ric rac, sequin, faux fur.

COSTUME ACCESSORIES can lift an average costume design and make it really individual. We can use wigs or hairpieces to transform a performer's appearance, makeup to age a performer up or down or accentuate or de-accentuate facial features, hats and headwear to draw focus to the performer's face, canes and walking sticks to shape how the performer moves on stage, special footwear to help the performer stand or walk in a particular way, handbags, briefcases or backpacks as an added character ingredient that may also be used in action and jewellery as a final finishing touch. Many of these elements require costume specialists such as wig-makers, hair stylists, milliners and makeup artists, and we will need to allow room in the budget for their contribution. They will work from detailed drawings and references, and will also need to be included in the costume fittings to check their work in the context of the complete costume.

DESIGN STRATEGIES: MAKE, BUY, STOCK OR HIRE

By this stage we will know the period of our production and the degree of stylisation we intend, and we will have considered the appropriate strategy for realising our designs: make, buy (new, second hand or vintage), adapt from stock, or hire (not a common option for theatre due to the wear and tear of the costumes over a whole season). If our production is quite real and contemporary it is likely that our costumes will mostly be bought. If the production is contemporary and stylised then it is likely that much of our design will be made. A period production might be partly pulled from stock, partly bought from vintage clothing sources, and partly made. Again, if our designs are stylised then more or even all of the show will be made. The strategies are very flexible and will vary from company to company and production to production. Some companies keep a well-maintained stock of costumes from previous productions which can be a real resource for designers. We can use our design eye to select, re-combine and adapt items from stock, usually at little cost to the budget. Typically our production is likely to be a combination of making, buying and adapting from stock and our costume supervisor will be able to advise on the best combination. In any case our costume designs will be a creative point of reference to what we want to achieve.

COSTUME-MAKING TECHNIQUES

There are many ways of making a costume. Each maker will have been trained in a slightly different way or will have adapted their own processes, however there are two basic approaches: by pattern and by draping. In pattern-making the costume-maker translates the design into flat pieces and when these are sewn together they form the desired shape. Patterns use seams and darts to shape the garment and the positioning of these are crucial to the fit and style. Pattern-making gives a very precise 'line' to the garment. Tailoring, which is a specialised form of pattern-making also uses techniques of moulding fabrics to the required form by using layers of interfacings, tailoring canvas and tailors' padding which are moulded using steam, and basted together to hold a specific refined shape. Draping is done by arranging lengths of the chosen fabric over a dummy or over the body of the wearer. The folds of cloth are pinned and then sewn into place, with excess fabric cut away. Draping produces a very fluid, sculptural effect (➡ *For an example of draping—Jennifer Irwin's 'Sun eclipse' dress, page 156*).

Whether our designs are made by pattern or draping it is likely that the cutter will *toile* the garment, especially if it is complex or the fit is precise. The toile is a draft version of the garment made from a cheaper fabric. Seams may be tacked or left open in the toile so that the fit of the garment can be adjusted in the fitting. Garments may be fitted once or twice, or if they are very complex many times to get the exact desired result. Body-hugging period costumes usually require several fittings.

It is very important to get the foundation of the garment correct before fitting the outer garments. The foundation may be a period-specific bra or corset, or body *padding* to change the shape of the performer's body. Common paddings are pregnancy, pot belly or hunched back, but any part of the body can be enlarged for character reasons: shoulders, bust, buttock… It is important to work with the performer when designing paddings so that they are correctly scaled to their body, and work with their characterisation.

The *costume fitting* will be with the performer who will be wearing the costume, the costume-cutter and -maker, the costume supervisor and of course ourselves as costume designers. When the performer is in the costume the early part of the fitting is usually devoted to the cutter/maker making the adjustments that they see need to be done for technical reasons, and it is often best to let them do their work before making our own contributions to the fit of the costume. It is always a good idea to work with the performer to make sure they can physically do everything they need to do in the costume (don't forget to ask them to sit) and that the costume is comfortable. It is also important to make sure the costume is taking shape in a way that meshes with their character development in rehearsal. This is usually a matter of good listening and good leadership.

Designers talk a lot about 'happy accidents' — it could be when a piece of fabric behaves differently from what was originally expected, or the colour in the dye pot reacts mysteriously to the properties of a fabric. Sometimes these mistakes prove to be better than we first imagined. By keeping our eyes open to all developments throughout the costume-build process we can embrace the 'happy accidents', even surprising ourselves.

Julie Lynch, designer

ART-FINISHING is the technique of using fabric paint, dye, printing (such as digital, screen or block printing) or abrasives to treat the fabric before being made up into the costume, or to treat the whole costume after it has been assembled. The art-finishing technique of breaking down usually refers to the aging of costumes to make them look more lived in. If we are designing a very realistic production in an intimate venue where the audience will be close enough to see fine detail we might use fine sandpaper to create naturalistic wear points on clothes that are intended to look lived in: the back of a collar, elbows and cuffs of tops, and knees, seats and bottoms of hems. This is especially important if we want brand-new purchased costumes to look real and care-worn. A more stylised production, or one where the design demands heavier breaking down might call for the cheese grater and dyed or spray-painted staining under arms, on hems or dirty hand smears down the front of shirts. Paint can also be used to subtly shape the garment by creating highlights and shadow areas. This requires skill and an understanding of how the lighting for the production will work with these painterly effects.

Case Study
Pygmalion — Stage 10:
Costume Realisation

Costume design, annotated drawing, first and subsequent toiles in calico,
finished costume and costume list for Mrs Higgins's Act 3 suit.

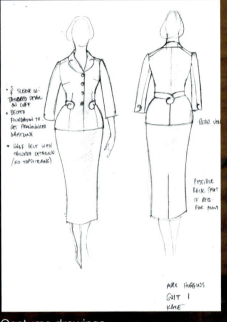

Costume drawings

Toiles and finished costume

PYGMALION COSTUME LIST 20.11.10

PERIOD: MID 1950s

Each scene has a strong colour accent, picked up where possible in key costumes.

NOTE Freddy is on stage for much of the night, and does not change.

ACT 1 (COVENT GARDEN) COLOUR STEEL GREY

- Melanie Zanetti — Eliza — cap, overcoat, cardigan, floral skirt, gloves, galoshes
- Robert Colby — Higgins — tweed norfolk jacket and trousers, brogues, tweed cap
- Bryan Proberts — Pickering — d/b overcoat over blazer, trousers, homburg, brogues, moustache
- Chris Sommers — Freddy — d/b suit, brogues
- Kerith Atkinson — Clara — pleated skirt, lace blouse, bolero, hat, handbag
- Carol Hill — Mrs Eynsford Hill — suit, fur cape/stole, hat, handbag
- Kaye Stevenson — ragpicker — overcoat, skirt, boots, gloves, beanie/hat
- Penny Everingham — duchess — opera evening dress, fur
- Chris Betts — bystander — overcoat, hat
- #1 Male — bystander — 2 piece suit, hat
- #2 Male — sarcastic bystander — 2 piece suit, hat, gabardine overcoat
- #3 Female — opera-goer — evening dress, fur
- #4 Female — bystander — overcoat over suit, hat

INTERLUDE 1

- Melanie Zanetti — Eliza — cap, overcoat, cardigan, floral skirt, galoshes

ACT 2 SC 1 (WIMPOLE STREET) COLOUR OXBLOOD

- Melanie Zanetti — Eliza — cap with flowers added, overcoat, cardigan, floral skirt, oversized high heels, manky fox fur
- Robert Colby — Higgins — tweed norfolk jacket and trousers, lab coat, cardigan, sandals
- Bryan Proberts — Pickering — blazer, trousers, brogues
- Penny Everingham — Mrs Pearce — skirt, blouse, apron, mop cap, lace-up shoes, wig?

INTERLUDE 2

- Melanie Zanetti — Eliza — (undresses completely)
- Penny Everingham — Mrs Pearce — skirt, blouse, apron, mop cap, lace-up shoes

ACT 2 SC 2 (WIMPOLE STREET) COLOUR OXBLOOD

- Melanie Zanetti — Eliza — kimono, '50s bra under
- Robert Colby — Higgins — tweed norfolk jacket and trousers, lab coat, cardigan, sandals
- Bryan Proberts — Pickering — blazer, trousers, brogues
- Penny Everingham — Mrs Pearce — skirt, blouse, apron, mop cap, lace-up shoes
- Chris Betts — Doolittle — dustjacket over waistcoat, cardigan, trousers, boots, scarf, cap

INTERLUDE 3

- Melanie Zanetti — Eliza — kimono, changing on stage into petticoat etc. for Act 3

ACT 3 (CHELSEA) COLOUR: DELFT BLUE

- Kaye Stevenson — Mrs Higgins — suit #1, shoes. Wig?
- Melanie Zanetti — Eliza — tailored outfit 1, hat, gloves
- Robert Colby — Higgins — tweed norfolk jacket and trousers, brogues
- Bryan Proberts — Pickering — blazer, trousers, brogues
- Chris Sommers — Freddy — d/b suit, brogues
- Kerith Atkinson — Clara — pleated skirt (variation on act 1), twin set, heels
- Carol Hill — Mrs Eynsford Hill — suit (variation on act 1), heels
- #3 Female — parlourmaid skirt, blouse, apron, mop cap, heels

INTERLUDE 4 (EMBASSY BALL AT AMERICAN EMBASSY)

Note some guests may be up-stage of gauze only

- Melanie Zanetti — Eliza — red satin ball gown
- Robert Colby — Higgins — tails
- Bryan Proberts — Pickering — tails
- Chris Sommers — Freddy (as footman) — d/b suit, brogues
- Kerith Atkinson — guest — ball gown
- Carol Hill — guest — ball gown
- Penny Everingham — guest — ball gown
- #1 Male host (American Ambassador) — tuxedo
- #2 Male (Hungarian diplomat) — tails, sash, cape, moustache
- #3 Female hostess (American Ambassador's wife) — ball gown
- #4 Female — guest — ball gown

ACT 4 (WIMPOLE STREET)

- Melanie Zanetti — Eliza — red satin ball gown
- Robert Colby — Higgins — tails, slippers
- Bryan Proberts — Pickering — tails

INTERLUDE 5

- Melanie Zanetti — Eliza — ball gown
- Chris Sommers — Freddy — d/b suit, brogues
- #1 Male — Policeman — Policeman uniform, helmet
- #2 Male — Policeman — Policeman uniform, helmet

ACT 5 (CHELSEA)

- Kaye Stevenson — Mrs Higgins — suit #2, shoes, hat, brunch coat, gloves added
- Melanie Zanetti — Eliza — tailored outfit #2, hat, gloves added
- Robert Colby — Higgins — tweed Norfolk jacket and trousers, brogues
- Bryan Proberts — Pickering — blazer, trousers, brogues
- Chris Betts — Doolittle — dust jacket over waistcoat, cardigan, trousers, boots
- #3 Female — Parlour maid — skirt, blouse, apron, mop cap, heels
- Chris Betts — Doolittle — morning suit, spats, top hat, cane

REALISING THE DESIGN

Anatomy Titus Fall of Rome: A Shakespeare Commentary (Designer Robert Kemp)

This chapter explores the final phase of the design process that brings our design to the audience, and all of the people in the production team that help us realise the design.

Realising a design is one of the most rewarding parts of this job. Working closely with skilled artists—watching your design come to life—this is truly exhilarating, and addictive.

Claude Marcos, designer

THE PRODUCTION TEAM

As we move into the final phase of our design process—design realisation—we will begin working closely with the production team. They will be specialists in their own craft, and will have much to contribute to the realisation of our designs. By definition they will know more about their own area of specialisation than we do and will be able to offer creative, technical and practical advice and expertise. Working together is a subtle combination of interdependence—we rely on them to enrich the production by giving their creative and technical best, and they rely on us for leadership, clear direction and openness so they are able to work at their best. If we get to know the capabilities of the production team while we are designing we will be able to design specifically for them—making the most of their high-level skills, sensitivity and intelligence, or keeping our design simpler when we are dealing with less-experienced artisans.

PRODUCTION MANAGER: Oversees the realisation of the entire production—costume, props and set design, lighting, audio-visual and sound design—to ensure that the production is achieved on time and within budget. They are involved from the outset, providing us with much of the technical information that is part of our initial checklist: key production dates, venue plans, casting information, production crew information and budgets. They review our designs as they progress and give feedback on feasibility. They budget and schedule production labour based on the finalised designs that we deliver, and give feedback on how best to realise the designs. They assemble a production crew for the production (if a company crew does not already exist). They supervise the build for all departments and chair the production meetings. They schedule and coordinate the *bump-in* of the production into the theatre and oversee the production through production week, right up to opening night, and if technical issues arise right through the season. They also coordinate the *bump-out* (the process of moving the production out of a performance venue). The production manager is a very important person for everyone in the creative and production team. We consult with them on all the 'big picture' aspects of the design realisation, and frequently on much of the detail too.

CONSTRUCTION MANAGER: Oversees the set construction team and the construction and painting of the whole set. They break the set down into components and budget each component in detail, right down to the screws and glue, using our construction drawings as the basis for the costing. We consult with them on all day-to-day aspects of the set build, and how the units of the set will fit together and work on-stage.

SET-BUILDERS: The construction team includes skilled and specialised carpenters and steel fabricators. They are allocated units of the set to build and usually construct a whole unit. We consult with them on specific construction detail within the scenic unit.

SCENIC ARTISTS: These include set painters and sculptors, and they are responsible for the final finish of all scenic units. Scenic art is more interpretive than other aspects of the set realisation, and we should expect to work closely with the painters and sculptors to develop the scenic art approach. Samples are often prepared early in the process, based on our model and reference material, and our feedback on these establish the techniques, textures and colours used by the scenic art team.

PROPS-MAKERS: Props (properties) include action or hand props used by the performers, furniture, costume props and set dressing. The props team are distinguished by their wide range of skills, which may include fine joinery, animatronics, sculpting and special effects. Often a **buyer** works within this production team to source items that do not need to be made, and we may go out with the buyer to select props and dressing for the production. Because props and furniture are often integral to the performances it is not uncommon for us to work closely with the props team to develop, adapt and modify props until they work perfectly for the rehearsed action.

COSTUME SUPERVISOR: Oversees the construction of all of the costumes, from design delivery right up to opening night, and manages the costume department. The supervisor budgets the designs, assembles the costume team for the production (if there is no in-house team) and allocates designs to each cutter or maker. We consult with them on all day-to-day issues relating to all aspects of the costume realisation, including accessories, make up and hair. The supervisor may also act as a **costume buyer** for the production, and we may accompany them on buying expeditions.

COSTUME-CUTTERS: They are specialised costumiers and include tailors. They are allocated a number of costume designs to realise, then devise the patterns and toiles and oversee the fitting and assembly of the costumes. In a smaller team they may also make up the garments. We work closely with the cutters on the interpretation of the designs and the specific detail of cut, fit and trim for each costume.

COSTUME-MAKERS: They assemble the garments under the direction of the cutter or tailor and our contact with the costume-makers may mostly be through the cutter, and at fittings where they are often present to assist the cutter.

MILLINER: A costume specialist who makes items of men's and women's headwear to our designs. Headwear is the kind of costume item that can complete a whole look. They use a wide range of shaping techniques to create the items of headwear which should be fitted with wigs or hairpieces as part of the final costume fitting process.

WIG-MAKER AND HAIR STYLIST: A specialist who makes wigs and hairpieces for the production and/or styles the hair or wigs. They work from our designs and through a number of fittings with the performer to develop the wig fit and styling. A wig may be fully hand-made, or more commonly will have an individual hand-knotted front added to a manufactured wig or hairpiece. Either synthetic or human hair is used, and the hair texture and colour will need to work with that of the performer.

MAKE UP ARTIST: A costume specialist who develops the make up style for each performer, to our overall concept. After an initial consultation during the production period they usually work closely with us and the performers in production week to develop and fine-tune the make up look under stage lighting and show conditions.

Sometimes when I have been asked to simplify my ideas due to budget constraints, the new idea is better, I call this 'Adversity Design'.
Julie Lynch, designer

During this phase of design realisation we are converting the creative imaginative ideas of our design into practical, working solutions. Every day we will be asked and will need to answer very specific questions about how this or that part of our design will work; we will need to be able to devise solutions to new problems; to find ways of integrating new ideas that have developed in rehearsal; to find ways to accommodate design elements that are cut because they no longer fit into the working concept for the show; to redesign existing parts of our design so they work better. Our task is to develop the best working design solutions for the production while maintaining the creative integrity of the design. Our decisions will be good decisions when they are practical and creative in equal measure.

DESIGN REALISATION: THE FINAL PHASE

During the process of finalising our designs and before design delivery we will meet with our director and co-designers to show them how the design is progressing, and for them to give feedback. We need to allow time for final revisions to be incorporated. Occasionally quite major revisions might be called for late in the day, and if this happens it is important to communicate with our production manager to make sure deadlines can be kept. I have designed productions (fortunately not many!) where the director has had a major rethink very close to the design delivery deadline. It is important to stay calm and work logically through all of the steps you have taken together in the design process and establish what is secure and what is in question. Often this process will in itself reaffirm the design for the director, and it will always help to identify the specific elements that need to be reworked. It may be more to do with how the element works than what it looks like. Sometimes a director will need to try an idea out in rehearsal before finally committing to it. If the design is not fully resolved at the time of delivery it is always best to inform the production manager so that the production team can work around the situation.

THE DESIGN PRESENTATION

13.1 The design presentation for *The Secret River*. The whole company have come to see and hear how this new production will take shape. Here the set designer and director use the scale model to describe how they visualise the production.

Once we have our whole design 'package' together we are ready to present. Normally the design will be presented to the production company several weeks or months before rehearsals start. The production company may be represented by the producer or company director, the production manager and other key staff such as the heads of the construction departments. The director will usually present the concept for the production (of which the design is an important part) and then hand over to the design team to present their work. It is an important opportunity to explain not only what the design is, but also the thinking behind it, so that the team that will be realising the design and the performers who will be working within and with it understand our choices, our design priorities and how it all works. This initial presentation will often be followed by other presentations for different members of the production team to talk through specific elements of the design, including the very important presentation to the cast on the first day of rehearsals. In all of these presentations we can use our model, costume drawings and other design material to show everyone exactly what we mean. We can refer to our designs in response to questions about the world of the production and how set elements fit together, character interpretation and costume cut and fabric choice, mood and atmosphere and scenic finishes, character doubling, practical electrics, wigs and makeup, masking… the questions will fly thick and fast because the cast and construction team will want to know *everything*—which is why we are so well prepared.

THE DESIGN DELIVERY 'PACKAGE'

- Scale model
- Scale floorplan
- Scale section/side elevation
- Scale working drawings for all constructed set and prop elements
- Props/furniture list
- Prop drawings and references
- References for scenic finishes
- References for special materials
- Set renderings

- Storyboards
- Scenic elements list
- Scene change plot
- Costume designs
- Costume construction drawings
- Costume plot
- Fabric swatches
- References for costume detail
- Costume schematics

BUDGETING

Once the finished design is presented, a detailed costing will be done by the production manager and heads of department—these costings are *very* detailed. Despite our best endeavours it is almost inevitable that the design will be over budget at this stage. The production manager is likely to have costed the ideal way of doing things, the best materials and the best-trained team. Our role now becomes one of finding the right approach that enables the director's concept and our design priorities to be met while bringing the show in on budget. If the design is less than one-quarter over budget it is a relatively straightforward process working through the budget line by line and working out where savings can be made. If the designs are substantially over budget this will usually involve some degree of redesign, and this will involve our director. Because we know our own design inside out we will know what elements can be simplified or possibly cut, where we need the detail and where it is less important. There are always ways to do things more economically and the production team will be supportive in this process—offering suggestions and research on different ways of doing things. Often this process of rationalisation will result in a stronger design, provided we lead the process with a strong sense of the design priorities.

THE PRODUCTION PERIOD

The production period in which the sets, costumes and props are realised usually corresponds with the rehearsal period. The designer's role through this time is to act as a bridge between the creative process of the production that is being made by the director and performers in the rehearsal room, and the creative process of the production being made by the costume-cutters and -makers, set-builders, props-makers, wig-makers, scenic artists, buyers… in the workshops.

13.2–13.5 The production meeting for *The Secret River*, chaired by the production manager, checks progress on every aspect of the production. The meeting provides the opportunity for sharing information and collective problem-solving. Part of the raked set floor is seen in construction, and being tested in the workshop by cast members. The raked floor needed to work as a water slide, and issues of drainage, waterproofing and the right amount of slip were trailled extensively during the construction phase.

We are the link that translates to the costume-, set- or props-maker how the performer is using an item so that it can be made to work for the performer; and we are the link reporting back to the rehearsal room how something has been made and how it works so the cast can successfully integrate it into their performance. Ours is a crucial role.

During this period we will usually need to do the rounds of all of the production departments several times a week, and if the show is a big one, we may be doing the rounds every day—moving from costume fitting to prop meeting to lunchtime conversation with our director to millinery consultation to a trip out with the buyer to production meeting to a run in the rehearsal

MOVING INTO THE THEATRE

PRODUCTION WEEK: The final phase of the production in which it moves out of the rehearsal room and workshops and into the performance venue.

BUMP-IN: The installation of the set, costume and lighting elements into the performance venue.

TECHNICAL SCHEDULE: A detailed plan for the whole production week, scheduling all crew and activities.

STAGE DOOR: The point of entry into the theatre for all production crew. Most venues require everyone to sign in when they enter at stage door.

BACKSTAGE: All those working areas in the venue that are out-of-bounds to the general public, including the stage, wings, dressing rooms and *green room* (a breakout space for the cast and crew).

FRONT OF HOUSE: Those areas in the theatre to which the public has access, including the auditorium and foyers, usually managed by the *front of house manager*.

MECHANISTS: The stage crew who will be part of the bump-in team and will operate the staging of the production. Supervised by the *head mechanist* and including the *fly operators*.

WARDROBE TEAM: Run the costume department in production week and performance and include the *head of wardrobe*, *dressers* and *wig/hair* and *makeup artists*.

TECHNICAL REHEARSALS: A series of highly structured rehearsals run by the stage manager in which every aspect of the production is plotted and rehearsed.

DRESS REHEARSALS: A series of performances without an audience in which the technical and performance elements of the production are coordinated, rehearsed and refined.

OPENING NIGHT: The final moment in our creative journey, and the beginning of the audience's experience of the production.

room to trial setup of part of the set in the workshop to discussion with the scenic artists about set finishes to… well, you get the picture. We are in the centre of things and the process relies on us knowing how each part of the design fits with each part of the production being developed in rehearsal. The more information we are able to communicate through our designs the better for everyone. Our designs continue to grow and develop through this process of realisation—the designs are not actually 'finished' until opening night. When changes to the design need to be made in response to the way the production is developing in rehearsal it is our role to seamlessly integrate the changes into the overall design without compromising the creative vision, and with as little impact as possible to the budget and the workflow of the production team. Our challenge throughout this period of design realisation is to shape the best creative and practical solution to every practical and creative problem.

THE PRODUCTION MEETING

Every week the production manager will call a meeting of all of the heads of department in the production team. The production meeting will include the production manager (who will usually chair the meeting), the director, set designer, costume designer, lighting designer, sound designer, AV designer, head of set construction, head of scenic art, head of props, head of costume, head of electrics, head mechanist, stage manager and the assistant stage manager (who will often write the minutes). The meeting is designed to bring everyone up to date on the progress of the production, and to draw on the combined collaborative experience of the whole team to solve problems holistically. The meeting will go through issues department by department and particular actions will be agreed on and minuted. The designers' role in the production meeting is to help negotiate and resolve the territory between production departments and rehearsal. Our opinion will often be sought, and equally we will often respond to the advice of others. After the production meeting there will usually be a number of follow-up meetings and discussions to resolve outstanding issues in more detail.

Have respect for the people you work with. You can't have a show without help from everybody you work with and they have a lot of knowledge to offer. Remember that!

Pip Runciman, designer

PRODUCTION WEEK

The final phase of completing our designs is production week (usually more like 10 days) in which all of the elements of the production come together on stage for the first time. The week begins with the bump-in (on-stage installation) of the set and lighting, which usually happen simultaneously—with the construction and electrics teams working around each other on a pre-planned schedule. When the lighting is all rigged and focused the lighting plot commences and each lighting state is created, plotted and cue points allocated in the stage manager's prompt copy. Sound states will be plotted in the same way. The cast are then brought in to the theatre and into their costumes on stage for the first time for the *technical rehearsals* in which the entire production is worked through moment by moment with each performance cue and lighting and sound cue run, replotted and run again until every element is perfectly synchronised. The technical rehearsals are followed by a number of *dress rehearsals* and these are expected to run as close as possible to show conditions. The final dress rehearsal will often include an invited or paid audience in what are known as *previews*. Finally the show will be fully run in, and will be ready for the opening-night audience.

Throughout production week we will be at the production desk in the auditorium with our director, plotting lights, taking notes during technical and dress rehearsals and then later following up on these notes with the production manager and heads of the production departments. This is the first time we will have seen all of the design elements complete, together and in stage light and

OUR FINISHED DESIGN:

- creates a world for the audience to imaginatively enter
- engages the audience and makes them want to watch
- helps to tell a story
- helps to motivate and shape action
- helps to create focus within a scene
- builds an atmosphere or mood
- helps the audience develop an emotional response

- communicates ideas, concepts or themes visually
- gives the production a tangible style
- tells us about the characters in the story
- uses detail to communicate information: when, where, who, what
- solves practical problems creatively and creative problems practically
- is realised on time and within budget
- illuminates the production.

there will be many details that we will want to adjust to make the stage picture perfect. This is also the first time the performers will have worked with all the sets and costumes and props and there will be design changes that we will need to make and oversee to get every element working perfectly. Frequently we will be among the last to leave the theatre checking and following up on issues backstage, and the first in to the workshops to give notes the next morning. We have been working for months on this production, and we will want to make sure that our attention to detail in this final phase does our work and the production justice. As production week progresses we should have less and less to do. The design will be complete and working to our satisfaction. We will be happy with how every element looks and works. We will have helped to create a world, engaged the audience, told a story, and communicated ideas, mood and character. Our work is done. It is an important time to thank all of those who have helped us realise the designs. It is also a time to take stock and reflect on our creative journey—what we have learned and what we have been able to contribute—and to prepare for our next creative challenge.

Case Study
Pygmalion — Stage 11:
The Final Phase

Production budget

Queensland Theatre Company						Wardrobe Costing		
Pygmalion						BUDGET		
Actor/role/scene	Notes	Stock fabric	make	buy	stock	alter	Price Incl GST	Price Excl GST	labour hrs
CHRIS SOMMERS							-		
Freddy	Hair						20	18	
Narrator	Make-up						0	-	
All acts	Underwear- Dark grey socks			x	x		$10	9	
	Dove grey, striped flannel 3 piece suit	x	x	x	x		1500	1,364	
	Meterage:							-	
	suit fabric- 4mtrs (140cm)							-	
	At $125 per mtr						500	455	
	Lining x 3.5 mtrs @ $12p mtr							-	
possible vintage	Mid-light grey fedora, dove grey band			x			180	164	?
	Black brogues			x	x	x	160	145	?
	Paisley tie- apricot, maroon, gold			x	x		30	27	
	Off white shirt x 2			x	x		160	145	
	Check vintage site from Gayle							-	
ROBERT COLEBY							-		
Higgins							-		
Act 1& 3	Hair						20	18	
	Make-up		x				0	-	
	Underwear- Off white socks?			x	x		10	9	
	Tweed Norfolk jacket & trousers- oxblood	x	x	x	x		1400	1,273	
	Meterage:							-	
	Fabric x 4 mtrs @ $240						960	873	
	Lining x 3.5 mtrs @ $12.50 per mtr							-	
	-with plaited leather buttons			x	x		50	45	
	Oxblood brogues			x	x		160	145	
	Tweed cap		x		x		80	73	
	Paisley bow tie- rust,cream,olive	x	x	x			35	32	
	Accessories- Pipe (PROPS?)			x	x			-	
	-watch?			x	x		25	23	
	-Ring?			x				-	
	Off white shirt with French cuff x 2			x	x		120	109	
	Cuff links			x	x		30	27	
	Clear plastic raincoat- 3/4 length			x	x			-	
Act 2								-	
	Knitted cardigan- fuchsia, leather buttons	x	x	x	x		300	273	
	Wool for cardigan-						150	136	
	Pants as above							-	
	Off white lab coat	x						-	25
	6mtrs off white cotton drill @ $15pmtr						90	82	
	Sandals			x				-	
	Off white socks			x	x		10	9	
Act 4	*Full tails:*							-	
	Black bow tie				x	x	25	23	
	White pique dress waistcoat		x	x	x		95	86	4
Possibly vintage	Dress shirt with studded front		x	x	x		75	68	4
	Black tails coat		x	x	x		50	45	3

Updated by Kirsten 3/9/09   Page 1 of 10   S

Production-meeting minutes

 queensland theatre company   *Pygmalion*

PRODUCTION MEETING MINUTES
Thursday 20th October 2011, Merivale Street Studio

In Attendance
Hilary Brown, Tony Brumpton, Stephen Curtis, Kylie Degen, Amanda Dinsdale, , Samantha French, Michael Gow, Staycee Johns, Michael Kaempff, Dan Maddison, Vicki Martin, Julian Messer, Jodie Roche, Tamsin Roseveare, Peter Sands, David Walters.

Apologies
➢ Roxane Eden

Wardrobe
➢ Tailored costumes will be ready next week. It has been suggested that the fitting happen next Friday Morning 28th November, before rehearsals.
➢ Wig meeting went really well between Michael Green and Stephen Curtis. Not many wigs needed to be purchased; those that did need to be purchased have been and wardrobe is awaiting their arrival.
➢ Michael Green has been given a folder with photos of the costume drawings.
➢ Michael Green has suggested that he may need another dresser on the show. This will be determined during the production week.
➢ A toupee may be used for Chris Betts, therefore his hair will not need to be coloured. It is still unsure if his hair will need to be cut.
➢ Vicki Martin and Stephen Curtis will have discussions on who they think may need a haircut and or colour. Michael Green will be able to trim all the gents' hair over at the theatre.
➢ There are still discussions about the moustaches.
➢ A character breakdown has been created by Jodie Roche and distributed. Jodie will keep everyone up to date on any changes.
➢ Melanie Zanetti's costumes will all need to be Quick change costumes.
➢ Jodie Roche will have more accurate Quick Change timings from tomorrow. At this stage there are no lighting fast changes but the changes will still be quick.
➢ Vicki Martin is still in negotiations with a makeup artist. The makeup artist working on Melanie at the Photo shoot on Monday is not available for the performance period.
➢ There will be no need to have a makeup session before the move to the Theatre. There was a suggestion that perhaps the Ladies be called in earlier on the first Tech to have a session.
➢ Vicki Martin and Michael Kaempff will discuss budget today.
➢ Hats are slowly going into the rehearsal room
➢ Melanie Zanetti will have 2x corselets. Kaye Stevenson is happy with her corselet.
➢ Toils will be sent into the rehearsal room to be used by the cast.
➢ There has been a hiccup on sourcing shoes. All shoes to be worn on the stage need to have a heel big enough so that it doesn't fall into the gap from the tracking system. Vicki Martin will start to call all Vintage shoe contacts to try and find shoes with a wide enough heel. Actors' avoiding these tracking areas is not a solution.
➢ Costumes that were suggested by Michael Gow for the Play Briefing on Monday will not be available. It was suggested that the Toils without any pins be used instead as the audience members come to see something that no other audience members will get an opportunity to see. Stephen Curtis, Vicki Martin and Michael Gow will discuss this further.
➢ The narrators will be wearing their bystander's costumes, except for Chris Hunter who will be wearing his footman Embassy costume before the Embassy Ball Scene.
➢ There will now only be 1x footman
➢ During the fittings today Stephen Curtis and Vicki Martin will discuss the wedding bands.
➢ Almost all costumes for the Embassy Ball will come from stock. Some items still need to be purchased. Michael Kaempff, Stephen Curtis and Vicki Martin will have a meeting this afternoon to discuss budget.

Set
➢ The Floor will not be taken over to QPAC until the Monday of Production week. (Monday 31st October). Michael Kaempff does not foresee a problem of bumping in on the Monday instead of the Sunday.
➢ Kylie Degen to contact Chair Co to get samples of the red fabric that the Red Club chair is covered in so that Workshop can experiment on the fabric with Designers Master paint. Stephen Curtis would like the chair to be painted with a Burgundy colour.
➢ The Tracking system will now all be operated from the PS of the stage so that the flyman can operator both the fly system and the tracking system.
➢ Jodie Roche will have a draft Scene Change Plot created Saturday 22nd October.
➢ The Glass top for the writing table has been ordered.
➢
Props

The production budget breaks down every element of the design into cost components; weekly production meeting minutes document discussion and required action on detailed aspects of the design realisation; the production schedule structures all crew and activities during production week.

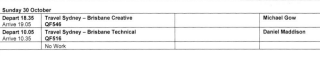

Pygmalion Production Schedule 271011JM.doc

Pygmalion
Playhouse QPAC
Production Schedule

Sunday 30 October

Depart 18.35 Arrive 19.05	Travel Sydney – Brisbane Creative QF546		Michael Gow
Depart 10.05 Arrive 10.35	Travel Sydney – Brisbane Technical QF516		Daniel Maddison
	No Work		

Monday 31 October

06.00	Load Semi at QTC Workshop	External Hire (ATS) – 45' Pan	PS JP TP JB
08.00	Continue to Pack Semi & Unload at QPAC Scenery Dock – Store Playhouse rear stage		PS JP TP SM DM JM
	Lx Pre-rig - O/H Stage	8 Lx (Including Head) 5 Mx (Including Head)	
	Sound Pre-rig - Stage & prepare signal runs	2 Snd	
12.00	Lunch Mx (not including HdMx & loader)		
13.00	Lunch Lx (+2Mx) & Snd		PS JP TP
	Mx Commence build (not including HdMx & loader)	3 Mx	
14.00	Lx Continue – rig FOH, Slots, Booms, Ladders	5 Lx (Including Head)	DM SK JM
	Snd Continue – Install Cricket/YamahaO1V96, run SM operations & commence line checks	2 Snd	SM DM
15.00	Projector Install with TDC		DM
18.00	Dinner Mx Lx		SM
	Snd PA tune TBA	2 Snd	DM
	Projector Line up		JR KD SJ
	SM mark-up furniture		
19.00	Mx Continue build	2 Mx (Including Head)	PS JP TP
	Lx Continue – rig FOH, Slots, Booms, Ladders & Set Lx	5 Lx	DM SK JM
	Snd Dinner		
	TDC Finish		
20.00	Snd Continue – Comms, Cue Lights etc.	2 Snd	SM
22.00	Finish All		

Tuesday 1 November

Depart 8.05 Arrive 8.35	Travel Sydney – Brisbane QF508		Michael Kaempff
Depart 14.25 Arrive 17.00	Travel Brisbane – Sydney Creative QF537		Michael Gow
08.00	Mx Continue build – Carpet runners, quick changes etc.	2 Mx (Including Head)	PS JP TP
	Lx Continue rig & Flash out	5 Lx	DM SK JM
12.00	Mx & Lx Lunch		
13.00	Mx Continue as required	2 Mx (Including Head)	
	Lx prep for Focus	5 Lx	DW DM SK
14.00	Lx Commence Focus	2 Mx (Including Head) 5 Lx	DW DM SK
15.00	Load Props / Furniture @ Merivale St Studio and deliver to QPAC Scenery Dock	QPAC Truck Driver + 1	JM JR KD SJ
18.00	Mx & Lx Dinner		
19.00	Lx Continue Focus	2 Mx (Including Head) 5 Lx	DW DM SK JM
22.00	Finish all		

Wednesday 2 November

Depart 09.05 Arrive 09.35	Travel Sydney – Brisbane Creative QF 512		Michael Gow
Depart 06.05 Arrive 06.35	Travel Sydney – Brisbane Creative QF500		Tony Brumpton
08.00	Lx prep for Plot	2 Mx (Including Head) 3 Lx (Including Head Lx Op & F/Spot Op)	DW JR KD SJ DM SK JM
09.00	Lx Plot	2 Mx (Including Head) 3 Lx (Including Head Lx Op & F/Spot Op)	MG (to join after 10.00) SC DW JR KD SJ DM SK JM
10.00	Load Alcohol @ QTC & deliver to QPAC OB Dock	QPAC Truck Driver +1	ST
	Load Wardrobe @ QTC & deliver to QPAC OB Dock		
	Set Up Wardrobe		VM HB KS AK EK

Page 1 of 6
Subject to change and alteration
Macintosh HD:Users:katywall:Desktop:Freelance:04 Currency Press:Handbook of Theatre design:The Handbook of Theatre Design - design brief, etc:Edited ms & Pics:Pics:15. Design Realisation:15A. Case Study #12:Pygmalion Production Schedule 271011JM.doc

Production schedule

---

queensland theatre company

Pygmalion

Rehearsal Report

Date: Tuesday 11th October

In Attendance: Ms Zanetti, Mr Coleby, Mr Probets

Rehearsal
* Worked through Act 4 (excluding the interlude)
* Mr Gow advised that Mr Sommers would not be required for rehearsals this afternoon.

Props
* Would it be possible to perhaps attach the bin to the bottom of the downstage OP table leg (to the OP side of the table)? Mr Coleby will throw Ms Zanetti's ring into this bin during Act 4.
* Due to the cut at the top of Act 4 (see below under "General"), the letterbox contents (pg 100) have been cut.
* We would like Ms Zanetti to be able to rip out one of the tapes of the reel-to-reel – we can discuss this further at this week's production meeting to see what is possible.

Sets
* Nothing to report.

Lx
* Nothing to report.

Sound
* Nothing to report.

Wardrobe
* Can Ms Zanetti please have a bracelet for the embassy ball & Act 4? This will be taken off with the necklace & ring.
* Mr Coleby will be taking Ms Zanetti's necklace off her during Act 4. Perhaps it could have a magnetic clasp, to make it a little easier?
* Mr Coleby will be removing his shoes & putting on the slippers onstage (Act 4).
* The slippers will be set offstage, prompt side.
* Ms Stevenson has a fitting tomorrow morning at 9am.
* Ms Zanetti has a fitting at 12.45pm tomorrow afternoon.

OH & S:
* Nothing to report.

General
* There has been a cut to the top of Act 4. The act will commence with Higgins' line "I wonder where the devil my slippers are?" (pg 101), & then we will cut to the bottom of pg 101, to Higgins' line "Oh, Lord! What an evening!". I will reflect these changes in the master script.
* Due to rehearsal photography taking place on Thursday, Ms Everingham, Ms Stevenson & Mr Betts are now called at 11.45am (as was originally scheduled).

Signed: Jodie Roche.

Queensland Theatre Company Production Department
Po Box 3310 South Brisbane Queensland 4101
Ph 07 3010 7600   Fax 07 3010 7699   Email mkaempff@qldtheatreco.com.au

Rehearsal report

Theatre is right up there with other wasteful industries. I think it is important that theatre—an art form that aims to show the 'other and the different'—also addresses the issue of sustainability. Not just from the 'we all must do our bit' point of view, but also from a creative perspective: to be creative with materials, to reinterpret what is around us, to see the old with fresh eyes. Creativity is the one thing that is going to get us out of the mess the world is in.

Joey Ruigrok van der Werven, designer

FURTHER THINKING
DESIGNING SUSTAINABLY

You may not feel that you are ready to start thinking about how your design practice will impact on the environment, but if you don't start thinking about it now, at the beginning of your career, will you ever?

As designers we design material things—the sets and costumes—and these things will be made from materials that are mined, milled, made chemically in large factories, made cheaply by third-world labour or made a long way away and need to be transported to where our designs are being realised. All of these processes potentially have negative impacts on the human and natural environment. With some care and forethought we can make a big difference to how big or small the impacts of our design will have.

There are a number of easy, practical measures we can take in our design process to design more sustainably.

LESS IS MORE: Economy of creative vision means that we aren't building more than we need to. The environment benefits and so does the audience as their imaginations get a more active workout.

RE-USE: Adapting design items from stock makes good sense all round: it is better for the environment than recycling and it is usually great for the budget. Basic design items such as levels, flats and cloths, or petticoats, corsets and shoes are easy to re-use, but we can also use our imaginations to adapt many other items from previous shows to our needs. It is a good idea to get in early, check stock and keep it in mind as we design so that the repurposed item becomes an integral part of our design. We can also design our costumes and sets thinking of how they could become good stock for future designers.

SUSTAINABLE MATERIALS: Timber grown from plantations rather than native forests, and natural fibres grown sustainably rather than chemically produced synthetics may be more expensive options, but they are usually better to work with for the cutters, builders and performers, and are more likely to be able to be re-used in future. Many companies and theatre workers will not use materials and products that are bad for their health, and neither should we. We can specify particular products, materials or processes that we know will be better for everyone and the environment. We can also opt to use materials that are made locally so that we are minimising the 'carbon miles' of our design.

RECYCLE: Set and costume items that cannot be re-used are usually taken to the tip as landfill. The production manager will consider recycling as part of the bump-out strategy, and we can help by making sure our designs can be easily broken down into recyclable components.

RE-THINK: At every phase of our design process we have choices about how we do things—these creative choices are in fact the subject of this book. We can see our role as sustainable designers to be part of the rich mix of creative choices that are open to us on every project.

APPENDIX A
FORMS, GENRES AND CONVENTIONS

DRAMATIC FORMS	GENRES	DEFINING QUALITIES/CONVENTIONS
DRAMA		
Comedy	farce	physical slapstick humour (lots of doors)
	black comedy	shock tactics to satirise social taboos
	stand-up comedy	performer plays direct to audience
	comedy of manners	satirises a very specific niche of society
	commedia dell'arte	an historic form of stock comic characters with stock gestures
	satire	a pointed social attack using scathing humour
Tragedy	epic	alienation techniques, audience as spectators, episodic action
	Greek	chorus representing society comments on the action
	Shakespearean	soliloquy, direct address, minimal scenery
	Theatre of the absurd	life has no meaning; an absurd situation used tragically
	melodrama	extreme, exaggerated emotions and atmosphere
naturalism		
	'slice-of-life'	fourth wall
	The 'problem play'	a topical social issue is the centre of the drama
	The 'well-made' play	plot twists, climax close to end, unexpected reversals of fortune
	Docu-drama/verbatim	often combine lecture techniques and dramatic re-enactments
Nōh (traditional Japanese drama)		masks, stylised language of movement
Kabuki (traditional Japanese drama)		stylised makeup, stock characters and situations, hanamichi

DRAMATIC FORMS	GENRES	DEFINING QUALITIES/CONVENTIONS
MUSIC THEATRE		
opera	There are many opera genres (e.g., *opera buffa*, *verismo*, grand opera, *romantische opera*, operetta)	music carries the story, characters sing their feelings
musical	'book musical', Bollywood, musical comedy, rock opera, jute box	characters break into song to tell the story and express their feelings
REVUE/VARIETY		
burlesque		caricature, parody and spectacle
cabaret		audience are part of the show; satirical song, dance sketch comedy
pantomime		stock characters cast against type (e.g., older male actor plays a witch)
PHYSICAL THEATRE: a hybrid form containing dance, acrobatics etc. in a dramatic context		
circus		a sequence of acts of amazing feats of skill
mime		no dialogue; only gesture is used to tell the story
DANCE: there are many dance genres (jazz, flamenco, tap etc.) which may set the style of a performance		
classical ballet		a formal language of movement established by classical tradition
classical ballet		a non-specific term for expressive dance that rejects classical conventions
PERFORMANCE ART: the artist as performer, highly conceptual performance		

APPENDIX B
VISUAL STYLE

An overview of some of the most common styles in art, architecture, fashion and design.

ABSTRACT EXPRESSIONISM	American post-WWII art movement characterised by anti-figurative, non-representational emotional intensity → Jackson Pollock, Willem de Kooning, Marc Rothko (painters)
ARTS AND CRAFTS	English and international design movement 1860–1910 inspired by mediaeval and folk arts and traditional craftsmanship → William Morris (interior designer), Charles Voysey (architect), Charles Rennie Mackintosh (designer)
ART DECO	International ornamental design and architecture style of the 1920s and '30s inspired by the streamlined lines of the industrial age combined with ancient Egyptian, classical Greco-Roman, Cubist and other influences → office towers and cinemas of the 1920s, product design
ART NOUVEAU	European decorative arts movement inspired by natural, organic forms 1890–1910 → Alphonse Mucha, Gustav Klimt (painters), Antoni Gaudi, Victor Horta (architects), Louis Tiffany (decorative arts designer)
BAROQUE	Italian art and architectural style of the 17th century adopted by the Roman Catholic Church as its 'house' style, characterised by exuberant dramatic forms designed to emotionally involve the spectator. The style has become synonymous with the word 'theatrical' → Peter Paul Rubens, Caravaggio (painters), Bernini (sculptor, architect)
BAUHAUS	Influential German design school 1919–1933 with the revolutionary philosophy that an object's form should proceed from its function. Architects, artists, industrial and decorative arts designers created pure unembellished forms with clean lines, influenced by the aesthetics of mass production → Mies van der Rohe, Walter Gropius (architects), Hannes Meyer (designer)
BRUTALISM	Architectural style and philosophy 1950s-'70s where a building's form is an expression of its structural materials; exposed poured concrete, raw, imposing geometric forms → Alison and Peter Smithson, Le Corbusier, Ken Woolley (architects)
CLASSICISM	A term used widely in the arts and philosophy referring to stylistic characteristics formulated by the cultural tastes of Ancient Greece, defined by qualities of balance, harmony and restraint. These principles were revived in the Renaissance and in neoclassicism → classical architectural orders: Doric, Ionic, Corinthian

CONSTRUCTIVISM	Post-WWI movement in art and architecture, associated with the socialist ideals of the Russian Revolution, defined by the machine aesthetic and an exploration of the raw material qualities of an object → Lyubov Popova, Vesnin Rodchenko (artist/designers)
CUBISM	Early 20th century abstract art movement that broke from the tradition of realistic representation by breaking forms up into angled planes and the simultaneous representation of an object from a number of viewpoints → Pablo Picasso, Georges Braque (painters)
DECONSTRUCTIVISM	Architectural philosophy of the 1980s in which the conventional form of a building is taken apart and manipulated leading to fragmented, unpredictable, highly sculptural forms → Daniel Libeskind, Frank Gehry (architects)
EMPIRE	French 19th century neo-classical decorative arts and fashion design style.
EXPRESSIONISM	Early 20th century movement in the arts and philosophy aimed at the subjective portrayal of intense, heightened emotion → Edvard Munch, Wassily Kandinsky, Marc Chagall (painters)
FAUVISM	Brief early 20th century art movement extending from post-impressionism, characterised by use of strong, vibrant colours → Henri Matisse, André Derain (painters)
FRUITS	Street-fashion phenomenon of the Harajuku district in Tokyo which sprang up in the 1990s and was characterised by bright colours and pattern: an eclectic mix of hippie, traditional Japanese and other influences → Shoichi Aoki (photographer)
FUTURISM	Italian early 20th century design and art movement that revered modern concepts of speed, technology, industrial objects → Umberto Boccioni (sculptor), Natalia Goncharova, Giacomo Balla (painters)
GOTH	A visually striking fashion and music subculture originating in the '80s drawing on a fascination with the mystical and macabre, incorporating punk, Victorian and mediaeval influences.
GOTHIC	Mediaeval ecclesiastical architectural style from 12th to 15th centuries characterised by the pointed arch, the flying buttress and the ribbed vault. In later revivals the style became identified as a romantic style → Chartres, Cologne, Amiens cathedrals
HIPPIE	Cultural movement originating in the USA in the mid '60s, incorporating beatnik, psychedelic art and 'flower-power' idealism. Fashion defined by bright patterns, Indian, Middle Eastern and African influences.
IMPRESSIONISM	French art movement of the late 1800s focused on capturing the transient moment and the effects of light and atmosphere using optical

colour-mixing and other painterly techniques → Claude Monet, Edgar Degas, Pierre-Auguste Renoir (painters)

MANNERISM	European art movement 1520–1580 reacting to the classical influences of the Renaissance, characterised by high stylisation and distortion and a sense of art imitating art → Caravaggio, Tintoretto, El Greco, Bronzino (painters)
MINIMALISM	Late 20th century art, design and architectural movement in which a form is stripped of all non-essential elements to its simplest, purest form, inspired by Zen philosophy, and summed up in Mies van der Rohe's adage 'less is more' → Tado Ando, Mies van der Rohe (architects), Ronald Bladen (sculptor), Mondrian (painter)
MOD	Subculture of the early 1960s with an obsessive fashion focus defined by the 'cool' aesthetic → Mary Quant (fashion designer), Teddy Boys, beatnik, Nouvelle Vague
MODERNISM	A general term applied to the philosophic imperatives of the 20th century that rejected 'traditional' realistic forms in favour of a simplified classical structure.
NEO-CLASSICISM	Influential art, architecture and design movement shaped by the ideas of the Enlightenment and a revival of the forms of Classical Greek and Roman art. It took many forms internationally: Adam, Regency, Georgian (English architecture and design), Empire, Beaux-Arts (French architecture), Biedermeier (Germany), Federal (USA) → Jacques-Louis David, Jean Ingres (painters), Antonio Canova (sculptor)
NEW LOOK	1950s fashion trend which reshaped women's clothing after the deprivations of WWII, defined by full skirts, cinched waists and a reawakening of colour and pattern → Christian Dior (fashion designer)
OP ART	Short for 'optical art', a brief 1960s painting movement defined by highly graphic optical illusions → Victor Vasarely, Bridget Riley, Arnold Schmidt (painters)
ORIENTALISM	General cultural term describing the fascination with and influence of Eastern cultures on Western art, at various times in cultural history (early 1800s, 1880s, 1920s).
POP ART	Visual arts movement of the 1950s–'60s drawing on mass culture, advertising and comics to create highly graphic artworks → Andy Warhol, Roy Lichtenstein (painters)
POST-IMPRESSIONISM	Collective term for French painters working at the beginning of the 20th century who developed their own individual expressive and painterly stylisations in response to impressionism, characterised by bold colour and expressive brushwork → Vincent van Gogh, Georges Seurat, Paul Cézanne, Paul Gauguin (painters)

POST-MODERNISM	A philosophical and cultural perspective of the late 20th century that rejected modernist formalism, characterised by the juxtaposition and reincorporation of disparate historic styles → Michael Graves, Robert Venturi, Peter Corrigan (architects)
PUNK	Anti-fashion subculture of the 1970s influenced by glam rock, biker, skinhead, bondage, military and mod trends, commercialised by → Vivienne Westwood, Jean Paul Gaultier (fashion designers)
REALISM	A visual arts and literature term that specifically applies to the French painting genre of the 1850s that rejected romanticism in favour of objective reality, and now broadly applied to arts that attempt to depict everyday, undistorted, true to life situations → Gustave Courbet (painter), Constantin Stanislavski (theatre director), Henrik Ibsen, Anton Chekhov (playwrights)
REGENCY	English early 19th century neo-classical architectural and design style → John Nash (architect)
ROCOCO	Decorative arts movement of the late Baroque characterised by ornate, highly decorative and sculptural forms with a playful, frenetic energy → Jean-Honoré Fragonard, Giambattista Tiepolo, Antoine Watteau (painters), Wessobrunner School (interior design)
ROMANTICISM	A late 18th century movement and now more broadly a stylistic term used in the arts and philosophy referring to aesthetic characteristics that reject rationality and order and give full expression to the artist's emotions, influenced by nature, dreams and the exotic → Caspar David Friedrich, Eugène Delacroix, JMW Turner (painters)
SURREALISM	A metaphysical arts and philosophy movement that grew out of the anti-art philosophy of the Dadaists in the 1920s. Artworks were created by tapping into the artist's unconscious, and appear like waking dreams → Salvador Dalí, Giorgio de Chirico, Yves Tanguy (painters)
SYMBOLISM	A movement in the arts in the 1880s that tapped into the spiritual and mystical (→ Odilon Redon, Gustave Moreau, painters), but more broadly a metaphorical technique that uses an object (symbol) in an indirect or suggestive way to stand in for a bigger, more complex idea.
TRIBAL	A loose trend in fashion that appropriates the traditional cultures of Africa, South America and Asia.
VICTORIAN	An English aesthetic associated particularly with the later part of Queen Victoria's reign (late 19th century) defined by a high level of ornamentation and undisciplined fusion of diverse decorative styles.

ENDNOTES

Please Note: majority of quotes from designers, directors, etc. are from personal correspondence with the author

i   National Museum of Australia: *Yiwarra Kuju: The Canning Stock Route,* Exhibition Notes, Sydney 2012

ii Ralph Myers, designer and Artistic Director Company B Belvoir, interviewed by Keith Gallasch in *Realtime Arts Magazine,* Issue 101, February/March 2011

iii Stanislavski, Constantin. 1963. *An Actor's Handbook: An Alphabetical Arrangement of Concise Statements on Aspects of Acting.* Ed. and trans. Elizabeth Reynolds Hapgood. London: Routledge, 2004, pages 64–65

iv Langer, Susanne K. *Feeling and Form: A Theory of Art Developed from Philosophy in a New Key.* London: Routledge & Kegan Paul, 1953

v   Behan, Dominic. *My Brother Brendan* (1965) quoted in *Oxford Dictionary of Humorous Quotations*

vi Julian Meyrick, director and theatre academic, in correspondence with the author goes on to say: 'That Aristotle, Horace, Schiller, Shakespeare, Coleridge, Stanislavski, Brecht, Grotowski and all the many other brilliant minds who have written about theatre have not given us a WORD for this KEY IDEA [the theatrical moment] ... well, it says something, doesn't it?'

vii Waites, James. Theatre blog http://jameswaites.ilatech.org/, 11 February 2012

viii Aronson, Arnold. 'Postmodern Design'. In *Theatre and Performance Design: A Reader in Scenography.* Eds. Jane Collins and Andrew Nisbet. New York: Routledge, 2010, page 147

ix Schopenhauer quoted by Meyerhold in 1906: Meyerhold, V. *Meyerhold on Theatre.* Ed. and trans. E Braun. London: Methuen, 1977

x   Phillips, Simon. *Richard III,* Program Notes, Melbourne Theatre Company, 2011

xi The objective of completely immersing the audience in the theatrical experience was developed to a high degree in practice by opera composer Richard Wagner, who went on to expound his theory of *Gesamtkunstwerk* or 'total', 'integrated', or 'complete artwork'. *Wagner, Richard. Oper und Drama*, Sämtliche Schriften und Dichtungen: Volume III/IV, 1852

xii Grotowski, Jerzy. *Towards A Poor Theatre.* Ed. and trans. T.K. Wiewiorowski. New York: Simon and Schuster, 1969, page 19

xiii Sam Strong, director: Blake, Elissa. *The Sydney Morning Herald, Spectrum,* 31 March 2012, page 6

xiv Hoghe, Raimund (1980) 'The Theatre of Pina Bausch'. *The Drama Review* 24, 1

xv Brook, Peter. *The Empty Space.* Harmondsworth: Penguin Books, 1990

xvi Morowitz, Charles. *Directing the Action: Acting and Directing in the Contemporary Theatre,* New York: Applause, 1991, page 46

xvii The idea of distancing the viewer in order to increase their degree of objectivity was applied to theatre by Brecht whose theories of *Verfremdungseffekt* or 'alienation effect' have had a profound effect on theatre since the World War II. Brecht, Bertolt. *Brecht on Theatre: The Development of an Aesthetic.* Ed. and trans. John Willett. Hill and Wang: New York, 1964

xviii Tony Assness, event and theatre designer: Blake, Elissa. *The Sydney Morning Herald, Spectrum,* 10 March 2010, page 4

xix Baugh, Christopher. 'Brecht and Stage Design: The Bühnenbildner and the Bühnenbauer,' in *Theatre and Performance Design: A Reader in Scenography.* Eds. Jane Collins and Andrew Nisbet. London: Routledge, 2010, page 189

xx Derek Nicholson coins this term in his essay 'Design Constrictions', in *Performance Design in Australia.* Kristen Anderson & Imogen Ross, Craftsman House, 2001, page 271

xxi Gay McCauley coins this expression in her essay 'A Taxonomy of Spatial Function', in *Theatre and Performance Design: A Reader in Scenography.* Eds. Jane Collins, Andrew Nisbet. London: Routledge, 2010, page 92

xxii Lennox, Annie. *Sunday Times,* April 1984

xxiii Wilson, Elizabeth. *Adorned in Dreams: Fashion and Modernity.* London: Virago, 1987, page 124

LIST OF ILLUSTRATIONS

7.13.–7.16.

Smith, Christina. Photoshop images for Malthouse Theatre Company's *Porn.Cake*, 2012.

7.17.–7.18.

Briscoe, Jo. Sketches models for Melbourne Theatre Company's *Madagascar*, 2010.

Pages 106.–107.

Clockwise from top left: photoshop sketch, Stephen Curtis; production photo from the Queensland Theatre Company's *Pygmalion*, 2011. Photo: Rob MacColl ©; photoshop storyboard, Stephen Curtis; production photo from the Queensland Theatre Company's *Pygmalion*, 2011. Photo: Rob MacColl ©; photoshop storyboards, Stephen Curtis, for Queensland Theatre Company's *Pygmalion*, 2011.

8. Using Space as a Design Tool

Page 114.

Robert Menzies, Lucy Taylor, Julie Forsyth, Matthew Whittet and Ross Williams in Malthouse Theatre's *Journal of a Plague Year*, 2005. Photo: Anna Tregloan ©

8.1. Humphrey Bower and Anna Houston in Perth Theatre Company's *Blackbird*, 2012. Photo: Richard Jefferson ©

8.2. Marcos, Claude. Floor plan for Perth Theatre Company's *Blackbird*, 2012.

8.3. Marcos, Claude. Section drawing for Perth Theatre Company's *Blackbird*, 2012.

8.4. Smith, Christina. Floor plan for Melbourne Theatre Company's *Blackbird*, 2008.

8.5. Smith, Christina. Storyboard image for Melbourne Theatre Company's *Blackbird*, 2008.

8.6. Greg Stone and Alison Bell in Melbourne Theatre Company's *Blackbird*, 2008. Photo: Jeff Busby ©

8.7. Smith, Christina. Section drawing for Melbourne Theatre Company's *Blackbird*, 2008.

8.8. Peter Kowitz and Paula Arundell in Sydney Theatre Company's *Blackbird*, 2007. Photo: Tania Kelley ©

8.9. Myers, Ralph. Floor plan for Sydney Theatre Company's *Blackbird*, 2008.

8.10. Myers, Ralph. Section drawing for Sydney Theatre Company's *Blackbird*, 2008.

Pages 126.–127.

Clockwise from top left: stalls floor plan, Stephen Curtis, based on a drawing by David Walters; photoshop storyboard, Stephen Curtis; production photos from the Queensland Theatre Company's *Pygmalion*, 2011. Photo: Rob Maccoll ©; section, David Walters; photoshop storyboard, Stephen Curtis, for Queensland Theatre Company's *Pygmalion*, 2011.

8.11. The amphitheatre in the Roman ruins of Palmyra in Syria. istockphoto. Michael Major ©

8.12. York Theatre plan. Image courtesy of the Seymour Centre, Sydney.

8.13. Marcos, Claude. Sketch for Malthouse Theatre Company's *The Trial*, 2010.

8.14.–8.15.

Marcos, Claude. 3D models and floor plans for Malthouse Theatre Company's *The Trial*, 2010.

8.16.–8.17.

Marcos, Claude. Floor plans for Malthouse Theatre Company's *The Trial*, 2010.

8.18. Ewen Leslie in Malthouse Theatre's *The Trial*, 2010. Photo: Jeff Busby ©

8.19. Arena di Verona, Italy. istockphoto. Stevegeer ©

8.20.–8.21.

Porta, Dan. Storyboard images for the Commonwealth Games, 2006.

8.22. Myers, Ralph. Floor plan for Sydney Theatre Company's *Blackbird*, 2008.

8.23. Sketch of the Swan Theatre, c.1596. By Arnoldus Buchelius (1565–1641) after the sketch sent to him by his friend Joh. de Witt: *Utrecht, University Library, Ms. 842, f.132r.* Courtesy of the University of Utrecht Library.

8.24. Interior Kabuki theatre 'Shibaraku' performance by Danjuro, c.1800 (woodblock print), Eiri, Rekisentei (fl.1790–1800) / Mead Art Museum, Amherst College, MA, USA / Gift of William Green / The Bridgeman Art Library

8.25. Open Air Comedy theatre (Corral de Comedias) (16th and 17th centuries). Corral scene and dressing side boxes surrounded by 54 wooden supports and beams. Almagro. Spain. SuperStock photo.

8.26. Tregloan, Anna. Floor plan for Malthouse Theatre Company's *The Ham Funeral*, 2005.

8.27. Tregloan, Anna. 3D model for Malthouse Theatre Company's *The Ham Funeral*, 2005.

8.28. Teatro Farnese, Parma, Italy. Image courtesy of Queensland Performing Arts Centre.

8.29. Interior of Farnese Theatre, Parma, Emilia Romagna, Italy, Europe. Nico Tondini/Robert Harding World Imagery Corbis ©

8.30. The court theatre at Český Krumlov, Czech Republic. Courtesy of Český Krumlov.

8.31. Joshua Brennan and Anna Houston in Perth Theatre Company's Tender Napalm, 2011. Photo: Richard Jefferson ©

INDEX

ACKNOWLEDGEMENTS

There are many, many people who have given me every kind of help and support in making this book. Chief among them, and I regret too numerous to individually name, are all of the performers, directors, lighting designers, set and costume designers and production teams in theatres, workshops and theatre companies all around Australia and beyond who have made the beautiful productions that I am privileged to include here.

Of these my warmest thanks go to all of the designers, directors and others who so generously shared their own ways of working and their personal reflections on the design process or who ransacked their archives to offer examples of their work: Andrew Bailey, John Bell, Kim Carpenter, Andrew Carter, Hugh Colman, Robert Cousins, Genevieve Dugard, Dale Ferguson, Sarah Giles, Shaun Gurton, Bill Haycock, Esther Marie Hayes, Jennifer Irwin, Judith Hoddinott, Robert Kemp, Julie Lynch, Claude Marcos, Julian Meyrick, Bruce McKinven, Ralph Myers, Jacob Nash, Dan Potra, Pip Runciman, Joey Ruigrok van der Werven, Michael Scott-Mitchell, Matt Scott, Tess Schofield, Alan Schacher, Christina Smith, Sam Strong, Rachael Swain, Anna Tregloan, James Waites and David Walters. Special thanks to Neil Armfield for a true hand of friendship; to Michael Gow, Michael Kaempff, Vicki Martin and everyone at the Queensland Theatre Company who joined me in creating the 'case study' production of *Pygmalion* which features in the book; to Jo Briscoe whose early hunting, gathering and thinking was so instrumental in its genesis and to Helen Zilko for her brilliantly critical support.

I would also like to express my personal gratitude to the Currency Press team, and most especially to editor Paul O'Beirne and designer Katy Wall for their tireless and talented shepherding and shaping.

To my partner Rosie Boylan, thank you for everything… for your careful readings, thoughtful comments and simply making the book possible. And to my parents, Helen and Peter whose nurturing love set me on course, this book is dedicated to you.

NOTES

NOTES